D1584236

10
SI

To Sharon, Crystal, Jason, and Travis

The
Corrections
PROFESSION

Harold E. Williamson

SAGE PUBLICATIONS
The International Professional Publishers
Newbury Park   London   New Delhi

For information address:

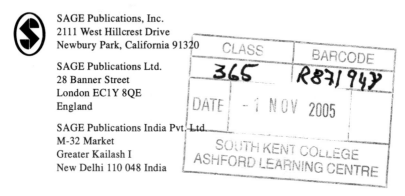

SAGE Publications, Inc.
2111 West Hillcrest Drive
Newbury Park, California 91320

SAGE Publications Ltd.
28 Banner Street
London EC1Y 8QE
England

SAGE Publications India Pvt. Ltd.
M-32 Market
Greater Kailash I
New Delhi 110 048 India

Printed in the United States of America

Library of Congress Cataloging-in-Publication Data

Main entry under title:

Williamson, Harold E.
    The corrections profession / Harold E. Williamson.
        p.   cm.
    Includes bibliographical references.
    ISBN 0-8039-3848-9. — ISBN 0-8039-3849-7 (pbk.)
    1. Corrections—Vocational guidance—United States. I. Title.
hv9471.W55   1990
365'.023'73—dc20   90-32898
                                                              CIP

FIRST PRINTING, 1990

Sage Production Editor: Kimberley A. Clark

Contents

The youth gets together his materials to build a bridge to the moon, or perchance, a palace or temple on the earth, and, at length, the middle-aged man concludes to build a wood shed with them.

Henry David Thoreau

The mass of men lead lives of quiet desperation.
Henry David Thoreau

Preface

This book was written for college and university undergraduate students who are considering lifetime employment in the field of corrections and are seeking information to facilitate informed choices. Students enrolled in practicum or internship courses in corrections will find the book useful in their attempts to understand their work environments. It is anticipated that students will also find the book to be of value to discussions and thought regarding the nature of the corrections profession. Corrections practitioners will find the book to be of value in focusing and placing their careers in perspective and in providing guidance for professional development. Other practitioners in the criminal justice system will find the book to be of value in understanding the corrections subsystem.

Corrections in the United States has developed primarily as dictated by political expediency. The principles upon which correctional practice rests have evolved with time, some are heavily based in tradition, and most are not articulated in any integrated way in a single source in the literature. The scope of corrections is too broad for a single, traditional textbook to include descriptions of all professional roles and activities. Therefore, intensive academic study and experience often are necessary for thorough understanding of the profession. Students seeking career guidance expect—and deserve—more than mere repetition of loosely formulated purposes of corrections; they need reliable information prior to their intensive studies. They are making choices that involve potential lifetime commitments to occupational activities. The need for advanced study and continuous development of knowledge dictates a level of commitment made with the most rational of decision-making processes. Whether or not the field of corrections in its present state is perceived to be a profession, the fact is that it is continuously evolving toward the professional end of the continuum.

When one considers that the average young person who now enters the corrections field can reasonably look forward to a 30- to 40-year career, the importance of commitment based on knowledge becomes apparent. In the 20 years that have passed since the late 1960s, corrections has become much more professionalized. The degree of movement toward professionalism that can be expected in the next 20 to 30 years can only be speculated. It is certain, though, that the complexity of the field will continue to increase, that even greater individual commitment will be required, and that the field will become more professionalized.

It is common to embark upon careers full of idealism and zeal. Frequently, as we mature in our professions, they become less fulfilling than they were initially, and we become disenchanted. It is sometimes difficult to see immediate positive effects of professional activity, and we sometimes decide—as Thoreau suggests—to lower our goals and do merely what we can, or to continue to perform at suboptimal levels in quiet desperation. At those times it is beneficial to recall the sense of commitment experienced at the most realistic times in the career and to review motivations for changes in perception and reasons for dissatisfaction. Unrealistic expectations and cynicism, at any career stage, have no place in human service work. To be effective the professional must be solidly grounded in optimistic reality, commitment, and belief. Realistic assessment of any profession is an absolute prerequisite to the long educational and training period and the total immersion of self into the life style of the profession.

This book is not a set of statements that seeks to establish a code of ethics. The American Correctional Association has established such a code, which is referred to in the text. I describe the fundamental duties, responsibilities, and general obligations of corrections professionals to society, clients, bureaucracies, and to self and others. The correctional ethic provides the basis for judgment, professional morality, and duty. It is defined by the degree of professionalism subscribed to by practitioners and the level of professional development of the field itself. I discuss the correctional ethos to the extent that I describe the distinctive features of particular groups of individuals.

In the course of my own career as practitioner and educator I have observed students and others, often ill-prepared, make choices that are wrong. They frequently do not know what corrections is all about and they are often unaware of career opportunities. Idealism, infatuation, misunderstanding, and acts of desperation for employment sometimes preclude rational choices regarding course of study, agency, and occupation. The motivation, expectations, and commitment they bring to their careers is sometimes improper for sustained satisfaction, acceptable performance, and career success. The opposite is also true—many who would enjoy corrections as a profession are turned away as a result of false perceptions and lack of knowledge. The general purposes of this book are to define the profession of corrections and to discuss the fundamental obligations upon which it is founded.

Most who read this book will use it to assist in deliberations regarding this choice of profession. Some will read it and decide to choose corrections; others will read it and turn from corrections. Either way, if it helps any student to make the right choice, both the individual and the profession will have benefited from that correct choice.

Books do not write themselves. Ideas do not first appear in their final form. Writing a book is a technical process; the development of ideas is a theoretical task involving the exercise of logic. The editors and numerous others have assured that I succeeded in the technical task and have assisted greatly in the theoretical task. The degree to which I am successful in accomplishing my primary goal—that of developing and presenting the theoretical ideas—will be determined by you, the reader.

The idea for this book stems from several sources. Egon Bittner's *The Functions of the Police in Modern Society* and Edward Shils's *The Academic Ethic* provided significant motivation and established, in part, the general pattern upon which this book is based. (I do not suggest that this book reaches the scholarly heights of the two aforementioned texts or that this volume is, or will be, in the same category as a classic.) Numerous students have, through their incessant questions and struggles to understand the corrections profession, forced me to refine my ideas. In addition, several practitioners have sought my counsel regarding their disillusionment—which can usually be traced to unrealistic expectations and motivations—with their careers. Perhaps this book will assist those who read it to gain more accurate perceptions of the corrections profession.

I would like to thank Gail and David Beach of the Federal Bureau of Prisons, Dr. Raymond Teske of Sam Houston State University, Dr. Robert G. Huckabee of Indiana State University, Dr. Lou San Marco of Baldwin-Wallace College, Warden Alton Braddock of the Louisiana Department of Corrections, and Professors Robbi Thompson and William F. Kitchens of Northeast Louisiana University for their diligent reading and appropriate comments on drafts. I would also like to thank Jana Bufkin, Jane Prichard, and Terri Foster for their proofreading and other timely assistance. Finally, I would like to thank Dr. G. Dale Welch for his assistance and encouragement throughout the duration of this project.

1

Introduction

Human choices are usually valid and appropriate only if made with relatively complete knowledge regarding the subject matter about which the decision is to be made. The course of human lives is sometimes determined by a series of seemingly inconsequential decisions, made at opportunistic times and often requiring little thought and planning. Yet this series of small decisions serves to constrain future choices or at the very least to increase the likelihood of particular choices in the future.

Career choices should be made with the utmost care. Few human activities are more influential in personal lives than those of career or professional activities. Career choice will influence educational alternatives; the degree of success—however defined—that will be ultimately attained; and the general quality of life for individuals and families. Locke (1976) has pointed out that a person's attitude toward work "can affect his attitude toward his whole life, toward his family, and toward himself. It can affect his physical health and possibly how long he lives" (p. 1334).

The pervasiveness of career influence on personal life dictates that career choices be deliberate and be made with full knowledge of self, personal desires, and the profession. Life transitions, social expectations, demographic shifts, and social changes have significant consequences for individuals throughout their professional lives. Most individuals do not consider these factors at a conscious level when making career decisions, yet their impact is real. Childhood and adolescence

---

AUTHOR'S NOTE: The word *corrections* will be used throughout this book as a singular term referring to the overall field or profession of corrections.

are characterized by physical and mental growth, both structured and unstructured. Growth continues through all life stages. When growth stops, the individual dies—either literally or figuratively. Career choices, like other choices, represent a selection of focused future behavior, denial of alternative courses of behavior, and reliance on continued growth and satisfaction from choices made with limited knowledge at a comparatively early age. As one matures in any profession, new experiences frequently become the exception rather than the rule. Therefore, it is necessary that individuals actively plan for continued growth in the professions that they choose.

Demographic shifts, or changes in the characteristics of society such as age and other factors, have significant implications for professional and personal satisfaction. An increasing number of women are entering the work force. Older workers are less mobile and less willing to change jobs. Work forces are aging, while the replacement pool of employees is shrinking.

> Between 1985 and 1995 the number of Americans between 30 and 55 will increase by more than 20 million, while there will be a decrease of nine million in the population of 15- to 30-year olds. The correctional work force recruited during the institutional expansion of the 1970s and the 1980s will become predominately middle-aged and will be looking for more opportunities for promotion and career development as well as higher salaries. (Benton, 1988, p. 108)

Retirement patterns are changing which will further constrain future professionals. The age for mandatory retirement in the United States is continuously increasing. Health care advances have extended life expectancy and improved the quality of old age. Fewer people are seeking retirement at the traditional retirement age and, instead, are choosing to continue working. The *baby boom* generation, born in the years following the end of World War II (1946-1962), and the *echo boom* (the children of those born during the baby boom years) will influence career progressions in the United States for the next 40 to 50 years. Because older employees will be around longer, younger employees are likely to find themselves in lower level and middle management positions for longer periods of time. It will become increasingly difficult for corrections to compete for the limited number of replacement employees available at the entry level.

Individuals with higher education usually have greater expectations regarding professional and personal growth. The increasing numbers of individuals possessing college degrees, beginning after World War II and continuing today, have resulted in a higher concentration of educated persons in society. In 1987, the proportion of adults in the United States with college degrees reached 19.9% ("In Brief," 1988). While 75% of all adults had high school diplomas, 23.6% of the men had four or more years of college. Thirty million Americans have some college credits; 18 million have bachelor's degrees; six million have master's degrees, and 768,000 have doctoral degrees (Schwartz, 1988). Higher education in the general population creates greater sophistication about professional matters and skepticism about professional practices. There is less mystery regarding professional practice, because there is a sharing of professional knowledge. At the same time, however, there is a greater willingness on the part of the public to use professional services (Wilensky, 1964).

These and other changes may force agencies to alter traditional employment patterns and to provide increased opportunities for professional growth and development. Individuals must also take greater responsibility for ensuring their own growth, development, and sense of satisfaction. Traditional orientations, lack of ambition, and limited preparation will result in professional and personal stagnation at earlier ages. Competition for upper level positions will increase. Therefore, those with traditional orientations and only basic preparation will suffer greater cynicism and discontentedness at earlier ages in the future.

Since the late 1960s or the early 1970s there has been a noticeable movement of individuals into second careers. Middle-aged professionals are increasingly willing to start over in new fields of endeavor, usually—but not always—related to their first careers. The implications for the future are that experienced people may be leaving corrections, and inexperienced mature individuals may be entering the field. There will be a greater need to retrain older workers, and more older employees will be found in the lower ranks. The dynamics of prison staff relations will change as the employee ranks lose their traditional characteristic of supervisors being older than new employees.

Adequate understanding of the corrections system requires a basic understanding of the principles upon which government in the United States is based. Further understanding of the design of the criminal justice system itself is also necessary for a thorough understanding of corrections. This chapter defines the basic principles of *federalism* and *separation of powers* and discusses the influence of these two concepts. It also presents an overview of the criminal justice system—police, courts, and corrections—as a system. The interrelationships of these three components are discussed briefly. Finally, this chapter contains a brief description of the corrections subsystem.

THE FOUNDATIONS OF CRIMINAL JUSTICE

The criminal justice system in the United States is a complex network of agencies at several levels that share power with each other and over specific jurisdictions. The system is designed so that there is a balance of power, with checks and balances, which precludes any one group or branch of government from accumulating too much power. The nature of this system is such that procedures are complex, sometimes ambiguous, and subject to influence from numerous sources but resistant to excessive influence from any one source.

The primary foundation of all criminal justice practice in the United States is the U.S. Constitution. The Constitution is considered to be a living document that is subject to court interpretations regarding specific requirements at any given time. State constitutions also form a significant part of the foundation for practice. A state constitution can provide more—but not fewer—rights than those provided for in the U.S. Constitution. In addition, state and federal laws provide a significant part of the foundation for practice. These constitutions and laws are (or were) made by the public through elected legislatures, are enforced by elected or appointed officials of the executive branch, and are interpreted by elected or appointed judges in local, state, and federal courts.

The two basic principles upon which the representative democracy in the United States is based are *federalism* and *separation of powers*. Federalism simply means that there are various jurisdictions—national, state, and local—that function to provide different rights, privileges, and services to the citizens of their jurisdictions. Separation of powers means that each government—national, state, and local—is further divided into three branches—executive, legislative, and judicial— which have separate powers regarding governmental matters and serve as a system of checks and balances in regard to the power exercised by each of the other branches.

Federalism

Federal is defined as "pertaining to . . . a form of government in which a union of states recognizes the sovereignty of a central authority while retaining certain residual powers of government" (American Heritage Publishing Company, 1970, p. 481). The United States Constitution is the basic document that defines the powers of the central government and limits those powers. The Tenth Amendment to the U.S. Constitution reserves other rights, powers, and duties not assigned to the federal government by the U. S. Constitution to the states. Interpretation of the U. S. Constitution by the federal courts has, over time, considerably expanded the powers of the central government from those limited powers envisioned by the founding fathers.

Separation of Powers

Each level of government—national, state, and local—is further divided into three separate branches: executive, legislative, and judicial. This latter division constitutes a system of checks and balances that is based upon the concept of separation of powers. Each branch of government has its unique duties, rights, and powers; the system is designed to ensure that no one branch gains excessive power and influence. Because each branch is responsible to different political constituencies, and members serve different lengths of terms in some cases and share powers with other branches, there is a consistency to governmental procedures that allows for slow, deliberate, and appropriate change. Radical shifts in public policy and governmental processes are rare. One consequence of the separation of powers—which some people view as negative—is that government tends to act slowly and its actions are the result of compromises.

The executive branch at the federal level consists of the president, his or her staff, and agencies directly under his or her control. Governors, their staffs, and agencies directly responsible to them constitute the states' executive branches. Mayors and the political heads of other local governments, their staffs, and agencies responsible to them constitute the local executive branches. The basic role of the executive agencies is to carry out the laws as established by the legislatures of their respective jurisdictions.

The legislative branch at the federal level consists of the U.S. House of Representatives, the U.S. Senate, and the staffs and agencies that report to them. Legislative branches at the state level are most often referred to as houses of representatives and senates in the case of bicameral (two house) legislatures; legislative assemblies in the case of unicameral (one house) legislatures. Legislative branches at local levels are referred to by various names, perhaps the most common being city councils and county commissioners. The basic role of various legislative branches at all levels is to make laws for their respective jurisdictions.

The judicial branch at the national level consists of many federal courts, some with limited and some with general jurisdictions. Limited jurisdiction refers to courts that hear matters related to a specific area (for example, tax courts). General jurisdiction refers to courts that hear cases involving violations of all federal laws, both civil and criminal. Federal level courts most commonly known to the general public are the U.S. District Courts, the U.S. Courts of Appeals, and the U.S. Supreme Court. The judicial branches at the state level consist of variously named courts. The most common names are district courts, superior courts, courts of appeals, and supreme courts. Local government courts consist of mayor's courts, municipal courts, county courts, justice of the peace courts, and certain other courts that have limited jurisdictions within the confines of local geographic areas. The functions of the courts, at all levels, are to interpret the laws of their jurisdictions and to conduct or review trial proceedings to ensure fairness, equal protection, and due process of law.

THE CRIMINAL JUSTICE SYSTEM

The criminal justice system is composed of police agencies, corrections agencies, and courts that function at the national, state, and local levels. Police and corrections agencies are, with minor exceptions, parts of the executive branches of governments.[1] Courts are the major components of the judicial branches of government. There are over 43,000 criminal justice agencies (see Table 1.1) which employ more than 1,300,000 persons (see Table 1.2).

TABLE 1.1: Criminal Justice Agencies in the United States

Agency Type	Local	State	Federal	Total
Police[a]	17,250	200	50	17,500
Courts[b]	13,221	3,887	107	17,215
Corrections	3,338[c]	4,916[d]	50[e]	8,304
Total	33,809	9,003	207	43,019

(a) Estimate. See Note 2.
(b) From Robin, G. (1987).
(c) From Bureau of the Census (1987).
(d) From American Correctional Association (1988). State numbers include 3,418 juvenile facilities.
(e) Landon (1989). Federal facilities do not include those in the community.

The Police

There are approximately 17,500 police departments[2] in the United States (Staufenberger, 1977). Some agencies (such as New York City at 30,000 sworn officers) are quite large. In cities with populations of more than 10,000, however, the median size of police departments is only 39 sworn officers. More than 60% of the total police personnel are employed by 280 departments (Staufenberger, 1977). The vast majority of police departments—approximately 17,250—are local (i.e., city or county) agencies that enforce the criminal laws within their respective jurisdictions. Each state also has one or more agencies—a total of approximately 200 in the United States—that have statewide jurisdiction over specific areas of criminal behavior. Some state police agencies have general police authority, which means that they are responsible for enforcing all criminal laws in the state; other state agencies may have limited police power in regard to certain types of crimes. In addition, there are approximately 50 police agencies at the federal level that enforce federal laws regarding criminal behavior.

In 1985 there were 737,741 police officers in the United States. Federal agencies employed 61,342; state agencies employed 107,606; and local agencies employed 568,793 (see Table 1.2). State police, local police, and sheriff's departments employed 757,508 persons in 1987 (Bureau of Justice Statistics, 1989). The police function is primarily a task of local government; in addition to the public police, however, there are approximately 1,100,000 private security personnel in the United States (Bureau of Justice Statistics, 1988c).

TABLE 1.2: Criminal Justice Employment in the United States, 1985

Agency Type	Local	State	Federal	Total
Police	568,793	107,606	61,342	737,741
Courts	115,967	61,082	15,455	192,504
Corrections	139,373	240,856	14,448	394,677
Total	824,133	409,544	91,245	1,324,922

Source: Jamieson, K. M., and Flanagan, T. J. (Eds.). (1987). *Sourcebook of Criminal Justice Statistics–1986*. Washington, DC: Bureau of Justice Statistics.

The Courts

Courts at the local, state, and federal levels are charged with the responsibility of interpreting the laws and of providing fair trials for those who come before them. Courts can be categorized as trial courts or appellate courts; some courts have both trial and appellate jurisdictions. A trial court is a court that hears the initial charges of criminal behavior, determines guilt or innocence, and imposes sentence. Appellate courts hear appeals from convictions in lower courts. Most appeals are "on the record," which means that only the record is reviewed. There is no additional trial procedure at the appellate level.[3] Courts at the local level usually hear cases involving misdemeanor offenses, conduct preliminary hearings, and so forth. Most felony cases are heard in state district courts (or their equivalent). Intermediate appellate courts and supreme courts (the highest courts) usually hear appeals only from the lower courts. Federal courts hear cases involving violation of federal laws or constitutional rights and certain other specified cases.

Corrections professionals are significantly affected by the courts' civil jurisdiction; both state and federal courts issue decisions that control the manner in which correctional processes must be conducted. The most significant action regarding inmates' rights, however, has resulted from suits filed in federal court under Title 42, United States Code, Section 1983 (42 USC 1983). Two results of courts' decisions issued within the last two decades have been increased bureaucratization of correctional agencies and increased professionalization of correctional staffs. Court insistence upon standardization of procedures and the provision of due process and equal protection has resulted in increased bureaucratization. At the same time, courts have imposed educational requirements, staffing requirements, and certification

TABLE 1.3: Courts in the United States

Type of Court	Local	State	Federal	Total
Trial	13,221	3,630	94	16,945
Appellate	—	206	12	218
Supreme	—	51	1	52
Total	13,221	3,887	107	17,215

Source: Robin, G. (1987). *Introduction to Criminal Justice* (3rd ed.). New York: Harper and Row.

mandates that have resulted in greater professionalization of the correctional staffs of almost all agencies.

There are 17,215 courts (see Table 1.3) in the United States (Robin, 1987). A court may have only one judge, or it may have several judges. The vast majority of these courts (13,221) are local courts that hear cases involving misdemeanors, traffic offenses, and other minor proceedings. Felony cases, serious misdemeanors, and appeals of state convictions are handled in the 3,887 state courts. There are 94 federal trial courts (Federal District Courts), 12 federal Circuit Courts of Appeal, and one U. S. Supreme Court. Although some states use appointing processes, most judges at the local and state levels are elected for specified terms in office. Judges at the federal level are appointed for life, and can be removed only for cause.[4]

Corrections

There were 3,338 jails in the United States in 1983 (Bureau of the Census, 1987). The rate of increase in jail populations was 21,000 per year in 1983—a rate which required the equivalent of one new 400-bed jail each week (Bureau of Justice Statistics, 1984). "The growth in the inmate population between 1978 and 1983 exceeded the availability of new bed space by 37,121" (Allen, Latessa, & Vito, 1987, p. 92). In 1986, there were 102 medium-to-maximum security prisons under construction in the United States, and more were planned (Carlson, 1988). "Furthermore, the U. S. Sentencing Commission estimates that the federal inmate population will increase from 42,000 to between 72,000 and 79,000 by 1992" (Corothers, 1987, p. 58). The Federal Bureau of Prisons expects to add 29 new institutions and renovate existing

TABLE 1.4: Correctional Facilities by Type and Client

Type of Agency	Adult	Juvenile	Total
Institutional	1,107	367	1,474
Community Corrections	391	3,051	3,442
Total	1,498	3,418	4,916

Source: American Correctional Association. (1988). *Juvenile and Adult Correctional Departments, Institutions, Agencies, and Paroling Authorities.* College Park, MD: The American Correctional Association.[5]

facilities to meet the demand for bed space (Rosetti, 1988). Jails hold over 240,000 detainees on any given day, a condition that places them at 9% over their rated capacity (Bostick, 1988). "More than 8 million people pass through our nation's jails every year—the number increases every year" (American Correctional Association, 1986, p. vi). The rate of incarceration in American prisons is expected to reach 300.78 per 100,000 in 1993—up from 235.47 per 100,000 population in 1988 (American Correctional Association, 1989a). Seventy-two thousand new beds were funded by government agencies in 1988 (American Correctional Association, 1989b). "Despite substantial construction efforts that added 122,317 new prison beds between 1978 and 1983, the shortfall in bed space during this time period still totaled 33,255" (Allen, Latessa, & Vito, 1987, p. 92).

In 1987, there were 1,474 corrections institutions (see Note 5) holding either juvenile or adult offenders (see Table 1.4). Approximately

TABLE 1.5: Correctional Population

Client Type	Probation	Parole	Institutions*	Total
Adult	1,958,167	272,465	621,927	2,852,559
Juvenile	74,574	48,502	75,618	198,694
Total (as of June 30, 1987)	2,032,741	320,967	697,545	3,051,253

*Does not include jail populations. Does include inmates committed to private institutions such as halfway houses and other community-based institutions. (Also, see Note 5.)
Source: American Correctional Association. (1988). *Juvenile and Adult Correctional Departments, Institutions, Agencies, and Paroling Authorities.* College Park, MD: American Correctional Association.

TABLE 1.6: Correctional Facilities by Jurisdiction and Type*

Agency Type	State(a)	Federal(b)	Total
Adult	1,498	50	1,548
Juvenile	3,418	—	3,418
Total	4,916	50	4,966

*Does not include local facilities.
(a) American Correctional Association. (1988). *Juvenile and Adult Correctional Departments, Institutions, Agencies, and Paroling Authorities.* College Park, MD: American Correctional Association.[5]
(b) Landon (1989).

one million inmates (see Table 1.5) were held in jail or prison. On December 31, 1987, there were 581,609 adult inmates being held in prisons (Bureau of Justice Statistics, 1988a). In addition, there were 3,442 community corrections agencies that supervised over two million clients. Travisono (1988a) makes the following observations regarding corrections in 1987:

(1) One out of 55 Americans were under some form of correctional supervision.
(2) The incarceration rate in the United States averaged 209 per 100,000 persons.
(3) Correctional budgets exceeded $9.5 billion; construction of prisons cost $4.5 billion; and construction of jails cost $6.5 billion.[6]
(4) Correctional employment increased by 15% over the staffing levels of 1986.

Whereas policing is primarily a local function, corrections is largely a state function. In 1985, the 394,677 correctional employees were distributed as follows: 14,448 at the federal level; 240,856 at the state level; and 139,373 at the local level (see Table 1.2).

THE CORRECTIONS SUBSYSTEM

Corrections is a subsystem of the criminal justice system. It is comprised of a large number of independent agencies related to each other primarily by function. It exists at the national, state, and local levels

TABLE 1.7: Correctional Employees by Type of Agency and Jurisdictions*

Type of Agency	State	Federal	Total
Adult	213,338	12,650	225,988
Juvenile	29,811	—	29,811
Total	243,149	12,650	255,799

*Does not include approximately 139,000 local employees.
Source: American Correctional Association. (1988). *Juvenile and Adult Correctional Departments, Institutions, Agencies, and Paroling Authorities.* College Park, MD: American Correctional Association

and serves juveniles, adults, or both in either institutional environments or in communities. Some jurisdictions have agencies that combine these functions in unique ways.

Institutional Corrections

Federal and state corrections agencies employ over 255,000 persons (see Table 1.7) involved in a wide range of activities. Appendix E contains examples of job titles ranging from an entry level security officer responsible for the custody of inmates to the director/commissioner who is responsible for the entire operation of the particular system. In addition to security personnel, each jail or prison must provide treatment personnel who perform functions related to medicine, dentistry, social casework, education, and counseling. A third group consists of maintenance personnel and technicians. The latter two groups are usually quite small, and perhaps even part-time or volunteer personnel in smaller jails and other small facilities. Larger facilities, such as most state prisons, however, have extensive, diversified staffs with varied job responsibilities.

Community-Based Corrections

The U. S. Department of Justice (1978) identified 774 agencies that supervised probationers, 157 agencies that supervised parolees, and 626 agencies that supervised both probationers and parolees (Allen, Eskridge, Latessa, & Vito, 1985) Community corrections assumes three basic forms: (1) probation, which in some areas is a local function and, in all cases, is actually a role of the judicial branch; (2) parole, which in almost all cases is a state function; and (3) community residential centers, which may be connected to the major prison system, the parole system, or a private organization.

In 1987 there were approximately two million probationers. These individuals were supervised in the community by probation officers, most of whom worked for local probation departments. In some states, probationers are supervised by state officers who also supervise parolees; however, in most jurisdictions, probation is conducted by local districts and agencies. In all cases, the probation officers answer to the court with regard to the behavior of probationers.

Parole, by definition, is supervised release after incarceration. In 1987, there were over 320,000 individuals in the United States on parole. Parole is almost exclusively the jurisdiction of the states; few, if any, local agencies supervise parolees. Parole is granted under varying conditions to those inmates who conduct themselves well in prison and prepare for reentry into society. The federal system and some states have eliminated parole as a discretionary function of a parole board.[7] Most states, however, have postincarceration supervision of some type for most prisoners. In some states, both juvenile and adult parole are supervised by the same agency, while in others the two functions are assigned to separate agencies.

Community residential centers are small facilities located in various parts of the community. They are usually referred to as halfway houses, group homes, or some similar name. Their functions are to supervise individuals in relatively free environments and to help inmates adjust to free society. Most clients living in such facilities hold jobs in the community and are outside of the facility for a specified period of time each day. Typically, these facilities are populated by inmates who are in the process of being released from prison. The residential centers may be a part of larger state agencies, local agencies, or may be private concerns.

Juvenile Corrections

Juvenile corrections is performed in both institutions (usually called training schools or reformatories) and communities. In 1985, there were 74,381 juveniles incarcerated in institutions (including group homes) and 74,574 being supervised in communities (American Correctional Association, 1988). Of those incarcerated, there were 49,322 confined in public custody institutions (Shover & Einstadter, 1988). In some states, juvenile institutions are administered and community supervision is conducted by the same agencies that handle adult prisoners; in others, separate agencies have jurisdiction over juvenile offenders.

Juvenile delinquency has constituted a problem in the United States for at least the last 100 years. The legal philosophy in the United States prior to 1966 was that of *parens patriae*, meaning that states acted as benevolent parents in determining what was "best for the child." Juveniles had few legal rights and did not enjoy the same constitutional protections that adult offenders enjoyed. Beginning with court decisions in 1966 and subsequent years, however, juveniles have been given the full range of constitutional rights and due process safeguards that are afforded to adults.[8]

SUMMARY

The criminal justice system is a complex series of agencies at three levels of government that perform complementary and complex activities under rules, procedures, and conditions specified by various public and private agencies and processes. Corrections is a significant component of this system. It employs almost 400,000 professionals, paraprofessionals, and nonprofessionals to supervise over three million convicted adult and juvenile felons and misdemeanants in communities and in institutions. Correctional processes are controlled by organizations, professional associations and standards, political bodies, courts, and public opinion.

The correctional subsystem has expanded considerably in the last 15 to 20 years. Prisons are currently being built at an unprecedented rate, and there are no signs of an immediate slowing of this rate. The number of persons being committed to prisons and to probation has increased significantly. Current construction, planned construction, and the expansion of community programs will continue in the foreseeable future.

Changes in American society will affect the work force and professional development of corrections into the next century. The society is becoming older, more educated, more complex, and less willing to tolerate traditional methods of correctional practice. Women are entering the work force in record numbers, and minorities are gaining more influence in public policy. Retirement patterns are changing, workers are remaining on the job longer or are retiring from jobs and seeking others, and traditional expectations of rising in the organization because of length of service are changing.

The fact that corrections is becoming more professionalized means—among other things—that the investment of time, energy, and money in the training and educational period required for successful career development is increasing. Valid career choices can best be made with adequate knowledge of the field. The remainder of this book is devoted to explaining the corrections profession in such a way as to facilitate these choices.

NOTES

1. An exception to this rule is that probation is usually a function of the courts. Although probation officers may work for state or local agencies within the executive branch, they answer to the courts with regard to probationers that they supervise. Another exception is district attorneys and/or their municipal and federal counterparts. The prosecutors are considered to be part of the courts (the judicial branch of government).

2. There is some confusion regarding the actual number of police departments. The total depends upon whether or not one counts the small one-man town marshal (or night watchman, in some cases) as a separate agency. The President's Commission on Law Enforcement and Administration of Justice (1967) stated that there were 40,000 police departments—37,750 local, 200 state, and 50 federal agencies. Hudzik and Cordner (1983), calling attention to *The National Manpower Survey of the Criminal Justice System: Volume II* (U. S. Department of Justice, 1978), point out that recent estimates indicate that there are between 17,000 and 25,000 police departments in the United States. Walker (1989) states that there are 19,691 separate law enforcement agencies in the United States. The Bureau of Justice Statistics (1989) indicates that there were 15,118 local police, sheriff, and state police agencies (general purpose) in the United States in 1987.

3. Any appellate proceeding which occurs from a court that is not a court of record will result in a "trial de novo." This means that a new trial is conducted in the appellate court and the fact of a lower court finding of guilt is not considered at all. For example, justice of the peace courts are not courts of record. A finding of guilt on a misdemeanor charge may be appealed to the next higher court, usually the state district court or county court-at-law. If that trial takes place in the higher court, technically it is not considered an appeal. It is the "trial de novo" which does not consider the fact that the justice of peace conviction took place.

4. Federal judges who are appointed to serve in territories and certain other judges in specialized federal courts are appointed for 10-year terms. However, judges who serve in Federal District Courts, Circuit Courts of Appeal, and the U. S. Supreme Court are

appointed for lifetime tenure and can be removed only by impeachment, retirement, or voluntary resignation. In most states, local and state judges are elected to terms in office which may vary in length from two to ten years, depending upon the court and the state in which it is located. Other states use a system of appointing judges. One such plan, known as the Missouri Plan, requires that judges be appointed by the governor through an established process and be subjected to unopposed election in a yes/no vote after a specified number of years.

5. The number of facilities includes (for adults) diagnostic/reception centers, institutions, community facilities, farms/camps, medical facilities, pre-release centers, work release centers, DWI centers, and others. For juveniles, the numbers include diagnostic/reception centers, institutions, community facilities/halfway houses, detention facilities, homes, camps, and others. Cole (1989) indicates that there are 694 state prisons and 2,900 juvenile facilities. The Bureau of Justice Statistics (1988c) indicates that there were 694 adult prisons, 209 state-operated community facilities, and 7,000 additional adult beds in private facilities in 1984. They also indicate 3,036 public and private juvenile custody institutions holding 83,406 juveniles.

6. As of July, 1988, local governments had allocated approximately $3 billion for jails currently being designed or constructed (Nelson, 1988). In December, 1988, local governments had actually begun construction on 200 new jails at a cost of $2 billion (Bostick, 1988).

7. The ten states that have abolished parole are California, Colorado, Minnesota, New Mexico, North Carolina, Florida, Connecticut, Illinois, Indiana, and Maine (Fox, 1985). The Crime Control Act of 1984 will result in the elimination of the federal parole system in the 1990s.

8. The only right provided to adult offenders that is not provided to juvenile offenders is the right to trial by jury (see *McKeiver v. Pennsylvania*, 403 US 528, 1971). All other rights (e.g., right to a speedy trial, right to confrontation of witnesses, subpoena rights, right to an attorney) are provided to juveniles.

2

Corrections Environments

Prior to the 1960s, corrections functioned largely independent of influence from external sources. The internal environments of both institutional and community corrections were defined by administrators. The general philosophy was of "out of sight, out of mind"; politicians, judges, and society were content to leave correctional matters to administrators. Although there were influential external groups that concentrated on prison reform, their efforts could be described as in harmony with the goals and procedures of the correctional establishment.

Beginning in the 1960s, greater social awareness, increased activism by numerous groups, the civil rights movement, judicial activity, public exposure of abuses in prisons, and other influences began to have significant impact upon corrections. Systems were forced to become open and interact with their social, political, and legal environments. The political environment changed dramatically (and will continue to change in the 1990s); systems, in response, became much more complex and were forced to become even more bureaucratic. Institutions and community corrections were subjected to change by both internal and external forces. The legal environment in which corrections functioned also changed dramatically in the 1960s. This chapter discusses the current social, political, bureaucratic, institutional, community, and legal environments of corrections.

James B. Jacobs's books *Stateville: The Penitentiary in Mass Society* (1977) and *New Perspectives on Prisons and Imprisonment* (1983) emphasize the dramatic changes that were occurring in the 1960s and 1970s as corrections entered the current open-systems phase of its existence. The changes that were required were at times dramatic. Prison populations and prison staffs changed, and the influence of external groups became pervasive. Prisoners became more vocal and less willing to accept their station in life. Court proceedings were initiated at a pace unprecedented in the American criminal justice system. Professionals such as teachers, social workers, doctors, lawyers, and others became interested in corrections and became integral parts of staffs in both prisons and community corrections agencies; their influence changed the way corrections conducted business.

The relationship between corrections and its external environments also changed. Civil rights groups and others had significant influence on correctional programming and on correctional procedures. Corrections was forced to be responsive to its external environment in many ways. Employees became much more independent and less willing to accept the traditional authoritarian organization. Increased mobility of employees, increased educational levels of the work force, an increased willingness to change jobs, and other factors forced corrections to compete for employees in a manner that had not been experienced before.

Criminal justice organizations are interdependent upon each other and upon their environments. They are often characterized by conflict within and between organizations, instability, and conflicting demands upon the resources of the organizations. An organization must adapt to its environments if it is to survive and remain viable (Duncan, 1972). Corrections is a dynamic and complex environment; individuals in complex, dynamic organizations usually experience uncertainty. Moreover, the uncertainty and degree of complexity is dependent upon the perceptions of organizational members and can change. People, to a great extent, create their own environments, which then control them (Brudney & Hebert, 1987; Weick, 1979). Prison overcrowding, court decisions, determinant sentencing, inmate unrest, and other pressures have resulted in changes in correctional environments—many of which have been resisted by corrections personnel (Cohn, 1987). Administrative ineffectiveness has also contributed to control from external sources.

THE SOCIAL ENVIRONMENT

The 1960s were turbulent times in America. Rapid and radical changes took place in all areas of society. President Lyndon B. Johnson's Great

Society programs, civil rights movements and laws, demonstrations, the war in Vietnam, court decisions, and other factors greatly affected the area of criminal justice and, more specifically, corrections. Greater emphasis was placed on community corrections (i.e., probation and parole) and on innovative institutional programming. Rehabilitation, based on the medical model of diagnosis and treatment, came to be the primary ideology of corrections.

Inmate and client groups changed from being members of an underclass that had no voice to, in some cases, a militant class that spoke loudly and was heard. The baby boom generation born immediately following World War II came of age. Crime increased and incarceration rates began a rapid rise. The middle and upper classes in society were more and more affected by correctional programs, because those individuals coming of age and committing crimes in the 1960s and 1970s were representative of the broad range of social classes—not merely the underclasses that had been the primary correctional population prior to the 1960s.

The change in ideology to a greater emphasis on treatment caused a significant increase in the numbers of professional persons involved in corrections. Professors, teachers, researchers, social workers, and others began to exert greater influence in correctional programming. There was a much greater concern shown for society and for the welfare of others. The prevailing opinion was that prisoners should be rehabilitated rather than punished. Through rehabilitation, society and the individual inmate would be far better served.

Court decisions became increasingly more influential (and prevalent) in the area of corrections. Civil rights laws and social unrest caused many court and administrative decisions that created great change and disorganization in corrections. The hands-off policy that had been practiced by courts with regard to corrections was replaced by a hands-on policy. Courts began deciding issues that affected every area of corrections, including major programming and day-to-day activities such as the number of hot meals that had to be served to prisoners and the amount of recreation time that must be provided.

Corrections prior to the 1960s, operating without significant influence from outside forces, was clearly a closed system.[1] The influence of social change, however—including the major effects of demography, social consciousness, gang activity, unemployment, and many other factors—forced corrections to become an open system. Corrections today is greatly influenced by its external social environment.

The internal social environment of the organization is also important. Research has indicated that the social environment of the organization is important to the mental health of the employee (Repetti, 1987). More specifically, the relationships that individuals have with supervisory personnel and with those within their immediate work groups can have significant and profound effects on their work performance, satisfaction, and personal mental and physical health. Therefore, corrections organizations have found it increasingly important to develop professional standards and ethics that provide an organizational environment conducive to effectiveness, efficiency, and employee morale. The complex, dynamic environment with ill-defined goals and procedures that is characteristic of many correctional organizations makes the social environment a critical factor.

THE POLITICAL ENVIRONMENT

Public administration, including correctional administration, is a value-laden practice. Administrators are often caught in the middle between elected officials who desire different things from agencies. Executive officers and legislative bodies frequently have different goals and different interpretations of laws (Cayer & Weschler, 1988). The public interest often is determined by persons outside agencies, by public officials, and by interest groups that have influence on agencies. The administration of a correctional agency must balance the competing interests, promote legitimate policies of appropriate processes, and cultivate outside support for the agency.

Since the 1960s, corrections officials have experienced rapid role change as a result of political interests. Politicians, traditionally content to leave corrections alone, began using crime, criminal justice, and corrections as mainstays in their attempts to win elections. Laws were passed, beginning in the late 1970s, that made prison terms mandatory for many offenses. Sentence lengths were increased in response to an infuriated public that became very conservative with regard to almost all social issues. Legislatures frequently passed laws without providing funds to meet the additional mandates; prisons became severely overcrowded and other correctional programs—such as probation and parole—were expanded. Officials who were accustomed to the daily management of a relatively stable environment found that the old methods no longer worked. The often chaotic environment that evolved in the late 1970s and the 1980s now forces correctional administrators to function in a dynamic and ambiguous environment.

The financial difficulties that arose during the 1980s, especially in the oil-dependent states, forced corrections to compete with other public services for scarce funds. At the same time that funding was becoming more difficult, the effects of crowding exerted pressure to increase budgets for building and other expenditures. Competition among public agencies for decreasing funds has forced politicians to prioritize services. The results have included some retrenchment among correctional programs or, at the very least, reduced growth rates and delays in needed changes. Paradoxically, longer sentences and mandatory sentences have, in many cases, resulted in inmates serving shorter sentences as correctional systems are forced to release inmates early to accommodate the huge influx of prisoners.

Corrections clearly is responsive to its political environment and to politicians. Many agency heads—approximately 80% (Cerrato, 1984)—are appointed by governors. All agencies must compete with other deserving public agencies for limited funds. Brudney and Hebert (1987) found that both governors (the executive branch) and legislatures (the legislative branch) had significant influence on state criminal justice agencies. However, one study indicates that governors do not exert sufficient power and influence in corrections (Abney & Lauth, 1983). Baro (1988) states that "top administrators perceive legislators as having more impact and more influence on their agencies than do their governors" (p. 468). Political solutions often are short-term and shortsighted, because politicians seek immediate resolutions to problems and their time horizons are very short; they want solutions that appear to be tough, are highly observable, get quick results, and will enhance their probability of being reelected.

THE BUREAUCRATIC ENVIRONMENT

Bureaucracy is a method of organizing in which routines are established and contingencies are clearly defined in advance. It is characterized by: (1) a hierarchy of offices; (2) a clearly defined systematic division of labor; (3) formal written rules of conduct and procedure that are applied uniformly; (4) impersonality in performance of duties; and

(5) neutral competence as the criterion for professional advancement (Nigro & Nigro, 1984). Professions have typically avoided the bureaucratic form of organization as much as possible because it tends to reduce creativity and not allow for variation among cases. The independent nature of corrections programs, however, has been eroded by court decisions, legislative mandates, and administrative expediency. Courts increasingly have ruled that procedures and operations must be standardized; all inmates must be treated equally and given the protection of due-process standards. The effect has been that agencies have become increasingly bureaucratized at the same time that they have become more professionalized.

"In the field of criminal justice, theorists have identified bureaucracy as the 'single most important variable in determining the actual day to day functioning of the legal system' (Chambliss & Seidman, 1971, p. 468)" (Rosecrance, 1987, p. 138). Professionals have been forced to find ways to practice their particular professions in the correctional environment and to comply with the requirements of bureaucracy; this has required change on the part of both the agencies and the professionals. Power bases[2] have been displaced (Rosecrance, 1987) and new power relationships have evolved. Bureaucratization has resulted in a decrease in the power to coerce and reward (Hepburn, 1985). Expert power has increased as the organizations have become more complex and as an increasing number of experts are entering corrections organizations. Legitimate power—that which is inherent in the position—and referent power have remained fairly stable. Wicks (1980) says that as the courts have forced better conditions in corrections, the informal power of correctional officers has been lost.

The bureaucratic form of organization has been identified as a most important factor in employee burnout. Brown (1987) states that

> one final area of role conflict is the professional–bureaucratic conflict. This may occur at the beginning of the new employee's career when he faces the reality of working within the confines of a bureaucratic organization that does not allow the freedom of operation that the idealistic employee envisioned. It can also occur later in the career when the employee has developed a sense of professionalism that conflicts with the constraints of the organization. Poole and Regoli (1983) noted that "one consistent finding is that as an organization's members become more professional, the likelihood that they will encounter role conflict, work alienation, anomie and the like increases." (p. 20)

Hummel (1987) identifies bureaucracy as the antithesis of effectiveness. He suggests that the bureaucratic form of organization is opposed to the fundamental nature of man. Bureaucracy causes employees to become uncaring individuals who deal with people as cases rather than as individuals with unique problems. These antagonistic relationships among the organization, the employees, and the clients create an unhealthy environment that functions inefficiently. Hummel makes several arguments that accurately define the nature of bureaucracy; however, there are many theorists who argue that bureaucracy can be efficient, does not need to be alienating, and that "professionals working in organizations are not, by definition, confronted with situations which reduce the level of professionalization" (Hall, 1968, p. 97).

Professional organizations frequently violate the principles of bureaucracy. Responsiveness to both positional authority and expert authority sometimes results in serving two masters (a violation of the unity of command principle). Individuals may be forced to choose between the two sources of authority and, as a result, become cynical. They may also become critical of the organization, ignore important bureaucratic details, and experience the stress of being caught in the middle. Rizzo, House, and Leitzman (1970) found that this type of environment contributed to employee attrition. However, Bartol (1979), like Hall (1968), challenges the idea of inherent conflict between professionals and organizations. Bartol's study found no relationship between role stress or turnover and professionalization. Rainey and Backoff (1982) suggest that there actually may be compatibility between professionalism and bureaucracy because bureaucracy emphasizes values, such as technical qualification of personnel, that are consistent with professional values. When professionals dominate the organization, there is even less conflict.

THE INSTITUTIONAL ENVIRONMENT

Prisons have always had internal problems with inmates and employees. Escapes, riots, inmate violence, theft, and other problems are endemic to any population such as that housed in prisons. However, prior to the 1960s, prisons were surprisingly predictable places. Highly regimented and controlled behavior kept the institutional environment relatively safe, predictable, and unambiguous.

The changes occurring since the 1960s have caused prison environments to change quite dramatically. Overcrowding, health problems (such as the Acquired Immune Deficiency Syndrome, or AIDS), drugs, violence among inmates, and the implementation of various treatment programs have served to decrease the stability and predictability of inmate populations. Institutions are becoming less predictable, less controlled, and much more complex in the 1990s than ever before.

Prisons can be categorized in several ways. Perhaps the most meaningful, for our purposes, is the minimum, medium, and maximum security classification. Minimum security institutions are characterized by campus-like atmospheres with relatively free movement of residents. Medium security institutions may or may not have perimeter fences—if they do, the fences are usually low and unimposing. Medium security institutions are not as regimented as maximum security institutions, but are more regimented than minimum security institutions. Maximum security institutions are the imposing facilities of television and movie fame; they are highly regimented facilities with wide arrays of security hardware. External fences are usually made of chain-link fencing and concertina (razor) wire and may include electronic monitoring and detection devices. Almost all maximum security facilities have external guard towers manned by guards with weapons.

Twenty-five percent of all prisons in the United States are maximum security, 39% are medium security, and 35% are minimum security (Bureau of Justice Statistics, 1988c). Of all inmates, 33% are housed in maximum security, 45% are housed in medium security, and 22% are held in minimum security institutions (Bureau of Justice Statistics, 1988c). Excessive overcrowding in most prison systems has, to a degree at least, reduced the importance of this categorization; inmates are now placed in the institutions that have space, with less emphasis attached to security levels. "Life in these prisons [all prisons] is very painful. On that score at least, prisons vary in degree, not kind" (Johnson, 1987, p. ix). The role of the correctional officer is, to a great extent, determined by the institution, its management, its policies and procedures, and its goals. Some correctional officers may function in unidimensional roles while others function in multidimensional roles. The varying roles that correctional officers must assume can cause confusion, apathy, and cynicism (Wicks, 1980) unless they have a thorough understanding of the institutions and the roles that they must assume.

Adjustment to prison life is problematic for many inmates. The social structure of the inmate populations of institutions is unique in many ways; a hierarchy evolves and unwritten rules of conduct govern inmate relationships with each other and with prison staff. Scarce resources create an exaggerated value system for desired items. Homosexual behavior is practiced by many inmates who do not view themselves as homosexual and who do not engage in homosexual behavior when a partner of the opposite sex is available. Extortion, lying, cheating, and stealing are, unfortunately, all part of institutional environments. "Violence is a tragic part of life behind bars . . . [and it differs in that it] is more prevalent and serious than that of the outside city counterpart" (McDougall, 1985, p. vii).

Most institutions strive to create routines whereby inmates are accounted for continuously and are, at all times, in the places to which they are assigned. Little latitude is available for personal choices of the inmates. Prison architecture is unique in that it allows maximum observation, but minimal movement without strenuous controls. Institutional design has changed since the 1960s, newer and renovated institutions are more open, are smaller facilities, and allow more space of all kinds for the inmate inhabitants.

There is an element of danger associated with working inside an institution. Lombardo (1981) found, in his study of New York correctional officers, that 50% identified physical danger and mental strain as a dissatisfying feature of their employment. Assaults on officers have increased since the 1960s: "When weapon and nonweapon assaults are included, a rough estimate is that 5 to 10 percent of all prison assaults are against staff members" (Hawkins & Alpert, 1989, p. 343). Between 1976 and 1987, there were 116 corrections-related deaths (Travisono, 1987b). From 1977 through 1986, there were 1,498 police officers killed (Bureau of the Census, 1988).

The institutional environment can have negative effects on employees. Perceived loss of control, a feeling of helplessness, and cynicism created by dealing with people in environments of conflict can have both short-term and long-term effects on individuals. (See Chapters 3 and 8 for more regarding the influence of corrections on the employees.)

THE COMMUNITY ENVIRONMENT

The political awareness and activism that began in the late 1970s have resulted in a more vocal public rejecting earlier correctional

methods. The community environment, never truly accepting of corrections programs, has caused legislatures to pass laws resulting in much
larger prison populations. Many community corrections programs have
been expanded in the past decade, not necessarily because the public
wanted it or liked it, but because the system simply could not hold the
prisoners who were being committed.

Community corrections programs, such as probation and parole, are
much cheaper than institutionalization. Many convicted persons do not
need the secure environment of a prison and, in some cases, imprisonment actually does more harm than good. Probation and parole impose
restrictions upon those committed to the processes; they are required to
meet specific guidelines regarding employment and personal behavior,
frequently have curfews imposed, and may face other sanctions such as
limited incarceration and restitution. Probation is more cost-effective
and has far less recidivism than does prison. The difference in recidivism, however, should not necessarily be interpreted to mean that
probation is more effective than prison. The process of selection is such
that only the good risks get probation; by definition, those who go to
prison are failures and are the poor risks.

Another difficulty encountered as a result of community consciousness is that of placing new prisons. The unprecedented amount of
construction that occurred in the 1980s (and continues into the 1990s)
is caused by public insistence upon lengthy prison terms for almost all
classes of offenders. However, communities generally object when
states suggest building prisons in their neighborhoods. Judges have
ruled, in some cases, that new facilities must be located within specified
distances of major metropolitan areas—the areas where community
rejection is highest. The economic difficulties encountered in many
states in the 1980s made communities more willing to accept prison
construction in their neighborhood. In fact, many communities now
actively seek the location of prisons as growth industries and for their
contribution to local economies.

THE LEGAL ENVIRONMENT

Prior to the mid-1960s correctional administrators could perform
almost any function with anonymity and immunity, and without concern
about courts. The civil rights movements in the 1960s had the effect of

extending the rule of law to prisons and to broad-based control over almost all phases of correctional activities. "Federal court decisions enlarged the scope of the prisoner's right of access to the courts and expanded [but did not totally recognize] inmate rights to religious freedom, uncensored mail correspondence, decent medical care, and procedural due process during prison disciplinary hearings" (Haas & Alpert, 1986, p. 207).

These victories for prisoners, however, have now given way to what some legal scholars are calling a "modified hands-off doctrine." Since 1976, the Supreme Court has sanctioned strict limitations on inmate free speech, freedom of association, and the right to sue state prison personnel in federal courts for the alleged deliberate destruction of a prisoner's personal property. The Court has minimized due process protections when prisoners are disciplined or transferred to more punitive facilities, and it has imposed a series of troublesome and time-consuming procedural obstacles to the access of state prisoners to federal courts. (p. 208)

Correctional employees, like employees of courts and of police agencies, must conform to the established law of the United States. Although federal courts may have shown restraint in the last decade regarding prisoner litigation, it is important to realize that corrections employees and officials are still held to a high standard of conduct. Both state and federal law can be used to hold corrections employees liable in civil proceedings and guilty in criminal proceedings. Since the federal courts have held that individuals are responsible not only for what they know but also for what they should have known, it is imperative that corrections employees apply professional standards to all their organizational behavior. Perhaps the single most important legislation affecting corrections professionals and, through them, corrections agencies is Title 42, United States Code, Section 1983. Originally established as the Civil Rights Act of 1871 (the Ku Klux Klan Act), Section 1983 establishes the liability of anyone who, while acting under color of law, infringes upon another's civil rights. Basically, this means that any relationship between an employee and inmate or client is covered by Section 1983.

Over 400 jails in 46 states were involved in litigation in 1988 (Bostick, 1988). Additionally, 35 states had one or more prison institutions under court order (American Correctional Association, 1988). In several states, entire correctional systems have been ruled unconstitutional and are under court order. There was an increase of 2,159% in inmate court filings between 1962 and 1987 (Thomas, 1988a). Mistreatment by correctional officers, abuse of discretion by staff, and failure to implement and follow established policies are major factors contributing to correctional litigation (Thomas, 1988b). The costs to state government have increased significantly as a result of litigation. Capital expenditures increase immediately following a court judgment and correctional expenditure as a percent of the total state budget increases (Straussman, 1986).

Corrections professionals have the added responsibility of effecting change in the law through legitimate means if the law in question is not in the best interests of the public and the correctional client. This change must be conducted in the public forum with adequate consideration for public desires and the professional requirements of correctional practice.

SYSTEM ENVIRONMENT

As a subcomponent of the criminal justice system, corrections is greatly affected by the other components. Corrections agencies have no choice of who is committed to their care and little or no influence regarding when individuals are released. The population size is dependent upon the number of criminals caught by the police, the number convicted and committed to the agency by the court, and the length of sentence imposed upon those who are committed. Release dates are frequently determined by parole boards which function under broad guidelines established by legislatures. Dates of release may be affected by such things as good time, the particular crime for which the inmate is committed, parole eligibility formulas, overcrowding in institutions, and other factors.

The criminal justice system is actually a loosely coupled system in that each subcomponent functions largely independent of the other subcomponents. All, however, are dependent upon each other (except for the police) for clients. The actions that each subcomponent takes regarding disposition of clients greatly affects the other subcomponents. The strong interrelationships require that agencies coordinate activity in order that each can plan to accommodate increased or decreased workloads and changed conditions. The amount of actual coordination that exists is minimal—almost accidental.

SUMMARY

For better or worse, the closed-system nature of corrections has changed forever. Correctional agencies could, prior to the 1960s, function largely as they desired with little or no influence from external sources. Politicians and the public were content to leave agency activity to the administrators. However, with the radical changes that began in the 1960s and which related to every area of society, that autonomy was lost. Social reformers, professionals from other areas, the courts, and the public became very concerned about what happened in America's correctional agencies. Inmates, once considered to have no rights, were granted many rights as a result of new laws, reinterpretation of old laws, and new policies and procedures specified by courts.

These changes have been a primary force behind the professionalization of corrections. The complexity of the system and its processes has increased and the scope of correctional responsibility has been redefined. Today correctional administrators must be responsive to many external pressures including politicians, courts, reform groups, and the public in general. Corrections must function as a part of the larger system of criminal justice; it is significantly influenced by the actions of courts and police. In addition, many internal pressures—such as the institutional environment and dynamics and the bureaucratic nature of the organizations—have changed the nature of corrections processes and organizations.

NOTES

1. A closed system is one that is dependent only upon itself. It functions without consideration for external pressures and requires that those external to the system who wish to conduct business with it must do so as it dictates. Open systems, on the other hand, are significantly influenced by their external environments. They must accommodate pressures from those environments and adjust their operational procedures to accommodate environmental change.

2. There are several types of power. Legitimate power, sometimes referred to as positional power, is power granted to individuals as a result of positions that they hold.

Expert power is power granted to individuals as a result of knowledge that they have. Referent power is power granted to individuals as a result of their associations with individuals or with entities that have influence over the person(s) granting the power. All power, no matter what specific type it may be called, refers to the ability to cause others to act.

3

Understanding Human Behavior

Corrections, in both institutions and communities, is human service work. As such, it is incumbent upon those charged with controlling human behavior to have an understanding of human nature. Stevenson (1987) identifies seven basic theories (or views) of human nature: (1) Plato's philosopher-kings and the rule of the wise; (2) Christianity; (3) Marxism; (4) Freud's psychoanalysis; (5) Sartre's atheistic existentialism; (6) Skinner's behaviorism; and (7) Lorenz's innate aggression. Each of these views of man's nature significantly influences the theories developed to describe man's behavior. A theory is simply a set of logical statements that, combined, explains some phenomena—in this case, criminal behavior. A valid scientific theory must—among other things—be based on factual evidence, be testable, and suggest some way of altering the phenomena that it describes. Many popular notions of criminal behavior do not meet these standards.

We all subscribe to theories of behavior, whether we recognize them or not. Human service workers must carefully analyze their beliefs and formulate sound perceptions. To do so provides direction to professional behavior and allows proper decision making in new and ambiguous situations. It also strengthens the ability to predict behavior and provides personal knowledge to combat burnout and cynicism.

It makes no difference what purpose is attributed to corrections. The ultimate goals are to control immediate behavior, change long-term behavior patterns (see Chapter 6) to be more conforming, and, at the very least, to make inmates or clients no worse during their incarceration or supervision. The accomplishment of these goals requires a true understanding of human behavior, not an ideological perception based on uninformed notions. We do not create our own reality, we must recognize it and deal with it as we find it. Merely believing or wishing something to be true does not make it true. Therefore, objectivity and understanding of the scientific method are prerequisite to understanding and changing human behavior effectively. Professional behavior and orientation require that one adopt a rational approach to understanding human behavior, which means among other things that one must be objective and accept the scientific method as the primary means of understanding. The scientific method is merely a way of studying phenomena that seeks "proofs" based on measurable characteristics and elements. Professionals must be willing to change their beliefs when they are shown to be wrong.

Human service professionals work in environments where human beings are in unpleasant and negative situations. For example, health care professionals deal with individuals who are ill or may be dying. Welfare workers deal with individuals who are economically and otherwise deprived, mistreated, or abused. Correctional workers work with individuals who are being held against their will in negative and unpleasant environments. All human service workers experience problems at one time or another in dealing with the unfortunate circumstances of their clients. Although the professional's role is a helping one, the constant exposure to unfortunate human beings can cause a person to become cynical, cold, and unemotional, or to develop other negative symptoms associated with such work. Inmates and clients who are committed to prison or community supervision are, as a group, a population that exhibits unpredictable, violent, or otherwise negative behavior. Corrections employees witness and deal with a wide range of maladaptive behaviors. Therefore, it is important that the individual have a basic understanding of human behavior in general and inmate/client behavior in particular.

This chapter addresses the nature of human service work and its effects upon those who work in human service professions. It also identifies the basic theoretical explanations of criminal behavior. Finally, it identifies and discusses some of the more prevalent maladaptive behaviors that correctional employees can expect to encounter.

THE HUMAN SERVICE PROFESSIONS

Human service occupations and professions exact a toll on those who work in them. Doctors, social workers, correctional employees, and other human service workers deal with individuals who are in unfortunate circumstances. In the case of correctional workers, the service of the professional is usually an unwanted intrusion in the life of the client. Therefore, hostility and open rejection of professionals and their work is not uncommon. Corrections professionals who understand human behavior—and, more specifically, inmate/client behavior—are better prepared to function normally and with minimal negative influences on their personal lives.

Those who work with people have many more problems than do those who work with objects (Farmer, 1977; Goffman, 1961). "As many as sixty-four percent of caseworkers in child welfare experience stress-related health problems" (Cournoyer, 1988, p. 259, referring to Lawton & Magarelli, 1980). There are several reasons for this, including a lack of clear criteria for measuring success (Edelwich & Brodsky, 1983; Ratliff, 1988) and a lack of a sense of accomplishment (Cherniss & Egnatios, 1978; Ratliff, 1988). (See Chapter 8 for more on stress.) Corrections officers in particular are required to establish authoritarian positions over others; there is danger, fear, and isolation associated with the profession (Skolnick, 1966). Order in a correctional institution frequently is based on informal and unofficial reciprocity of inmates and officers, rather than force (Sykes, 1958). In addition to working with involuntary clients, the correctional officer also experiences role ambiguity (e.g., Manning, 1983) and contradictory role demands (e.g., McCabe, 1986). The conflict between the correctional goals of security and rehabilitation, relationships with management, and relationships with other workers can cause cynicism in corrections employees (Farmer, 1977).

Many officers endorse the rehabilitation goals of institutions and agencies (Jacobs, 1978; Johnson & Price, 1981; Teske & Williamson, 1979). They also view inmates as human and react to them in humane ways. Human relations training and orientation is critical to the personal well-being of the officer:

Prisons are less total and primitive than they once were. And basic officer training, even of the most stripped-down variety, features some human relations components and the assumption that custody over human beings requires at least a modicum of tact, sensitivity, and awareness of the pressures that circumscribe and stunt the lives and hopes of prisoners. (Johnson & Price, 1981, p. 350)

The stress that is inherent in correctional positions must be dealt with positively if it is to not have negative consequences for the professional. Chapter 8 deals with interpersonal relationships in correctional environments and discusses the management of related stress.

BASIC EXPLANATIONS OF HUMAN BEHAVIOR

There are numerous theories that attempt to explain human behavior. Each is successful in explaining some behavior but none will explain all human behavior under all circumstances. The various explanations of behavior should be used if appropriate, but must not be used where it is obvious that they do not apply. The three basic categories of explanations are biological, sociological, and psychological. This section will describe these categories briefly.

Criminological theories should be the foundation of criminal justice and correctional policies. "The traditional view is that policies are derived from theories, while theories are based on empirical research to discover facts. It appears that, more often than not, this sequence is reversed in criminology" (Vold & Bernard, 1986, p. 356). Individuals frequently adhere to particular theoretical explanations because they are consistent with their preferred crime policies.

There are many ways to classify human behavior. As a result, there are many different types and categories of explanations. The two basic schools of criminology are the *classical* and the *positivist* schools. The classicists basically believe, among other things, that individuals are responsible for their own behavior. There are few, if any, extenuating circumstances that would absolve one from absolute and total responsibility for committing a crime. Even children as young as age 7 were initially held totally responsible for wrongful acts. The positivists, on the other hand, believe that individuals are responsible for their behavior to an extent; however, the conditions and circumstances of their lives combine to create predispositions to certain types of behavior. The positivists place some of the blame for criminal behavior on society. It is important to note that neither classicists nor positivists believe that crime should be allowed to occur; they differ primarily in their approaches to the resolution of the crime problem. Classicists hold individuals totally responsible and punish them. Positivists hold individuals responsible for having made a wrong choice and provide treatment to improve their chances of not committing criminal behavior in the future.

The biological, psychological, and sociological explanations of crime addressed in this chapter are largely positivist in orientation. The distinctions between the classicist and positivist schools as discussed above have become somewhat blurred as newer perceptions of human nature have emerged. The *new classicists* of today often combine elements of both the classical and positivist schools to arrive at a positivist explanation, with responses containing both positive and classical elements.

Biological

Biological theories place the cause of behavior in the biological makeup of the individual. Chemical imbalances in the body or genetic abnormalities are used to explain criminal and other abnormal behavior. There is little doubt that the biological explanation is satisfactory in some cases. Tumors, endocrine imbalances, and other biological problems may cause abnormal behavior in anyone, criminal or noncriminal. Such abnormal behavior may or may not be dangerous or criminal in nature.

The first major theorist proposing a biological explanation of crime was Cesare Lombroso, an Italian physician, who proposed that many criminals were indeed "born criminals" in the sense that they were throwbacks to a lesser evolved man. In fairness, Lombroso's explanation also considered sociological factors and was much more complex than indicated above. Recent research efforts seeking biological or genetic explanations of crime involve studies of twins and the XYY syndrome. The twin studies take as their premise that, if two individuals are genetically alike but reared in different environments, any differences in their behavior would signify social causes. Likewise, similarities of behavior would signify biological or genetic causes. Although some studies support the genetic explanation, they are not strong enough to be accepted as valid explanations of most criminal behavior.

The XYY studies concentrate on the genetic structure. A normal male contains one chromosome contributed by the female—an X chromosome—and one contributed by the male—a Y chromosome. During fertilization there can be aberrations of chromosomal contributions—XXY and XYY. The XYY male is one whose genetic structure contains one female chromosome (the X) and two male chromosomes (the Y chromosomes). These individuals usually exhibit physical characteristics that set them apart from normal males. They are frequently quite tall, but are not "supermales" in the sense of being extremely masculine. There is a higher incidence of XYY males in prison than there is in the free population. Scientists, however, have discounted the XYY as a causative factor in crime and have explained the excessive presence of such males in prison populations as being related to their physical characteristics, which usually make them easily identifiable and easier to apprehend.

Psychological

Psychological theories explain human behavior in terms of imbalances in thought processes. They seek to explain abnormal behavior as a function of neuroses, psychoses, personality disorders, retardation, or learning disabilities. Neuroses are unrealistic fears or unusual behavior that, unless extreme in nature, seldom create serious problems for the individual or for society. When the neuroses become extreme, however, they can cause undesirable behavior.

Psychoses are much more serious psychological illnesses that can seriously incapacitate the individual and cause strange—and sometimes bizarre—behavior. These individuals are those that are out of touch with reality. They hear, see, feel, and believe things that can be totally outrageous and unreal; the consequences of their behavior can be very damaging. Organic psychoses are those mental disturbances that are induced as a result of chemical imbalances or actual damage to the brain or other parts of the nervous system—for example, brain tumors. Functional psychoses are those that are real in their effects but have no identifiable organic causes. The result may be behavior equally as abnormal as that manifested by the organic psychosis patient, but the treatment is generally much more difficult. In the case of organic psychoses, the organic cause can frequently be removed or treated by physicians or psychiatrists. In the case of functional psychoses, however, the cause cannot be determined, and only the symptoms may be treated through the use of drugs and other therapy.

The individual who has had perhaps the most influence in the area of psychological explanations of crime is Sigmund Freud. He and those who followed him placed great emphasis upon elements of personality as primary factors in explaining deviant behavior. "According to such theories, crime is a form of substitute behavior which compensates for abnormal urges and desires. . . . Psychological explanations of criminality have, however, played a major role in criminal justice policy during the twentieth century. Correctional policies emphasizing rehabilitation have been largely based on the the belief that personality is linked to behavior" (Cole, 1989, pp. 48-49).

Sociological

Sociological explanations of human behavior seek the causes of behavior in the structure and the processes of society. These theories usually maintain that human behavior is learned or caused through some process(es) or event(s) that occurred during the socialization of the individual. Factors such as family background, education level, religious affiliation, marital status, socioeconomic status, race, and other more sophisticated and abstract social measurements are used to explain behavior patterns.

> Sociological explanations of criminality emphasize that offenders are molded by societal forces, not born. Among the several theories that have arisen from this foundation, three deserve special mention: social structure theory, social process theory, and social conflict theory. (Cole, 1989, p. 49)

Social structure theory places the source of crime in the social structure itself. The stratified nature of society is such that some cannot obtain the benefits of society. Those without wealth, power, and status are economically and educationally deprived, live in poor housing areas, have only the basics of life, and are unable to influence governmental agencies. The lifestyle practiced by the lower class contributes to criminal behavior. Opportunity and capability of achievement are differential in society; those who are frustrated and denied opportunity may turn to criminal behavior. Society does not always provide clear and convincing guidelines for behavior, which may result in some members of society feeling free to commit criminal behavior. Rapid social change basic to the structure of society can cause conditions wherein the norms that regulate behavior are weakened (e.g., the sexual revolution of the 1960s and drug use of the 1980s) and more members of society participate in previously avoided behavior.

Social process theories concentrate on the processes of socialization. We all have the capability of becoming criminal, and these theories claim that the circumstances of life are the primary determining factor. There are three basic types of social process theories: (1) social learning theories; (2) social control theories; and (3) labeling theories. Learning theories argue that most behavior—both criminal and noncriminal—is learned. The actual process of learning is explained in different ways by different theories. Learning may take place under a variety of conditions, in a number of places, and from numerous sources. The common elements of most theories are that all persons learn how to commit crime and how to rationalize criminal behavior. Some, when faced with circumstances which for them are serious, will commit criminal behavior. Social control theories concentrate on the institutions of society that instill a basic desire to avoid criminal behavior. Churches, peer groups, and schools, as well as individuals, all act to instill in each individual control mechanisms which, if appropriate, will keep the person from committing crime. If these influences are inappropriate and the control mechanisms are not instilled, the individual is likely to commit criminal behavior. Social labeling theories concentrate on the processes by which individuals are labeled as criminal. The basic idea is that if one is treated as capable of committing criminal behavior, or in a discriminatory or stigmatizing way, that the individual is more likely to commit the criminal acts or other deviant behavior. Labeling places the responsibility for criminal behavior both with the individual and the social processes through which the person is labeled criminal.

Social conflict theory explains crime as a consequence of competing power groups in society. Some theories, such as Marxist theory, are radical and propose that the only way to eliminate crime is to eliminate the capitalist economy. The radical theorists see criminal law as a means by which the powerful elite controls the poor.

INMATE/CLIENT BEHAVIOR

Inmates in prisons and, to a lesser extent, individuals under supervision in the community manifest a broad range of behavior with a higher frequency of abnormal behavior than that found in normal populations.[1] It has been estimated by some that approximately 20% of those in prison suffer from mental illnesses—including, psychosis, neurosis, and psychopathology (Bromberg, 1961; Lillyquist, 1980). Wilson (1980) estimates that the number of prisoners with serious mental disorders range from 20% to 35%. Bentz and Noel (1983) found that 32% of those admitted to prison had psychiatric disorders, and an additional 43% showed mild to moderate symptoms of such disorders. This is not to suggest that criminals are necessarily more abnormal than the general population; it may merely indicate that there is a greater likelihood for persons who manifest this type of behavior to be under correctional supervision than there is for those who do not exhibit abnormal behavior. The range of behavior encountered in correctional environments includes normal behavior (which is most common), behavior resulting from problems of adjustment, behavior resulting from personality disorders, behavior resulting from mental illness, and behavior resulting from mental retardation. In addition, many clients under correctional supervision exhibit abnormal sexual behavior and are prone to suicidal behavior. Other abnormal behavior may be caused by substance abuse and certain biological illnesses.

Because of changes in mental health laws, increasing numbers of individuals with psychological problems are being lodged in our nation's jails rather than being treated in mental hospitals (Whitmer, 1980). In a study of 486 admissions to the Philadelphia prisons, two thirds of the subjects were identifiable as psychiatrically disturbed and in need of specific mental health treatment services; 34 percent were identifiable by all indicators of psychopathology; 11 percent needed immediate inpatient psychiatric care. (Guy, Platt, Zwerling, and Bullock, 1985; Kennedy & Homant, 1988, p. 442)

Jail and prison populations are unique in many ways. Allen and Simonsen (1986) describe the jail population as follows: 43% were serving sentences, while 57% were pre-trial detainees. One-fourth had been denied bail. Ninety-three percent were male, 41% were nonwhite,

50% were 19 to 29 years of age, 70% were under age 30, and 43% were unemployed. Those with an income during the year preceding their arrest averaged $3,255 per year. Thirty percent were charged with violent offenses, 41% with property offenses, 9% with drug offenses, and 20% with other crimes.

Allen and Simonsen (1986) also describe the following characteristics of prison populations: 57% had committed crimes against people; 43% had committed property crimes. Ninety-five percent were male. Most were undereducated (one-half never finished high school), unemployed, poor, had no skills, came from broken homes, and were drug and alcohol abusers. Many had medical and psychological problems. Between 15% and 25% were considered dangerous. Fifty percent had been drinking at the time of their offenses; 33% were under the influence of drugs. Sixty percent earned less than $6,000 during the year preceding their arrest.

Beck, Kline, and Greenfeld (1988) indicate that 40% of the juveniles held in state-operated institutions were being held for violent offenses. Forty percent were under the influence of drugs when they committed their offenses, and 60% used drugs regularly. "More than half . . . reported that a family member had been incarcerated at some time in the past" (p. 1). Incarcerated juveniles were mostly male (93.1%), had come from one-parent families (54%), had been on probation before (82.2%), had been in institutions before (58.5%), and had prior use of drugs (80%). Whites represented 53.1 % of the population; blacks, 41.1%; and other races, 5.7%. Many had been arrested more than five times (43%) and some had been arrested more than 10 times (20%). The single largest crime category for the current admission was property offenses (45.6%) followed by violent offenses (39.3%), public order offenses (7.2%), drug offenses (5.6%), and status offenses (2%).[2]

Normal Behavior

Imprisonment involves the loss of many freedoms. The pains of imprisonment include the loss of status, the deprivation of sexual satisfaction, deprivation of material gain and status, and other losses (e.g., Johnson & Toch, 1982; Sykes, 1958). Inmates have real concerns regarding privacy, structure, support, safety, emotional feedback, activity, freedom, and autonomy (Toch, 1977). Imprisonment also involves a process that sociologists refer to as *prisonization* or *institutionalization* (Clemmer, 1958). Inmates become indoctrinated in the rules of conduct required by the institution and the informal, but strong, rules of conduct required by the inmate society. This is a constant source of stress and strain for those in an atmosphere of deprivation, ruthlessness, and regimentation. Fortunately, most inmates adapt to the demands of the institution and continue to exhibit acceptable behavior.

Adjustment Problems

Many inmates, including those who are normal in every way, experience temporary adjustment problems when committed to an institution. The rules, regulations, procedures, routines, and inmate society can cause great concern on the part of some inmates. These adjustment problems usually are not serious and do not last very long. During the time required for adjustment, however, the inmate may experience considerable anxiety and exhibit minor maladaptive behavior such as withdrawing from others, inability to concentrate, minor depression, or rule-breaking, and other behavior that detracts from the ability to get along in the regimented institution. "Inmates who have continual emotional difficulty adjusting to prison can create serious custodial problems" (Adams, 1985a, p. 33).

Inmates may have difficulty getting along with other inmates. Acts of violence and other conflicts are not uncommon in prisons (Adams, 1985b; MacKenzie, 1987). Interpersonal conflict with others may create problems at any age; MacKenzie (1987), however, suggests that younger offenders usually have more conflicts with other inmates than do older offenders. She also found an inverse relationship between age and aggressive behavior (younger inmates exhibited more aggressive behavior than did older inmates). MacKenzie (1987) suggests that the expression of anger may differ over the lifespan of the individual, and that fear of others and fear of being victimized contribute to conflicts with both guards and inmates:

> At any age, increased anxiety was accompanied by increased conflicts with guards. . . . Only for those under thirty was increased anxiety accompanied by increased conflicts with other inmates. (p. 442)

Personality Disorders

The individuals in this category are not out of touch with reality in the classical sense. In fact, many of these individuals—especially antisocial personalities (psychopaths or sociopaths)—are normal in most ways, except that they do not care about others. They do know right from wrong, but they choose to commit unacceptable behavior anyway. The major categories of personality disorders include: (1) antisocial personalities; (2) personality pattern disturbances; and (3) personality trait disturbances (American Correctional Association, 1983).

Antisocial personalities have been called sociopaths and psychopaths at different times and by different people; all three labels mean the same thing. The existence of this type is rare in its pure form. Fox (1985) estimates that 20% of the inmate population are psychopathic; however, Mobley (1986) indicates that 30% to 50% of the overall inmate population manifest some symptoms of antisocial personalities. Therefore, correctional officers can expect to encounter these individuals. Antisocial personalities typically have long histories of conflict with moral codes and with the legal establishment. They frequently are unable to postpone gratification and, instead, live for the moment. They may be very intelligent, be good planners, communicate very well, and—at first glance—be very likable individuals. Their instability and inability to adjust to routine expectations of normal life, however, make them capable of dangerous acting-out behavior at any moment. These persons are sometimes pathological liars and are capable of manipulating others. They are frequently very clever actors who can convince others of their sincerity.

Treatment for antisocial personalities is not very effective. The defect in personality that causes these people to be the way they are is not readily nor easily understood by psychologists and psychiatrists. There is some evidence, however, that maturity alone (that is, age) tends to reduce the prevalence of acting-out behavior among antisocial personalities. It may be that they merely tire of being in opposition to the mainstream population at all times. Whatever the cause and whatever the cure, correctional officers must be constantly alert when dealing with this type of individual.

Another disorder is that of personality pattern disturbances. "Some of the types of Personality Pattern disturbances encountered in correctional work are the inadequate personality, schizoid personality, cyclothymic personality, and paranoid personality" (American Correctional

Association, 1983). Inadequate personalities are apparently normal except that they are unable to cope with their environments and frequently lack self-esteem appropriate to normal functioning. They may readily accept the routine of institutional life, because it makes no demands on them as responsible and independent adults. Cyclothymic personalities include those who show periods of depression and of exaggerated well-being (manic-depressives). The schizoid personality is frequently aloof and avoids contact with others, preferring instead to be a loner. Paranoid personalities are characterized by exaggerated suspicion of everything and everyone; they believe others are after them, and can be hostile, vindictive, and dangerous. In prison, paranoid inmates frequently are troublemakers (American Correctional Association, 1983).

The two personality trait disturbances most prevalent in prisons are the emotionally unstable and passive-aggressive personalities (American Correctional Association, 1983). Emotionally unstable persons panic easily, have poor judgment, may anger easily, and may exhibit explosive behavior; they rarely develop close relationships with others because of their unpredictiveness. Passive-aggressive personalities consist of three types: (1) passive-dependent; (2) passive-aggressive; and (3) aggressive. A passive-dependent individual cannot make decisions, is frequently helpless, acts like a child, and "clings to institutions, agencies or individuals for emotional support and decision making" (American Correctional Association, 1983, p. 88). Passive-aggressive individuals cannot express hostility directly; they choose, instead, to express hostility indirectly by manipulating others, refusing to work, completing assignments reluctantly, and so forth. The aggressive type lacks control, and may explode and attack physically or choose to ridicule others overtly. An aggressive inmate is generally prone to emotional outbreaks of irrational behavior.

Mental Illness

Mental illness includes two basic types: neuroses and psychoses. Neuroses are milder forms of mental illness where "the person is in contact with the real world but extreme anxiety usually interferes with an ability to deal effectively with it" (American Correctional Association, 1983, p. 88). The primary symptoms of neuroses are vague feelings of unease, anxiety, or phobias that can interfere with the ability to

carry out normal daily behavior. Neurotic individuals may be obses-
sively concerned about aspects of their health or situations. They may
also exhibit compulsive behaviors that are often inappropriate and not
well-thought-out; examples of compulsive behavior are stealing and
setting fires. Neurotics are generally unhappy individuals who can
become depressed and attempt suicide. As a general rule, neurotics are
less likely to commit crimes due to their fears. Crimes of a compulsive
nature, however, are frequently committed by neurotics. "The obses-
sive-compulsive neurotic suffers from an inability to stop himself or
herself from thinking irrational thoughts (obsessions) or performing
irrational acts (compulsions)" (Lillyquist, 1980, p. 73).

Psychoses are generally much more severe mental illnesses involving
a loss of touch with reality. These individuals are those that we think of
in everyday terms as being "crazy" or "on cloud nine." Psychotics may
be totally unable to understand the realities of life and have severe
inability to perceive events or situations accurately. Many have great
difficulty in remembering events, rules, or anything else. Organic psychosis is induced by biological problems or chemical imbalances in the
body; an example would be the psychosis induced by some brain
tumors. Treatment of organic psychoses usually involves the removal
of the organic impairment or treatment of the impaired body system or
organ. Surgery and drugs are used to treat organic psychoses, with
varying effects depending upon the type and cause of impairment.
Functional psychoses are those which have no organic base. These
psychoses are very hard to treat, because there is no clearly recognized
cause of the problem. Drugs are frequently used to control the behavior
of functional psychotics.

Psychotics, regardless of the basis of the disease, usually exhibit
behavior that is bizarre and unpredictable. They may also suffer from
delusions—that someone is controlling them, voices are speaking to
them, they are important or grand persons, someone is reading their
minds, and so forth. Emotional reactions are very exaggerated and
distorted. The perceptions of psychotic individuals are inaccurate, and
they can be dangerous to themselves and to others. Those who are
psychotic at the time of trial will likely never go to prison; rather, they
will be committed to a mental institution. Those who become psychotic
in prison or correctional environments, however, can cause difficulties
for the correctional officers. Inmates with histories of psychiatric disorders have higher than average rates of rule-breaking behavior

(Adams, 1983). Psychotics must be isolated immediately and confined to medical care in order to protect them and those with whom they come into contact. Correctional psychiatrists usually commit these individuals to long-term care in mental institutions if the prognosis for control of their psychotic episodes is poor and the necessary treatment periods are long. In many cases, however, drugs such as lithium can control psychotic episodes very effectively.

The literature suggests that 0.3% to 40% of inmate populations are neurotic; 1% to 7% are psychotic (Adams, 1985a; Monahan & Steadman, 1983). When dealing with the mentally ill, it is very important that correctional officers not overreact; they should take note of the inmates' behavior and be especially observant of behavioral changes. To react to a mentally ill inmate as a malingerer can cause further damage to the inmate. When marked behavioral change occurs, an officer should immediately inform appropriate authorities such as physicians, psychiatrists, psychologists, or appropriate security personnel.

The immediate control of mentally ill inmates can be important. It is critical to not do anything to further upset an inmate who is mentally ill. Often, a show of force—not the use of force—is all that is necessary to gain control of a situation. Force should be used only in accordance with institutional policy. The most logical and easiest way to gain immediate control of some mentally ill patients is to take advantage of their illusions. This approach must be used only in those situations where immediate control is necessary; not for treatment of the illness or as a routine interaction pattern with the inmate. An example of this procedure may be telling an inmate who hears "voices" that the voices are actually telling him or her to go to sleep. An example: The author of this text was called to a scene one night where a mentally ill inmate was calling a baseball game in a very loud voice. He was disturbing others and the officer on duty could not get him to be quiet and did not know what to do. The author, upon arriving at the scene, suggested to the inmate that it was raining. The inmate turned immediately, stuck his hand in the commode, flicked water in the air, said "Game called because of rain," laid down and went to sleep. A report was made the following morning to the psychologist. Force, or a show of force, would not have been as effective in gaining immediate control of the situation and in fact may have aggravated the situation. Officers, however, should never "play" with inmates in this manner.

Mental Retardation

It has been estimated that 10% of the prison population is mentally retarded (Brown & Courtless, 1971). A score of 70 or less on a standard IQ test is generally considered to indicate mental retardation. Mentally retarded individuals are *not* mentally ill. Whereas mental illness denotes some type of disordered and distorted malfunctioning of the mind, mental retardation refers to those who have below-average intellectual abilities. Mentally retarded individuals have great difficulty, depending upon the degree of retardation, in learning from experience and being able to cope with everyday life. They are usually not dangerous in the traditional sense; they may, however, as a result of not knowing any better, expose themselves or others to dangers that should be avoided.

Mentally retarded persons are frequently very docile individuals who are very susceptible to suggestions by others. They seek to be liked and accepted. As a result, many inmates will encourage mentally retarded inmates to do things that are against the rules. Officers must protect the mentally retarded from abuse by other inmates and should never make fun of, ridicule, or take advantage of the mentally retarded in any way. The tendency since the 1970s has been to "mainstream" the mentally retarded by placing them with normal populations. Most jurisdictions, however, still separate in some manner those who are grossly retarded. It is important to remember that retarded inmates cannot function and perform as independently as the normal inmate. They can, however, adequately perform tasks that they understand.

Sexual Behavior

Most correctional environments are unisexual. That is, they are either male or female—not both. As a result of the deprivation of normal sexual outlets, many inmates engage in types of sexual behavior that typically they would avoid if they were free citizens. Masturbation is not at all uncommon. Homosexual behavior in prisons is a matter of great importance; it can create serious problems and instigate violence of different types.

Some inmates are homosexual upon entry into prison. For these inmates, the opportunities for consensual homosexual conduct are ever present. There also are inmates who do not define themselves as homosexual, but because of sexual deprivation and the environment they choose to participate in homosexual conduct. Upon release, many of these inmates return to heterosexual relations and do not continue in homosexual relationships. It is not uncommon for individuals in prisons to be homosexually assaulted. Weak, effeminate inmates are easy prey for stronger inmates, who usually approach these individuals by offering protection or similar help. Eventually, they trade their protection for sexual services, and may even prostitute the individual. Homosexual behavior causes violence—including homicide—among inmates; it should be discouraged in all possible ways. Although known homosexuals are segregated from the general inmate population, homosexual behavior still occurs frequently. The prevalence of such activity, and the presence of the AIDS virus, have prompted some states (e.g., Vermont, Mississippi, and New York) to issue condoms to inmates (Baker et al., 1989).

It is important that correctional officers understand that many inmates who are homosexually assaulted will not inform an official; they will have been threatened, and may be in real danger. Therefore, the officer must be constantly alert for behavioral change that may indicate an individual has been assaulted. Many such inmates will become very depressed, withdrawn, and will exhibit uncharacteristic behavior. For example, they may make every effort to remain within the sight of officers, whereas they had not done so in the past. They may attempt suicide or engage in rule-breaking behavior in an effort to cause officials to isolate them from the general inmate population. The alert officer does not always accept inmate behavior on its face value; however, not all unusual behavior is related to sexual assault. Good judgment, patient and alert observation, understanding of human behavior, and knowledge about the inmates under their control are primary characteristics of good correctional officers.

Suicidal Behavior

The age-adjusted suicide rate for the national male population in 1985 (all races) was 18.8 per 100,000 (Bureau of the Census, 1988). Several studies have found the suicide rate to be significantly higher in jails and prisons[3] in both adolescent and adult populations (Kennedy & Homant, 1988). The American Correctional Association (1983) identifies three reasons why suicidal behavior is more prevalent in jails and prisons than in the normal population: First, there is a higher incidence in prisons of those prone to suicidal behavior than there is in the general population. Alcoholics, drug addicts, sex offenders, and antisocial personalities tend to be more suicidal than the normal population. Because there is a high concentration of those individuals in the jail and prison population, a natural consequence would be higher suicide rates. Secondly, the general situation in which offenders find themselves is such that they are more prone to suicide at that time than at other times in their lives. Third, the authoritarian environment of prisons, the dehumanizing aspects of imprisonment, the embarrassment and shame, and isolation from family and friends make incarceration a particularly crucial time for the individual, who may resort to suicide.

It is difficult to create a profile or to specify the type of inmate who may commit suicide. The early period of incarceration is a particularly important period. Inmates who have not yet adjusted to their new situation in life, the prison environment, and the circumstances of their incarceration may be particularly prone to suicidal behavior. Traumatic periods during inmates' incarceration—such as denial of parole, the death of family members, and so forth—may also be events which predispose some to attempt suicide. There usually is a behavioral pattern change—which the alert officer may observe—that will signify the increased likelihood of suicidal behavior. There are many myths regarding suicide; the inmate who speaks of it should be taken seriously, and appropriate treatment officials should be notified immediately. In many instances, those who are at high risk for suicide attempts will be segregated, and all items which could contribute to a suicide attempt will be taken from them. Officers must refrain from any behavior which may prompt an inmate to commit suicide. For example, offering to let an inmate who has threatened suicide use your knife is not a good approach to preventing suicide. Probably the most common method of suicide chosen by inmates is cutting; the second most common method is hanging. Other methods, such as drug overdose, are also used. Officers should watch for any unusual behavior and look for suspicious items in an inmate's possession. In addition, inmates who give away valued possessions should be carefully watched.

Biologically Induced Erratic Behavior

Certain diseases may cause chemical imbalances in the body that trigger erratic behavior. Physical dependence upon alcohol and drugs often creates withdrawal symptoms which may involve physical and mental reactions. Two diseases in particular—epilepsy and diabetes—can cause behavioral change and erratic, irrational behavior. Epilepsy is a disturbance of brain function that can cause convulsions and "fits," loss of motor function and control, loss of awareness, and related psychological problems. The seizures and physical manifestations vary by type and by individual, but in all cases there is some physical or mental dysfunctioning. Individuals with epilepsy may froth at the mouth, convulse, or merely lose their memory of an event and time. It is important to recognize that these individuals may harm themselves during the more violent attacks and may accidentally harm others. Epileptic seizures and the abnormal behavior associated with them are medical problems that should be treated immediately by medical personnel.

Diabetics suffer from insulin imbalances as a result of pancreatic malfunctioning. They may have too much insulin (and not enough sugar in their blood), or too little insulin (and too much sugar in the blood). There are different types of diabetes that require varying medical treatments. The correctional officer may observe strange, lethargic, disoriented behavior or individuals may look, act, and smell as if they are drunk. Mistaken identification of the problem can result in death for the inmate. Diabetes requires appropriate and immediate medical attention to avoid the negative effects of insulin shock or diabetic coma. Diabetes is controlled through the injection or ingestion of insulin, control of blood sugar levels, exercise, drugs, and diet. Diabetics who are treated appropriately and take care of themselves can function normally and will not exhibit abnormal behavior associated with the disease.

Other Special Populations

There are other types of prisoners in the population that deserve mention as special populations. Elderly offenders are becoming more of a consideration as lengths of prison sentences increase and life-without-parole statutes are passed. Medical populations may need special care, have limiting disabilities, or be stigmatized by their diseases (e.g., Acquired Immune Deficiency Symdrome, or AIDS). There also are inmates who need protection for one reason or another.

Although elderly offenders do not exhibit unusual or aberrant behavior to any degree greater than other offenders, this population is rapidly becoming a special consideration in correctional agencies. Inmates are being sentenced to and are serving longer periods of time in confinement. Some states have life-without-parole statutes which, if not altered, will result in a comparatively large population of elderly inmates. Although the crime-prone years are generally recognized as being the teens and twenties, there may be an increase in the number of older individuals committing crimes and being committed to prisons and to other correctional programs.

A population made up of elderly offenders has different needs than does a generally younger population. Medical care, housing conditions, diets, recreation programs, work programs, and other types of correctional activity and programming may need to be altered and/or designed specifically for an older population. Correctional officers must recognize that elderly inmates are usually more limited in their capacities, desires, and motivations than are younger offenders.

Special medical populations, such as those with Acquired Immune Deficiency Syndrome (AIDS), must be protected from other inmates and from themselves. In addition, it is necessary that they be provided medical care as needed. It is important to note that AIDS patients do not require constant hospitalization; other inmates, however, may harm them if they are placed in the normal population. Staff must also be protected from the AIDS patient. Inmates will sometimes throw urine and other bodily wastes on officers and other inmates. Officers may be exposed to blood in the case of accident, suicide, or assault; blood is a transmitter of the AIDS virus and must be avoided.

There is much that we do not know about AIDS. At this time, if it is contracted it is terminal; there is no known cure. It can reside dormant in individuals for long periods of time. In addition, persons can be AIDS carriers and not have the disease. Tests are not always accurate; it is necessary for a period of time to elapse from the point of contracting the virus before it will show up in tests. The virus can be transmitted during this stage, even though it cannot be detected by tests. In 1989, there were 3,136 AIDS cases in prisons. The number of cases increased by 60% in prisons in 1988, whereas it increased by 76% in the general population in 1988. Less than 3% of inmates entering federal prison in 1988 tested positive for the virus (Baker et al., 1989).

Other special-situation inmates may require protection from inmates. Sex offenders, especially child molesters, need protection from the inmate population; ex-policemen, ex-judges, and ex-prison employees also must be protected. Inmates may have enemies within the inmate population who have the ability and desire to cause them bodily harm. The behavior of these individuals, with the possible exception of sex offenders, most often will be normal in every respect. Officers, however, must be aware to keep them separated from those populations, groups, or individuals which put them at undue risk.

SUMMARY

Human service workers experience pressures not present in other types of work. The unfortunate and unpleasant circumstances and situations of their clients often cause human service workers to experience great stress, accompanied by burnout and cynicism. Correctional employees provide their services to an unwilling clientele who often reject their services. In order to control immediate behavior and to change long-term behavior patterns, the correctional employee must have an adequate understanding of human behavior.

Three basic types of theories attempt to explain criminal behavior. Biological theories explain such behavior as resulting from genetic deficiencies or malfunctioning. Earlier biological theories essentially stated that criminals were biologically inferior humans who were born criminals; contemporary biological theorists explain criminal behavior as a result of genetic deficiencies associated with chemicals and hormones of the body. Psychological theories explain crime as resulting from mental defects or diseases. Sociological theories ascribe crime to the social structure, social processes, or social conflict. No single theory adequately explains all criminal behavior. Each type has advantages and disadvantages, and each is undoubtedly applicable in some circumstances.

Most inmate behavior is normal. However, the nature of institutions and the prevalence of psychological abnormalities among inmates create a wide range of behavior that correctional officers must confront. Inmates experience normal problems of adjustment to the institutions and to life situations encountered while incarcerated. Mentally ill inmates, mentally retarded inmates, and those exhibiting psychopathology (personality disorders) can engage in strange and bizarre behavior. There also are special populations that need protection from themselves or from others. Some special populations, such as the elderly, are normal in most respects except that they have special needs and their general behavior patterns are different from other inmate populations.

NOTES

1. "Most departments of correction allow for mental health treatment beds for 2% to 4% of the inmate population" (Mobley, 1986, p. 13).

2. A status offense is an act that when committed by a juvenile is sufficient to warrant incarceration or correctional control, whereas if an adult committed the act it would not be considered a crime and would not warrant correctional control.

3. The suicide rate in Texas jails in 1981 was 137.5 per 100,000. This compares to 12.6 per 100,000 in the general population in Texas (Kennedy & Homant, 1988).

4

The Professional Status
of Corrections

Any occupation wishing to exercise professional authority must find a technical basis for it, assert an exclusive jurisdiction, link both skill and jurisdiction to standards of training, and convince the public that its services are uniquely trustworthy.

—*H. L. Wilensky*

"Professionalization occurs in degrees . . . [and] is relative to time and space" (Kearney & Sinha, 1988, p. 572). Professions can be viewed as established, emerging, or marginal. Established professions that clearly deserve the title are those such as medicine, law, and the clergy. Emerging professions are those that are in the process of changing from an occupation to a profession. Marginal professions are those that have moved along the continuum toward professionalization, but have stopped short of becoming a fully recognized profession. Pavalko (1971) places pharmacy and police work in the category of marginal professions. Since the mid- to late-1960s, however, police work has moved into the category of emerging professions. Kearney and Sinha (1988, referring to Mosher & Stillman, 1977) state that

> in government, occupations generally accepted as professional include social work, teaching, librarianship, city planning and city management, the police, the military, foreign affairs, and educational administration. (p. 572)

Corrections was identified as an emerging profession by Wilensky (1964). Significant advancement has been made since that time.

Although corrections has not achieved the status of a fully developed profession, the diversity and complexity of roles and the broad scope of correctional activity has generally required that corrections professionalize to a great extent, especially in positions above entry level. Barber (1965) identifies the following as characteristics of an emerging profession:

(1) Its level of knowledge and community orientation is not clearly defined or recognized by the profession itself or by others.

(2) There is significant variation among members regarding the level of knowledge and orientation toward the community interest.

(3) The leaders of the profession acknowledge deficiencies, but explain them away as being a necessary stage in the development of the profession.

(4) A code of ethics is published at this stage of development.

(5) A professional association is developed to regulate the profession, educate the members, communicate with the public, and to defend the profession against those who would infringe upon its right to regulate and perform its functions.

(6) Behavior that constitutes professional behavior is defined.

Bucher and Strauss (1961) also discuss the characteristics of emergent professions. They indicate that the profession at this stage is not homogeneous. There are many identities, values, and interests among the members who have different perceptions of proper methodology, technique, and so forth. Members do not communicate well and they segment clients, thereby creating further divisions within the profession. Various segments of the profession are in different stages of development. Codes of ethics and professional associations are not necessarily evidence of homogeneity and consensus, but rather of power distributions among the groups.

Hall (1968) identified professions as containing both structural and attitudinal components. The structural components include the creation of a full-time occupation, training schools (education), professional associations, and codes of ethics. Attitudinal components include use of the professional association as the major referent of the group, providing a service to the public, belief in self-regulation, a sense of calling to the field, and belief in the autonomy of the members and the group.

Rainey and Backoff (1982) identified three levels of professionalism as being: (1) professionals; (2) public service professionals; and

(3) general public administration professionals. Corrections agencies are composed of all three types. The predominant concern of those advocating professionalism in corrections, however, is the public service professional. Public service professions are those advanced, specialized occupations that are located almost entirely in public agencies (Mosher, 1982). The primary differences between professionals and public service professionals identified by Rainey and Backoff (1982) are:

(1) Public service professionals have the characteristics of all professionals, except that they score lower on the various scales than do traditional professionals.
(2) Autonomy, identification with fellow professionals, and self-regulation desires and expectations are somewhat weaker, or are different.
(3) The knowledge base, service ethic, sense of calling, and attributes toward self-regulation and autonomy are influenced by identification of the profession with service in government. The knowledge base is more likely to include knowledge about the organization and institutional setting.
(4) The service ethic is more likely to include a conception of and belief in public service.

This chapter discusses the movement toward professionalization of corrections in the United States. The nature of professions is described. Professional development in corrections is analyzed in reference to the eight characteristics upon which professions are evaluated along the occupation-profession continuum model developed by Pavalko (1971). The inherent commitments to professional behavior, to the organizational functions and goals, and to self and others also are discussed briefly.

THE NATURE OF PROFESSIONS

The trend in the United States during the last 30 to 50 years has been toward professionalization. More and more groups are striving to achieve professional status. The emphasis on professionalization in government—including corrections—is expected to continue. Because professionalization is a matter of degree and can be viewed as a continuum, it is necessary to distinguish the elements of professions from those of occupations. The primary elements of a profession are: (1) a systematic body of theoretical knowledge acquired through lengthy academic study and not possessed by those outside the profession; (2) community interests rather than self-interest as a motivator of professional behavior; (3) self-regulation; and (4) a system of rewards.

> These characteristics and collective claims of a profession are dependent upon a close solidarity, upon its members constituting in some measure a group apart with an ethos of its own. This in turn implies deep and long commitment. (Hughes, 1965, p. 4)

Specialized knowledge is usually obtained through intensive study, practice, or a combination of the two. The professional is then able to provide unique services in a near-monopoly fashion to individuals or to a public that accepts the monopoly and recognizes the importance of the services (Barber, 1965). The nature of the knowledge possessed by the professional in some professions (e.g., medicine) is quite clear; in the case of other professions (e.g., corrections), the body of knowledge is not so clear.

The primary motivator of professional behavior is the well-being of the client. Although Houle (1980) suggests that corrections agencies may have difficulty in identifying their "clients" because it is unclear who actually benefits from correctional service, McDougall (1985) states clearly that it is the inmate or individual being supervised who is the correctional client. Professionals maintain objectivity in regard to their clients by remaining detached and avoiding personal involvement with the clients. Because their primary interest is the best possible outcome of each particular case, professionals' methods, concerns, and processes are not always compatible with the requirements of bureaucracy. Many professionals (e.g., those in private practice) have maintained almost total control over their own time; in recent years, however, more and more professionals are working in organizations and are therefore subject to the pressures of bureaucratic organization. The public sector has become the largest employer of professionals (Cherniss & Kane, 1987; Mosher, 1982; Von Glinow, 1983). Government employed 15.5% of the civilian work force in 1980—a relative growth of 13% in the 10 years from 1970 (Cherniss & Kane, 1987). Physicians, lawyers, and the clergy—the traditional professions—have also become very dependent upon organizations such as hospitals, government agencies, clinics, and law firms. Almost all correctional activity is performed in an organization.

The self-regulating nature of professions is provided by a "self-generated and maintained set of ethical principles which direct the vocation to serve society and to safeguard the public when it accepts without understanding the advice or service offered" (Mayhew, 1971, p. 2). According to Mayhew, a profession constitutes "a group with an ethos of its own that enables the individual practitioners to feel a deep and lifelong commitment to the practices and life-modes of the profession" (p. 2). Mayhew further states that

> Professionals govern themselves through codes of ethics, protect themselves and try to increase their effectiveness through professional association. Then, too, professionals have well-recognized systems of regards [sic], both monetary and symbolic which glorify good practice. (p. 18)

Early in the history of this country, professional education was restricted primarily to those with the means to acquire advanced education. Professions such as law and medicine typically involve very extensive (and very expensive) education; under these conditions, professionalization of any field tended to place that field under the control of elite groups in society. Increased availability of education to all of American society has eroded the influence of elite groups on all professions. The fact that bureaucracies today contain individuals from all strata of society precludes domination by any single elite group representing particular political or professional attitudes. "The expansion of the professions in government is both inevitable and desirable in an increasingly complex, technological society" (Kearney & Sinha, 1988, p. 577). Kearney and Sinha also state that although "certain biases are reflected in professional membership, by no means is the attainment of professional standing restricted any longer to the well-born or well-heeled white male" (p. 576).

PROFESSIONAL DEVELOPMENT IN CORRECTIONS

The last 15 to 20 years have been a period of instability in corrections. One response to the external pressures and to the lack of clearly defined goals has been the professional development of the field.

> However, front-line criminal justice staff have neither initiated nor been primary beneficiaries of increased professionalism. . . . In fact, profession-

alization has been promoted and mandated by those at the top of criminal justice bureaucracies to protect their autonomy from external control and to enhance their power in the governmental process. . . . Further, professionalization of the ranks, as it has been defined by correctional administrators, often has heightened worker frustrations, thereby contributing to a growing rift between management and staff. . . . [T]he upgrading of criminal justice line personnel has not involved their systematic acquisition of attributes identified in the literature as essential elements of a professional occupation. (Jurik & Musheno, 1986, pp. 458-459)

The occupation-profession continuum introduced by Pavalko (1971) can be used to evaluate the status of professional development in corrections. It includes all of the components of, but is more detailed than, those general characteristics discussed earlier in this chapter. The conceptual model contains eight dimensions: (1) theory or intellectual techniques; (2) relevance to basic social values; (3) training periods; (4) motivation; (5) autonomy; (6) sense of commitment; (7) sense of community; and (8) codes of ethics. The eight dimensions represent desirable—indeed, necessary—qualities of a profession. The higher a profession scores on each of the eight components, the more professional the field is said to be. The following sections analyze and comment on the development of corrections along these eight dimensions.

Theory or Intellectual Techniques

To focus on skills alone when evaluating a profession can be misleading. Some nonprofessional occupations actually involve higher-order skills than some professions. Greenwood (1957) makes the following distinction: "The skills that characterize a profession flow from and are supported by a fund of knowledge that has been organized into an internally consistent system, called a *body of theory*" (p. 46). Acquisition of a professional skill involves mastery of the theory. It is also important to note that professionalism is based on *rationality*, which is the opposite of *tradition*. Those who hold a professional orientation are willing to consider challenges to conventional wisdom and to ideas that they currently hold. They will change those ideas based upon rationally supported evidence.

Professions are based on systematic bodies of knowledge and theory that validate them and provide the basis for their practice. Such knowledge may be scientific, but it may also be nonscientific and normative in nature (Pavalko, 1971). Wilensky (1964) states that the knowledge base of a profession must not be too narrow or too broad. Rather, it should consist of information and knowledge gained from formal study (i.e., in classrooms) and from practice: "Many new or aspiring professions face this barrier [to exclusive jurisdiction] because they are grounded mainly in human-relations skills or some program of reform" (p. 149) and are not adequately grounded in theory. Corrections is a unique profession in that it incorporates theoretical aspects of many distinct disciplines such as psychology, sociology, public administration, and other policy and behavioral sciences. A further characteristic of the knowledge base of a profession is that it is tacit (Wilensky, 1964), which means that there are some elements of the knowledge that cannot be explained—we simply know it to be the case, but have a hard time explaining why we know it to be the case. This kind of knowledge comes from practicing the profession.

A large body of knowledge has been developed since the mid-1960s. Many academic journals which publish corrections-related articles have started since 1960; journals in other fields, such as psychology, also have started publishing many more articles related to corrections. The number of books concerning corrections has increased tremendously in the past three decades. The support provided by the Law Enforcement Assistance Administration (LEAA), which began in 1968, was a primary contributor to a significant increase in research and expansion of the theoretical knowledge base.

The majority of the journal articles published are empirical or scientific in nature. Most monographs published are also based on scientific research being conducted. The nature of the articles and books are both descriptive and theoretical; however, a large portion of the monographs and a significant—but smaller—portion of the journal articles are normative (describing how things should be) in nature. They typically deal with material related to the administration of corrections, the political nature of the system, and the cultural aspects of criminal behavior and inmate control. Trade magazines (as contrasted to academic journals) usually publish anecdotal, normative information. At most, the trade magazines contain descriptive articles. Most academic journals, on the other hand, concentrate on statistical, scientific research. Both types of publications serve valuable purposes; the trade magazines are designed for a general audience, whereas the academic journals are designed for professionals with advanced knowledge in specific areas.

The absence of a unique body of knowledge has been suggested by some studies. Lawrence (1984) found that probation officers were uncertain of their professionalism because of the absence of a base of scientific knowledge; however, that base of knowledge is constantly being expanded. The multidisciplinary nature of corrections makes other knowledge bases appropriate and important. Indeed, professionalization in some cases requires indoctrinating other professionals into the unique environment of corrections, and indoctrinating corrections professionals in the knowledge bases of other professions and disciplines. Professionalization has involved the utilization of appropriate knowledge from related fields such as psychology, sociology, political science, public administration, social work, and others.

Relevance to Basic Social Values

The second characteristic that Pavalko (1971) identifies is that of relevance to basic social values. The concept of justice is clearly a basic social value in American society; there is virtual unanimous agreement that corrections is necessary and central to the concept of justice. Pavalko states that "work at the professional end of the continuum is regarded as that which has the greatest applicability to the most intense crises that persons face" (p. 19). Crime, for those who experience it as victims, is usually a very intense experience—especially for victims of violent crime. Being exposed to a correctional environment, especially for the first time and no matter how deserved, is also an intense crisis in the lives of the inmates or clients and their families.

There has been significant disagreement over the last three decades regarding the effectiveness of corrections programs. There are also differences of opinion as to how the business of corrections should be conducted. Factors such as overcrowding have necessitated early release, in some cases, of serious offenders in some jurisdictions. The intense public concern about crime that began in the late 1970s has resulted in significantly longer sentences and the tendency to convict and to incarcerate more and more individuals. Fear of crime has consistently rated as a top concern of the average American citizen (Karmen, 1984).

The public interest and social values must be considered if an organization is to provide a service for the public: "The public service orientation still requires the consideration of the public interest, political purposes and professional requirements" (Stewart & Clarke, 1987, p. 168). Particular care must be exercised to identify correctly the clients of corrections programs. The primary client of corrections is the inmate, probationer, or parolee (McDougall, 1985). However, it is impractical to allow either the public or the inmate client to dictate the level of service to be provided by corrections programs or agencies. It is necessary to take into consideration the wishes, needs, and desires of both groups. A balance must be struck that provides for the competing basic social values and professional requirements to assure that the greatest service is provided to the different clients. "There is a fine line between being *sensitive to the public's needs* and *catering to one's clientele*" (Hammond & Miller, 1985, p. 17, emphasis in original).

The Training Period

"Training is defined as the systematic acquisition of skills, rules, concepts, or attitudes that result in improved performance in another environment" (Goldstein, 1986, p. 3). The Declaration of Principles adopted by the American Prison Association in 1870 stated that

> special training as well as high qualities of head and heart is required [sic] to make a good prison or reformatory officer. Then only will the administration of public punishment become scientific, uniform, and successful, when it is raised to the dignity of a profession and men are specially trained for other pursuits. (Gill, 1958, p. 8)

The training dimension of professions consists of four subdimensions: (1) the amount of training; (2) the extent to which training is specialized; (3) the degree to which the training is symbolic and ideational; and (4) the content of the training. The training period involves both educational (theoretical) instruction and training (practical) instruction.

Higher levels of professionalization require greater amounts of training and usually involve increased specialization when compared to lesser professionalized activity. Higher levels of professionalization also involve the learning of more abstract knowledge and information.

Professionalization is ideational to the extent that its learning involves the manipulation of ideas and symbols. Again, higher levels involve greater amounts of training that stresses the manipulation of ideas and/or symbols rather than the manipulation of objects or things. It is not uncommon for the initial training period to involve four or more years in college. Advanced education—graduate school—also becomes important in specialization and advancement in most professions.

The training period also involves the learning of the professional subculture. Although some have questioned the value, or indeed the presence, of a subculture in corrections (e.g., Kauffman, 1981; Klofas and Toch, 1982; Lombardo, 1981), correctional officers such as police, tend to form unique social structures within the correctional environment. They tend to form friendships among the other correctional workers, tend to be very supportive of each other, and associate frequently with other correctional workers. They also tend to form networks between and among agencies. In some respects, correctional workers still represent a closed system, though not as closed as the police. The training at this stage involves learning the art of correctional practice. Relationships and interaction with inmates and officers are emphasized. Poole and Regoli (1980a, 1981) found that positive relationships among officers reduce cynicism and alienation. Cullen, Link, Wolfe, and Frank (1985) and Lombardo (1981) suggest that officers do not derive satisfaction from relationships with the officer subculture; because the training stage is so crucial, however, agencies must be very selective about the officers chosen to serve as mentors.

Rising educational levels, job requirements, competitive pressures, and court orders regarding performance of job roles are causing the amount of required training to rise continually. The first training school for correctional officers was opened by the Federal Bureau of Prisons in New York in 1930 (Schade, 1986). Almost all correctional agencies now provide entry level training that ranges from two weeks (in one state) to over 24 weeks (in 10 states); classroom training ranges from one week to 16 weeks (American Correctional Association, 1989b). Courts have mandated that in-service training must meet court-ordered standards and, in some cases, consist of a specified number of hours each year. Many universities and colleges provide training and education for all or some areas of corrections. Academic (as contrasted to training) courses concentrate on the higher-order abstractions that establish the theoretical base of the profession. The American Correctional Association has correspondence training courses that many institutions and individuals use on a regular basis. Training courses tend to be very specific and to address the unique concerns and aspects of corrections and/or community programs, both in general terms and terms specific to the jurisdiction. The National Institute of Corrections provides, through its National Academy of Corrections, specialized training programs for corrections professionals. These include courses designed and delivered by the National Academy of Corrections staff, by consultants, and by the Federal Bureau of Prisons.

Motivation

People enter occupational or professional activity for numerous reasons. Professions, more than occupations, stress the ideal of service to the client and public as the primary goal, with self-interests being a lesser consideration. The system of rewards for most professions is sufficiently great to allow professionals to give lesser concern to their own survival and basic self-interests. Pavalko (1971) says that "the professional does not work to be paid as much as he is paid in order that he may work" (p. 21).

Entry level pay is low in many correctional agencies. Progression from entry level, however, provides for (sometimes rapidly) increased pay and benefits. In 1988, the pay for beginning corrections officers ranged between $10,837 and $26,784 (see Appendix D). The average pay for several groups in corrections is contained in Appendix E. The median salary in 1988 for entry-level correctional officers was $19,438 (up almost $2,000 over the median salary in 1986); for chief administrators, the average salary was $66,410. The salary distribution for all corrections employees in 1988 was as follows: 38.3% made $20,000 or less; 61.7% made more than $20,000; and 21.6% made more than $30,000 (American Correctional Association, 1989). These salary figures (which do not represent total family income) compare to a median family income of $30,853 in the United States in 1988 (Bureau of the Census, 1989). Thirty-four percent of the families in the United States in 1986 had both husband and wife working (Bureau of the Census, 1988). Seventy percent of the women in their twenties work; 20% of them have college degrees (Benton, 1988).

Motivation for entry into corrections employment is often one of convenience. That is, the job is available and the individual either wants to work in a particular geographic area or merely needs a job to survive.

Some have even suggested that correctional officers seek the job because it is not challenging (Wicks, 1980). Others suggest that the correctional officers see their jobs as worthwhile endeavors (Johnson, 1987). Shannon (1987) found that 59% of those in corrections chose the field because of economic necessity; 18% chose the field as a second choice, and 22% had chosen the field as a first choice. Jurik and Halemba (1984) found that the primary reason for seeking correctional employment varies by sex. Women listed the following reasons: interest in human service work (55%); entry position for other jobs in the department (16%); salary (13%); interest in security work (10%); no alternative work available (3%); and others (3%). Males, on the other hand, listed their primary reasons as follows: interest in human service work (23%); entry position for other jobs in department (21%); job security (20%); no alternative work available (14%); interest in security work (10%); salary (8%); fringe benefits (2%); and others (2%).

A study by Cherniss and Kane (1987) considered three aspects of the work experience—job satisfaction, job characteristics, and aspiration for intrinsic fulfillment through work—to determine how public sector professionals perceive their work environments. They found that "professionals perceived their jobs to possess lower levels of intrinsically fulfilling characteristics than did blue-collar workers" (p. 130). They also "found that the high status public employee experiences less autonomy, variety, task identity, and significance than lower status workers in the same organization" (p. 133). They state, however, that "the lower ratings given by the professionals may be influenced by higher expectations regarding professional jobs" (p. 133). Cherniss and Kane conclude that professional employees adapt to less intrinsically motivating jobs while maintaining job satisfaction and intrinsic need satisfaction.

Motivation for remaining in the profession may be different from motivations for entry. Klofas (1986) indicated that human service roles became more important among older correctional officers and those with more seniority. Therefore, many may come to like the profession and remain for intrinsic reasons. Other factors such as the nonportability of pensions, owning their own homes, not wanting to leave the geographic area, having to take a job that pays less, and so forth, keep some from leaving the profession. These *sunk costs* make it important for career decisions to be well thought out and based on adequate knowledge about the profession.

Autonomy

Autonomy means that the profession and the individual professionals are largely independent of external control. There are two dimensions of autonomy. The first is that professions control their members and other matters that relate to the work of the profession. The second dimension refers to the autonomy of the individual practitioner; each controls his or her own time and methods and is subject to approval, disapproval, control, and censure by peers—that is, other professionals—who possess the same body of knowledge.

Accreditation and licensing procedures assure that only those qualified actually perform services. The public is incapable (because it does not have the knowledge) to judge a professional's expertise on technical matters. At the same time, corrections has no accreditation or licensing of individual practitioners.[1] The public is often very opinionated regarding the technical matters of corrections, and believes that it does have the knowledge to evaluate professional performance. Those opinions, however, are based on uninformed popular notions regarding the treatment of criminal offenders. A major task of professionalization in corrections is to establish credibility with its public.

Corrections does not yet control its members in a professional sense; control of members is vested in agencies, rather than in any professional organization. The American Correctional Association (the primary professional organization, founded in 1870 as the American Prison Association) had a membership of more than 24,000 in 1988 (American Correctional Association, 1989a). Thus, only 6.07% of the 395,000 correctional workers were members of the primary professional association. In 1988 there were 29 other professional associations, 32 state organizations, and 4 regional associations affiliated with the ACA (American Correctional Association, 1988).

With few exceptions, individual practitioners in corrections do not control their own time, working conditions, or performance factors related to their profession. Physicians, lawyers, and some other professionals maintain a relatively high degree of professional autonomy while working in corrections although they must function within parameters specified by the bureaucracy. By far the majority of correctional workers are controlled by the bureaucratic environment that is characteristic of every correctional organization, and by the rules and procedures for practice set down by courts and legislatures. The higher one goes in the organization, the greater the degree of autonomy that is granted. The corrections professional, however, never reaches the degree of autonomy that individual practitioners (such as physicians or lawyers in private practice) reach.

The relationship of employees to the organization can preclude autonomous activity. For example, Lawrence (1984) states that probation officers lack autonomy because of their relationships to the court. Cherniss and Kane (1987) found in their study of public agency professionals that "professionals rated their jobs as significantly lower in . . . autonomy" (p. 125). Ineffectiveness with client relationships can cause emotional and physical exhaustion (Gerstein, Topp, & Correll, 1987) and may be an indicator that autonomy needs are not met (Toch & Grant, 1982). Professionals who are denied the ability to use independent judgment and to influence their professional environment frequently become disenchanted and frustrated. Whitehead (1987) argues that "supervisors must allow room for autonomy by being responsive to what workers want, that is, by allowing for staff participation in decision making" (p. 6).

Several authors have concluded that "public service professions are characterized by less professional autonomy and lower levels of self-regulation" (Kearney & Sinha, 1988, p. 576). Although expectations for autonomy and intrinsic fulfillment are usually higher among professionals, those in public organizations often find that they are in routine jobs, under close supervision, and must comply with rigid bureaucratic standards (Sarason, 1977).

> The crux of the issue of autonomy for salaried professionals is whether the organization itself is infused with professionalism (as measured, say, by a large percentage of professionally trained employees and managers) and whether the services of the professionals involved are scarce (as measured by a large number of attractive job offers from the outside). (Wilensky, 1964, p. 147)

In today's increasingly complex and highly regulated society, professionals can expect to continue experiencing strain in their needs for autonomy. Corrections is not unique in this situation. All professionals, whether in private practice or working for an organization, are experiencing the same constraints on autonomous behavior. Maximum autonomy can only be gained with maximum professionalization. Correctional organizations will grant, and be granted, more autonomy as professionalization increases.

Sense of Commitment

Professionals have a sense of commitment to their professions that is usually not present among those in occupational groups. The work is viewed more as a "calling" than as a temporary—or even permanent—means to mere survival. Professionals have a love for their work that is above that of employment merely to receive a paycheck. "Those individuals [who express a] . . . strong belief in sense of calling appear to experience less role conflict and less work alienation" (Poole & Regoli, 1983, p. 66) than those who do not express such beliefs. Poole and Regoli (1983) also state that "the results of the research offer support for the contention that commitment to a professional ideology lowers role conflict, work alienation, and anomie among correctional supervisors" (p. 62).

The sense of commitment at the lower levels of corrections is not great. High turnover (employee attrition) rates are evidence of a lack of commitment. Archambeault and Archambeault (1982), referring to the National Manpower Survey (U. S. Department of Justice, 1978), report that turnover rates ranged between 17% and 28% and averaged 19.1% among state agencies for the period covered by the survey. The turnover rate was reported by *Corrections Compendium* (1983) to be 16.2% overall and as high as 40% in some agencies. Benton (1988) found correctional employee attrition to be 24.7% in 1985. As workers move up in the organization from entry-level positions into more professionalized roles, the sense of commitment becomes greater and turnover becomes lower. Baro (1988), however, notes that "states also have serious problems in stabilizing middle prison management" (p. 469), indicating further that turnover rates among wardens have, for 50 years, ranged between 17% and 20%.

Some have argued that persons with higher education can be expected to leave correctional service at high rates; the assumption is that such jobs are boring, repetitive, unchallenging, stressful, and problematic. A study by Jurik and Winn (1987), however, did not find that educated employees left corrections at a rate that was any higher than that for less educated individuals. They did find that "perceived promotional opportunities, policy input, attitudes toward superiors, general job satisfaction, and the perceived working conditions" (p. 12) were negatively correlated[2] with correctional officer turnover.

Entry level work in correctional institutions should be perceived as an apprenticeship period. That some will leave corrections at this stage should come as no surprise; in fact, it is commendable that some learn quickly that the profession is not for them and move on to other careers. Although turnover is commonly thought to be a bad thing for agencies, it is functional at the same time. It is undesirable for an agency to have no turnover. "Turnover functionality, which considers both turnover frequency and the performance level of leavers and stayers, is more critical to organizational effectiveness than is turnover frequency" (Hollenbeck & Williams, 1986, p. 606). Thus, some turnover at the entry level is desirable; the high rates indicated above, however, are undesirable. These rates are partially explained by the motivation of the applicants, lack of commitment to the work, and uninformed notions about correctional work. Entry level work is at best semiprofessional and therefore fails to satisfy many of those with professional orientations. Those who do not have the education, training, and professional orientation needed to achieve higher levels of work often become very frustrated with their organizations. Organizational problems add to that frustration, and many leave the profession without giving it a chance. Organizations in the future will be more professionalized and should attract appropriately oriented people. The fact that commitment has not reached professional levels can be partially attributed to the fact that corrections is an *emerging* profession that has not reached a high level on the occupation-profession continuum.

Sense of Community

A strong sense of community develops in professions. Those who belong to the profession have a strong commitment to it, and few leave. Members share values on a wide range of subject matter and develop similar lifestyles. Role definitions are agreed upon, and a common jargon (language) develops that is shared by all members of the profession. The professional community has power over its members and the social limits are clear. In addition, the professional community controls the next generation of professionals through selection and socialization.

Professional groups tend to have greater influence in criminal justice agencies than in some other types of governmental agencies. Brudney and Hebert (1987) state that

given the comparatively low social standing and resources of the clients of criminal justice agencies, it is not surprising to find that clientele groups rank low in influence. . . . In contrast, like personnel in human resources agencies, criminal justice staff usually have extensive training and socialization in their professions, and in fact, the level of influence of professional associations over both types of agencies reaches its peak. (p. 195)

The sense of community is fostered by common interests, goals, problems, and the similarity of members' orientation. Similarities of education and training and common work experiences also contribute to cohesiveness and sense of community. The unique knowledge (theory or intellectual) base sets the group apart and creates a commonality of interests not experienced by nonprofessional groups.

As stated earlier in this chapter, there is some question as to the extent to which correctional officers form a subculture. While some argue that they do create a subculture, others argue that they do not. Farmer (1977), however, points out that there is limited support for the idea that "off-duty social contacts among officers . . . were important in producing a sense of community (social system) among the officers. Such contacts were further necessary for the maintenance of the correctional officer subculture so common among guards" (p. 239). Hawkins and Alpert (1989) point out that, although early research found the existence of officer subcultures, research conducted within the last ten years does not support their existence. The demise, if indeed that is the case, of the traditional officer subculture may set the stage for the development of a new, more professional, subculture that will be more conducive to the general professionalization of the field.

Code of Ethics

All professions have a clearly defined code of ethics. Prior to 1975, a code of ethics for the corrections profession did not exist (McArdle, 1988). The current Code of Ethics (see Figure 4.1) was adopted by the American Correctional Association in August, 1975, at the 105th Congress of Corrections.

The purposes of an ethics code are to bind the professionals to ethical behavior and to set the standards of acceptable behavior. Many professional organizations, such as medical and legal associations, have authority to revoke professional licenses or otherwise impose sanctions on those who violate their code of ethics. As individual practitioners of corrections are not licensed, neither the American Correctional

Figure 4.1. Code of Ethics

The American Correctional Association expects of its members unfailing honesty, respect for the dignity and individuality of human beings, and a commitment to professional and compassionate service. To this end we subscribe to the following principles.

Relationships with clients/colleagues/other professions/the public—

- Members will respect and protect the civil and legal rights of all clients.
- Members will serve each case with appropriate concern for the client's welfare and with no purpose of personal gain.
- Relationships with colleagues will be of such character to promote mutual respect within the profession and improvement of its quality of service.
- Statements critical of colleagues or their agencies will be made only as these are verifiable and constructive in purpose.
- Members will respect the importance of all elements of the criminal justice system and cultivate a professional cooperation with each segment.
- Subject to the client's right of privacy, members will respect the public's right to know, and will share information with the public with openness and candor.
- Members will respect and protect the right of the public to be safeguarded from criminal activity.

Professional conduct/practices—

- No member will use his or her official position to secure special privileges or advantages.
- No member, while acting in an official capacity, will allow personal interest to impair objectivity in the performance of duty.
- No member will use his or her official position to promote any partisan political purposes.
- No member will accept any gift or favor of such nature to imply an obligation that is inconsistent with the free and objective exercise of professional responsibilities.
- In any public statement, members will clearly distinguish between those that are personal views and those that are statements and positions on behalf of an agency.
- Members will be diligent in their responsibility to record and make available for review any and all case information which could contribute to sound decisions affecting a client or the public safety.
- Each member will report, without reservation, any corrupt or unethical behavior which could affect either a client or the integrity of the organization.
- Members will not discriminate against any client, employee, or prospective employee on the basis of race, sex, creed, or national origin.
- Members will maintain the integrity of private information; they will neither seek personal data beyond that needed to perform their responsibilities, nor reveal case information to anyone not having proper professional use for such.
- Any member who is responsible for agency personnel actions will make all appointments, promotions, or dismissals only on the basis of merit and not in furtherance of partisan political interests.

(Adopted August 1975 at the 105th Congress of Correction)

Source: Reprinted with permission of The American Correctional Association

Association nor any other association has the ability to impose sanctions on persons who violate the code.[3] Corrections practitioners are subject only to the disciplinary procedures of their agency. It is possible for a practitioner to violate every part of the ACA Code of Ethics and, to the extent such actions are tolerated by the agency, not face any sanctions.

INHERENT COMMITMENTS

Professionals in corrections work in bureaucratic environments. Their work activity is dictated to a great extent by legal mandates created by legislatures and courts, as well as professional standards dictated by many professional groups. Being a part of government requires commitment to basic democratic principles and to the republican form of government as practiced in the United States. Corrections professionals must subscribe to a public service ethic that places the public trust as a primary factor controlling behavior. In addition, the general ethics of all professional activity, which dictate concern for the primary client—the inmate/probationer/parolee—must also prevail on balance with other clients' interests. Correctional officials, like all government officials, perform their work in the light of public scrutiny. Government is currently the single largest employer of professionals; this trend will continue with beneficial results.

> There are four principal advantages of professionalism in government. First, it promotes bureaucratic responsibility and accountability through professional norms and standards that guide administrators' behaviors and provide democratic decision rules for allocating public goods and services. Second, it serves as an antidote to the common ailments of bureaucracy. Third, professionalism aids cooperation and understanding between the scientific and political estates. Finally, it provides an important source of intrinsic motivation for professional employees. (Kearney & Sinha, 1988, p. 575)

Many who work in corrections are members of other professions; lawyers, accountants, physicians and other health care personnel are examples. This trend will continue, with increased numbers of other professionals being employed by corrections agencies. The numbers of corrections professionals will also increase. All have inherent commitments to their professions, to their organizations, and to themselves.

Commitment to the Profession

The primary commitment of professionals is to their professions. They must believe in the basic purposes and methods of their professions and critically assess their own achievement against high standards of professional performance. This commitment dictates primary concern for the outcome of individual cases. Activity, however, must be conducted with consideration of legitimate concerns for the organizations involved and for other cases. In the absence of a clear course of action with predictable positive results, the physicians' credo, "first, do no harm" must be remembered. Kearney and Sinha (1988) state the following about *professional* responsibility:

> It has two dimensions: (1) the professional's dedication to and confidence in his/her expert knowledge and skills, and (2) the utilization of that knowledge and those skills in accordance with certain standards and norms set forth by the profession in the context of what Friedrich (1935:38) referred to as the "fellowship of science." (p. 575)

Dedication to and confidence in expert knowledge implies that the individual believes in the thing that is being done and expects it to achieve some desirable goal. Murphy (1988) states that correctional officers must have a sense of pride, adopt professional standards, believe in what they are doing, and do what is right. As Greenwood (1957) indicates, professional work is an end in itself—not just a means to an end. It involves total personal involvement in both the formal and informal structures that make up the profession.

Utilization of knowledge and skills in accordance with professional standards certainly implies that the individual must know those standards and apply them properly. It further means that individuals must remain current in the field; they must read, attend to other types of professional development, and be open to scientific learning. The application of the scientific method implies objectivity and systematic study. Scientific principles must be applied only for valid purposes and not be used for self-interest or unethical purposes. The rational approach of professionals means that they must be willing to abandon tradition when it is shown to be ineffective.

Commitment to the Organization

Corrections is practiced in organizational environments. A large majority of the organizations are public agencies, although some private organizations are now conducting some correctional services. Several prisons across the country are run by private companies; other private companies are providing surveillance for probationers and parolees. Private organizations also have existed for many years in the area of juvenile corrections. Private practitioners who function in corrections are limited to consultants, contract professionals (such as physicians), and employees of private companies. However, government continues to have the major responsibility for correctional practices, even if contracted to private firms and individuals (Stewart & Clarke, 1987). Therefore, organizations have many legitimate interests regarding professional practice. All activity must contribute positively to outcomes in which the organization has interests, and each activity must be compatible with other organizational interests.

Reichers (1986) identifies three classifications of variables that are related to organizational commitment: (1) psychological variables, such as job satisfaction and identification with organizational goals and values; (2) behavioral variables, such as irrevocability of job choice; and (3) structural variables, such as long-term association with the organization and the nonportability of benefits. It is important that the individual identify with (and support) the goals and values of the organization in order that psychosocial conflict be avoided. Individuals who experience role stress in the organization usually are not committed to the organization (Fisher and Gitelson, 1983; Reichers, 1986). Reichers (1986), however, found that the length of service with the organization did not have any relationship to organizational commitment. Those with lengthy service were equally as committed, or uncommitted, to the organization as those with shorter service. Bateman and Strasser (1984) found that organizational commitment is a necessary prerequisite to job satisfaction, rather than an outcome of it. Professional attitudes have also been shown to result in greater organizational commitment (Bartol, 1979; Poole & Regoli, 1983).

Success—especially for those professions such as corrections that require organizations for their practice—requires that professionals support the organization. Changes to the bureaucratic structure must be made from inside the organization, if necessary, to ensure optimum professional performance.

Commitment to Self and Others

It is critical for professional and personal success that individuals be satisfied with their professions and organizations. As indicated earlier in this chapter, people choose jobs for many reasons. Extrinsic factors have to do with such things as pay, benefits, and so forth. Intrinsic factors relate to the nature and content of the work itself. O'Reilly and Caldwell (1980) found "some evidence . . . which suggests that decisions made under external constraints, that is, decisions based on a concern for family and financial considerations, are inversely related to job satisfaction and commitment" (p. 563).[4] They further found that intrinsic factors were more important than extrinsic factors in determining satisfaction and commitment. The point here is that choice of profession is critical to personal well-being and satisfaction. Individuals have obligations to themselves, to families and friends, and to their clients to be as well-adjusted and happy as possible. Being in the right profession and making satisfactory progress is central to that adjustment, well-being, and happiness.

SUMMARY

The field of corrections has been in the process of professionalization for many years. The present emphasis began in the mid-1960s and continues today. The key characteristics that define a profession—knowledge base, relevance to basic social values, training and educational period, autonomy, motivation, commitment, sense of community, and code of ethics—are all present in sufficient degrees to validate the professional status of the corrections field. As a public service profession, these characteristics are less pronounced than in the traditional professions. Although many entry level positions in corrections could, at best, be described as semiprofessional, positions above entry level usually require professional orientation and preparation.

The knowledge base of corrections includes subject matter from a variety of fields. The base has expanded significantly since the mid-1960s as new journals have appeared and as more books are written on the subject. The education and training needed for some positions and for advancement in the field can be extensive, and involve one or more college degrees. The training and education period necessary for adequate professional preparation depends upon the particular component of corrections and the particular career path (e.g., security, treatment, or administration) that the individual wishes to pursue. A four-year college degree should be the minimum that an individual who wishes to reach middle to upper management positions should possess. Treatment-oriented positions frequently require advanced college degrees (masters and/or doctoral degrees) for maximum achievement in career growth.

The training period for familiarization with agency policy and routine techniques is important but relatively short. The first 12 to 18 months should usually be viewed as an apprenticeship period during which the new employee, regardless of educational preparation, gains on-the-job experience, learns the art of correctional practice, and becomes familiar with the professional subculture. Chapter 5 analyzes in more detail the need for education and training and the development of educational and training programs.

Corrections is clearly relevant to basic social values. Although there may be considerable disagreement as to the particular methods by which corrections is to accomplish its ill-defined goals, there is broad public agreement that corrections is a necessary institution. The current unprecedented expansion of correctional systems—including the building of new prisons, expansion of existing prisons, and expansion of community corrections programs—is evidence of the public's perception of social relevance. Corrections has taken increasingly larger shares of total state budgets in the last 15 to 20 years. The willingness of the public to support such costs reinforces the fact that corrections is central to the basic social values of society.

Corrections professionals do not possess the degree of autonomy held by private practitioners of traditional professional specialities. They are controlled by organizational and political demands, professional mandates, court decisions, and by public opinion. Motivation for seeking correctional careers varies considerably. Those functioning at the entry level (e.g., guards) are motivated by many factors, including security, need, and opportunity. Those in positions beyond the entry level, however, usually have a sense of motivation based on service to clients and to the public. Commitment for those beyond the entry level is usually quite high, and the sense of community among those committed individuals is usually quite strong.

Control by professional organizations is not as fully developed as in most traditional professions. The American Correctional Association developed a code of ethics for the profession in 1975; however, there is currently no licensing or certification process through the professional association for individual practitioners. The only licensing or certification currently required of individuals is that granted by other professions, such as the medical and legal professions, and—in some specific positions—a degree granted by an accredited college or university. There is a certification process for institutions and agencies; but it is not required at the present time that agencies and institutions be certified. There is, however, some indication that it may become either a practical or real requirement in the future as court decisions and other factors (such as the general increase in educational levels of society) cause increased professionalization.

Corrections professionals work in organizations and have inherent obligations to them as well as to the profession. It is also important that individuals continue their professional commitments and growth and that they be satisfied with the profession in order that they may be well-adjusted. The remaining chapters look at these elements in more detail.

NOTES

1. The American Correctional Association, after merger with the Committee on Accreditation for Corrections, does have a program whereby correctional institutions may be accredited if they meet the standards as specified by the ACA/CAC. There are numerous standards that relate to every area of jail and prison operation and structure. Bostick (1988) states that, by the year 2000, ". . . jails that do not receive accreditation cannot be assured of autonomy and longevity" (p. 6).

2. A correlation is a statistical indicator which establishes the relationship between two variables. A positive correlation means that as one variable increases, the other also increases. A negative correlation means that as one variable increases, the other decreases. The actual correlation between education and turnover in the study was −.02. This slightly negative correlation is not statistically significant, but there was a slight indication that those with higher education left employment at a lower rate than did those with less education.

3. Other professionals who work in corrections, such as physicians and lawyers, may have sanctions imposed upon them by their respective licensing associations and by their other professional associations. For example, the American Medical Association and the medical associations of the various states, along with licensing associations, can revoke, or cause to be revoked, the license of physicians and surgeons who seriously violate the code of ethics. The American Bar Association, the bar associations of the various states, and the licensing associations/agencies in each state similarly control the behavior of attorneys.

4. An inverse relationship refers to the fact that two variables correlate in a negative way (see Note 2 above). In this case, the inverse relationship between extrinsic motivators and commitment simply means that those who chose the job because of outside pressures were not as committed to the organization or as satisfied with their jobs as were those who chose the job for intrinsic reasons.

5

Preparation for the
Corrections Profession

That corrections is an emerging public service profession which is moving toward the professional end of the occupation-profession continuum has been established. "Never has there been such a demand for professionally competent and motivated staff." (Rosetti, 1988, p. 34) The past 20 to 25 years of research and correctional activity has created an increasingly complex body of knowledge. Extended periods of education—for example, bachelor's and master's degrees—are becoming more important as selection criteria and/or practical requirements for promotion and professional advancement; it is not too uncommon to find practicing professionals who hold a doctoral degree. Successful careers in corrections clearly require greater commitment to professionalization than was necessary as recently as 15 years ago. Though entry level requirements are still comparatively low in some places, advancement often requires higher education, commitment to professional values, and exemplary performance. "Therefore, management has encouraged the recruitment of college-trained staff, preferably individuals who have completed bachelor's degrees" (Jurik, 1985b, p. 525).

Correctional careers require that individuals be of good moral character and not have been convicted of any felony or misdemeanor offenses that involve moral turpitude. An offense involving moral turpitude is usually interpreted to mean misdemeanor theft or similar, less serious crimes that may reflect an untrustworthy character. Almost all agencies conduct a background investigation designed to determine if the individual is a good candidate. Some agencies require psychological examinations and polygraph examinations. Although the use of psychological testing is questioned by some (Wahler & Gendreau, 1985), Benton (1988) found that 24% of the states do use psychological tests to screen entry level candidates. However, fewer than 24% use the tests in filling other positions involving promotion or lateral transfer within agencies.

Coordination of work in complex organizations is frequently best accomplished when members of the organization are like-minded (Gulick, 1937). "In pursuit of this 'singleness of purpose,' organizations often hire individuals with similar backgrounds and schooling so that all will have a similar approach to the organization's tasks" (Hammond & Miller, 1985, p. 16). For most of correctional history in this country, employee selection has been based on the similarity of personal background characteristics. Little or no formal education was required or desired; primarily rural, uneducated, white males were hired to contain prisons and to keep inmates incarcerated. Today, however, primacy is being placed on education to the exclusion of personal characteristics. Similarity in educational backgrounds is important, but it must also be emphasized that the broad scope of corrections requires diversity in educational background. Perhaps the useful similarity is not so much in terms of education in a particular discipline as it is that advanced education in one or more of several disciplines is required.

INITIAL PREPARATION

The scope of corrections is broad. All types of professionals, semi-professionals, and nonprofessionals are involved in many different activities. Therefore, it is difficult to identify one path that should be chosen in order to best prepare for the profession. Perhaps the single criterion that most employees in corrections share is that they work with or on behalf of convicted persons who, in most cases, do not want to receive the services or to participate in the processes of the agency.

There are three types of skills necessary for satisfactory performance in any profession, career, or job (Warrick & Zawacki, 1984). First, technical skills involve performing the task, that is, manipulating the things that are necessary to do the work. Second, human skills involve getting along with other people, learning to supervise and coordinate the work of others, and generally understanding human nature. In corrections, because the basic activity is supervising people, human skills are exceptionally important. In fact, it could be said that human skills *are* the technical skills of corrections employees.

The third type of skills, necessary for promotion and professional advancement, is conceptual skills. These skills involve the ability to understand the "big picture" and to develop and implement programs designed to achieve selected goals. Those who aspire to upper management positions in corrections must refine their conceptual skills in order to be able to compete.

Although "management has encouraged the recruitment of college-trained staff, preferably individuals who have completed bachelor's degrees" (Jurik, 1985b, p. 525), in many agencies the entry level position (e.g., guard) does not require any college credits. Although a high school education or its equivalent may be the only prerequisite to obtaining employment, the practical requirement for advancement may be much higher—either as a prerequisite to certain jobs, or as a practical issue where many competitors do possess college degrees. Technical and human skills are products of education, but perhaps the most important product of a college education is the development and refinement of conceptual skills.

EDUCATION

"Perhaps no issue in corrections is as important as the training, educating, and recruiting of qualified staffs for the various systems" (Allen & Simonsen, 1986, p. 470). "In personal growth for job improvement in corrections, the three most important factors are education, education, and education" (Travisono, 1987a, p. 4). Prior to 1960, 9.2% of adult correctional officers had a college education at the time of entry into corrections; in 1974, 28.1% had a college education; and in 1982, 34.5% had been to college (Archambeault & Archambeault, 1982). Probation and parole officers are generally better educated than institutional officers; prior to 1960, 82.1% entered employment with a college education and in 1974, 83.1% had been to college. Considering all probation and parole officers working in 1960, 82.4% had been to college; in 1974, 91.2% had been to college (Archambeault & Archambeault, 1982). In one study of Ohio correctional workers, Shannon (1987) found that 48% of all officers had some college education. Forty-three percent (43%) of those who had been to college had majored

TABLE 5.1: Criminal Justice Higher Education in the United States by Region, 1983–84

Region	Total Programs	Under-graduate Degrees Offered	Graduate Degrees Offered	Under-graduates Enrolled	Grad-uates Enrolled	Under-graduate Degrees Granted	Graduate Degrees Granted
Northeast	172	432	93	34,636	1,447	8,805	328
Midwest	242	669	68	28,476	2,176	4,394	322
South	341	792	131	40,127	1,645	6,503	395
West	181	511	52	24,184	958	3,201	141
Total U.S.	936	2,404	344	127,423	6,226	22,903	1,186

Source: Nemeth, Charles P. (1986). *Anderson's Directory of Criminal Justice Education, 1986-87.* Cincinnati, OH: Anderson Publishing Company.

in criminal justice or corrections. Staufenberger (1977) states that there were 184 colleges offering police-related programs in 1966-67; by 1974 that number had reached 1,030. Nemeth (1986) identified 936 criminal justice programs in the United States, and 5 in Canada; the total enrollment in the 941 college programs was 134,908 students. Table 5.1 contains the enrollment and program information by region of the United States (see Appendix B for state listings).

In 1971, the number of bachelor's, master's, and doctoral degrees awarded in criminology, law enforcement, and corrections was 3,050 (Shover & Einstadter, 1988). Table 5.2 contains the numbers of degrees conferred in 1985-86; over 25,000 students were awarded criminal justice degrees during that year. An additional 1,166 were granted degrees in criminology, and a large but unknown number of students who received degrees in other fields will actually seek employment in corrections.

The importance of education cannot be overstated. Cherniss and Kane (1987) refer to several studies (Bartol, 1979; Gurin, Veroff, & Feld, 1960; Mannheim, 1975; Van Fossen, 1979) that support the "view that there is more job satisfaction and less job-related strain as one climbs up the occupational, educational, and organizational ladders" (p. 126). Other studies have supported the idea that education reduces burnout and stress (Brown, 1987; Carroll & White, 1982). The importance of education is underscored when one considers competition for

TABLE 5.2: Degrees Conferred in 1985–86

Degree	Criminal Justice	Criminology	Total
Associate's	12,096	—	12,096
Bachelor's	12,704	1,097	13,801
Master's	1,074	69	1,143
Doctorate	21	—	21
Total	25,895	1,166	27,601

Source: National Center for Education Statistics. (1988). *Digest of Education Statistics.* Washington, DC: U.S. Government Printing Office.

promotion and other professional and career development. As indicated in Chapter 1, Schwartz (1988) reported that 30 million Americans have some college credits, 18 million have bachelor's degrees, 6 million have master's degrees, and 768,000 have doctorates. Hepburn (1985) found that 56% of guards (not other correctional workers) had stopped formal education at or before completion of high school. The average years of education was 12.8 years; 16% had completed two or more years of college, and 11% had not finished high school. Jurik (1985b), however, found that 55% of the officers in her study had two- or four-year degrees and 76% had more than 13 years of formal education. In a survey of 9,472 respondents,[1] the American Correctional Association found that 72.9% had bachelor's degrees or higher, 40.7% had master's degrees or higher; and 16.6% had high school educations or their equivalent (American Correctional Association, 1986). In a study of probation and parole officers in New York and Indiana, Whitehead (1985) found that only 4.8% had less than an associate's degree; 5.8% had less than a bachelor's degree. Thus, approximately 95% of the probation and parole officers had one or more college degrees. Probation and parole frequently require a college degree for entry into the field (Abadinsky, 1977; Allen, Eskridge, Latessa, & Vito, 1985; Lawrence, 1984).

Education pays off in several ways. It gives added security and ability to compete for jobs and promotions, lessens the dependence of individuals on the organization, and pays off with added income.

Those who earn a bachelor's degree average $1,841 [per month] while those who attend college but drop out earn only $1,169. High school graduates average $1,045 while high-school dropouts earn only $693 per month. (National Neighborhood Foot Patrol Center, 1988, p. 13)

THE APPRENTICESHIP PERIOD

Corrections is a service industry staffed, to a great extent, by public service professionals. The general requirement is that all employees start at the basic level, because organizational knowledge is a critical component of the knowledge base of public service professionals. Exceptions are made for those with advanced professional skills such as doctors, lawyers, teachers, and others with refined technical abilities. The period from entry level to advancement is dependent upon performance and preparation. The general familiarization period for most professionals does not extend beyond one or two years at the entry level. After that, advancement usually occurs, sometimes rapidly, to progressively responsible positions. Adequately prepared and highly skilled individuals can move rapidly into upper management positions.

The rapid expansion of corrections within the last two decades and its projected further expansion indicate that the field is indeed a growth industry. The apprenticeship period should be used to learn all that can be learned about the particular agency in which the employee is located and about particular career patterns that are available. At this stage of development in the profession, it is generally better to seek employment with a large agency and plan to stay with that particular agency. The tendency for agencies to promote from within the organization limits the opportunity for movement from one agency to another in middle management positions. As the profession matures, the ability to move between agencies at all levels should increase.

FUNCTIONAL ROLES

Archambeault & Archambeault (1982), referring to the *National Manpower Survey* (U. S. Department of Justice, 1978), indicate the following division of employees in corrections: 7% are in management roles; 34.2% are in correctional officer roles; 8.8% are child-care workers; 11.1% are probation and parole officers; 11.15% are professional staff; and 27.8% are clerical, craft, and support personnel.[2] These various roles can be placed into four categories: (1) custodial surveillance; (2) support; (3) treatment; and (4) administrative. The first three categories require both technical and human skills.[3] The fourth category, administrative, requires technical, human, and conceptual skills. This section defines these roles and identifies the basic requirements of adequate preparation for each. Chapter 7 will identify the responsibilities and tasks associated with roles in each of the four categories.

Custody and Surveillance

Institutional correctional officers provide custody and ensure the safety and security of the institution; they are frequently considered the single most important group in the prison. Their constant contact with the inmate population gives them the power to enhance or destroy the efforts of professionals. Observation of inmate behavior is crucial in that it can provide many cues to future behavior, amenability to behavioral change and intervention programs, and other important factors about inmates or inmate populations. The American Correctional Association (1983) states that

> the role of today's correctional officer is more involved than simply providing custody. There are many tasks required and officers must understand the philosophy and function of the correctional institution . . . the limits of responsibility and amount of authority . . . their job in relationship to other employees . . . [and] court and legislative decisions. (p. 8)

The educational requirement for entry level prison custodial personnel is usually a high school diploma or its equivalent. Probation and parole officers are usually required to have at least a bachelor's degree in criminal justice or a related field; many probation and parole agencies require a four-year degree to establish minimum eligibility for employment (Abadinsky, 1977; Allen, Eskridge, Latessa, & Vito, 1985; Lawrence, 1984). Federal probation officers, as a practical matter, are usually required to have a master's degree (Allen et al., 1985). In addition, many probation/parole agencies have additional requirements such as experience, entry examinations, and so forth.

The surveillance role of officers working in community corrections is similar to the custody role of institutional officers. Surveillance is more difficult in the community because it is only one (perhaps even a subordinate) role of the probation/parole officer. Clients are usually free to move within their communities, and their actions are not easily observed. Some community agencies employ officers whose only role is surveillance; that, however, is an exception. Most probation and parole officers have dual roles. They not only observe offenders' behavior but also engage in counseling, assisting clients regarding employment issues, and broker community services such as drug programs, among other tasks.

Support

Support roles include both professional and nonprofessional roles. Some require limited preparation while others require extensive preparation. Examples of support roles include secretarial and clerical staff, construction workers, computer operators and programmers, engineers, accountants, lawyers, maintenance workers, and similar occupations or professions.

Large correctional agencies with multimillion (in some cases, over one billion) dollar budgets have need for all types of professionals. Agencies responsible for institutions require large numbers of employees. They provide almost all (and, in some cases, more) of the services that are found in a city. Maintenance operations, construction, industrial, and other types of activity are found on a large scale in many state correctional systems.

The preparation necessary for these varied roles depends upon the specific role. Accountants, attorneys, architects, engineers, and the like need to be certified and/or licensed in accordance with the requirements of their particular professions. There may be an additional need to understand the unique aspects of practice in the correctional environment, but this usually can be accomplished with brief orientations at the time of employment.

Many support roles—such as maintenance, mechanical repair, truck driving, equipment operation, some construction activity, and others— do not require extensive academic preparation. Though highly skilled in many cases (perhaps even more skilled than some professions) these occupations do not possess the attributes of professions. Each, however, may involve extensive experience and knowledge regarding the practice of that particular occupation. These comments are not intended to devalue the support roles, but to indicate the variety of roles available and the wide range of preparatory requirements.

Treatment

Treatment roles usually require extensive preparation in one of several professions, as well as familiarity with corrections. Examples of roles in treatment include social caseworkers, teachers, counselors, psychiatrists, psychologists, physicians, dentists, and other health care professionals with various specialties.

Social caseworkers, depending upon the specific job which they hold, may be required to hold master's degrees in social work. School teachers usually are required to meet the certification standards of their states. Counselors, depending upon their specific jobs, may also be required to hold advanced degrees in appropriate disciplines. Psychologists are subject to the licensing requirements of their states and the particular jobs that they hold. Some psychologists in prison systems, for example, do not actually administer therapy; rather, they may administer tests or perform other similar tasks. These individuals may or may not be required to hold a license. Psychologists who conduct therapy are usually required by state law to obtain licensure and certification as clinical psychologists; doctoral degrees are usually required. Psychiatrists, physicians, surgeons, dentists, and other health care personnel are required to meet the strict guidelines of educational, licensure, and certification requirements of their states.

Many agencies also have positions in treatment programs that do not require professional status. These positions, however, are usually clerical, security, or paraprofessional in nature. Such individuals are not actually involved in the administration of the treatment; rather, they work in support roles in programs that administer treatment.

Administrative

Administrative roles in corrections require that individuals be familiar with corrections and with the specific organizations in which they work. A thorough understanding of the organization is necessary in order that each individual be able to perform the technical skills required. Most administrators are also supervisors, and make decisions regarding the welfare of both clients and employees. Higher level administrative positions involve the development and implementation of policies that comply with laws, court decisions, and legislative intent, and are consistent with sound correctional practices.

Administrative positions range from limited roles (such as personnel officers at particular institutions) to agency heads who have responsibility over all institutions and all programs in their agencies. The specific skills required in each of the positions depends to a great extent upon the positions themselves. All administrative positions involve leadership roles. The leadership components of each role may vary as to the reference groups toward which they are directed and their significance, but such components are always present.

Administrative roles also involve political components. Agency administrators must interact in political environments that define their missions and provide their resources. In order to be competitive and to operate their agencies in an effective and efficient manner administrators must be able to articulate goals and processes and justify particular courses of action. These goals and processes must be consistent with legislative intent, legal mandates and requirements, and public concerns. Legislatures, judges, and the public are sometimes uninformed about correctional programs and processes, and may require inconsistent actions; administrators must assure that the legislative, judicial, and public mandates are implemented in ways that are consistent with professional correctional practice.

The necessity of combining effective and efficient operation of a professional corrections agency with competition for limited resources, legislative mandates, judicial mandates, and public pressures makes it imperative that the administrator have refined conceptual skills. It is important that higher level administrators be well educated, experienced, and mature individuals. The American Correctional Association lists the general characteristics of commissioners/directors and administrators/deputy secretaries as being in their mid-40s with 10 to 15 years' experience and holding master's degrees (American Correctional Association, 1986).

CAREER DEVELOPMENT AND PROGRESSION

Few individuals are content to remain at entry or journeyman levels of work throughout the entire course of their careers. Most want to advance along the administrative or line supervisory hierarchy to more responsible positions with increased responsibilities, rewards, and satisfaction. Higher level positions in criminal justice agencies involve a greater presence of professional attributes.

Because almost all criminal justice functional roles involve the supervision of people—either employees, inmates, or clients—human skills are perhaps the most important of the three types of skills required. Technical skills are necessary in order to be able to operate hardware and understand procedures. Conceptual skills, and therefore education, gain increasing importance as one ascends the ladder of agency responsibility.

It is important to become fully knowledgeable regarding potential career options and career paths. Various line and staff roles exist for which a variety of specialized knowledge may be required. It is very important, however, that all individuals who work in a corrections agency (with the possible exception of the traditional professions of law, medicine, and clergy) be knowledgeable regarding the basic work roles of the agency or a similar agency.

Professionals have stronger growth needs than do other types of workers (Cherniss & Kane, 1987). Continuing education and training is important for many reasons, including the facts that the missions of professions change (Houle, 1980) and that new knowledge is always being accumulated.

> The professional does not earn his status once and for all. Rather, it is a continuous process in which his claims to competence are being tested every day in interaction with others and he can lose the respect of others. (Bucher & Stelling, 1977, p. 123)

Houle (1980) indicates that many professionals do not continue educational development in the manner required. Self-growth is important, however, and can help to reduce job dissatisfaction (Brown, 1987). Continuing education and training is a lifelong process that is the primary responsibility of the individual.

> The burden for continuing education does unquestionably fall on the incumbent. . . . A true professional's essential task is not to apply a specific fact or principle to a particular case but to deal with it by use of a synthesis of all relevant knowledge. (Thomas, 1983, p. 9)

The application of all relevant knowledge requires that individuals seek continuing education and training opportunities in their primary fields and in related areas. Continuing education and training must be multidisciplinary in their approach (Lawrence, 1984). Corrections professionals must pursue both educational and training opportunities that have direct application and those that do not have direct application. In one study (McGowan, 1980), two-thirds of the professionals interviewed stated that public professionals must be aware of developments outside the organization.

> The public professional, to function properly, must know how to integrate professional goals with those of the organization. This individual must continually update skills as the technology changes and must have some understanding of the formal and informal networks. (McGowan, 1982, p. 348)

Both training and education are critical. Each has a different role, and each should be a continuing process. Education concentrates on the development of theoretical knowledge, which allows one to understand processes and to make decisions in ambiguous situations. Training, on the other hand, is designed to impart specific skills that have direct application in more concrete (and less ambiguous) situations. Houle (1980) identifies the following as the goals of lifelong professional education:

- Clarifying function and mission of the profession
- Mastery of the theoretical knowledge
- To increase the capacity to solve problems
- To gain the use of practical knowledge
- Self-enhancement
- Formal training in new techniques
- Credentialing
- Creation and perpetuation of professional subculture
- Legal reinforcement of professional procedures
- Public acceptance
- To promote and ensure ethical practice
- To determine and reinforce penalties for unethical practice
- To improve relations with other vocations
- To improve relations with users of services.

Continuing Education

A primary role of education is to instill in individuals the desire, capability, and ability to continue learning throughout life. The world in which the corrections professional functions is continually changing. New discoveries are made, new laws passed, new judicial rulings issued, and new technology is developed on a continuous basis. Adequate development of all skills—technical, human, and conceptual—requires increased amounts of education as society changes and the complexity of the profession and its knowledge base increases. Because higher order skills require more education than lower order skills, those who wish to compete adequately and rise to higher level positions must continue to pursue continuing education opportunities conscientiously.

The consequences of continuing education are positive. It serves to provide growth and development for employees, keeps them current regarding developments in the field, and serves to stimulate new procedures for goal accomplishment. Poole and Regoli (1980b) argue that "the exposure of officers to higher education may cultivate a flexibility of job definitions and goal redefinitions that could serve as a safeguard against ossified and inappropriate work procedures" (p. 220).

Education is available from many sources. Informally, one can continue the educational process in a self-directed way. One alternative that many professionals pursue when burned out in their fields is to pursue educational alternatives in other fields. More and more adults are returning to college campuses to pursue basic or advanced education in many different fields of study. In addition, many professional associations offer seminars that could appropriately be considered as educational endeavors. Colleges and universities offer professional and continuing-education seminars in corrections and many related fields.

Sixty-one percent (61%) of the states offer reduced or remitted tuition for those returning to college to pursue criminal justice education; 24% offer expense stipends, and 6% offer scholarships (Benton, 1988). Jurik, Halemba, Musheno, and Boyle (1987) found that 24% of the respondents in their survey were enrolled in one or more college courses. Usually, costs are comparatively low, and some agencies may pay all or most of the costs. Most agencies will send individuals to seminars if there is a relationship to the agency work that the individual does or plans to do. Although most of these seminars are actually training-oriented courses, some also serve educational functions.

Training

> Relevant training is the lifeblood of any career development effort. It offers the opportunity to develop skills necessary to climb up the career ladder. Training refreshes and revitalizes critical thinking and creativity. It can unify an organization and empower its staff to create change and improvement. (Sheridan, 1988, p. 87)

Although education is an important prerequisite to career development and progression, training is an essential function required for minimal performance of duty. Education is designed to broaden the breadth and depth of knowledge, but not necessarily to teach particular skills. Training, on the other hand, is designed to impart specific knowledge and abilities (technical skills) that can be immediately translated into more effective performance. "Training can serve to invigorate staff by providing ideas of new, different, more sophisticated, or more advanced ways of performing work responsibilities" (Shapiro,1982, quoted in Brown, 1986, p. 6). "Staff need to be trained and retrained, both to increase their efficiency and to expand their career capabilities" (Travisono, 1987a, p. 4). All correctional agencies provide preservice training to one extent or another (see Chapter 4 for further discussion of correctional training). Basic familiarity with the rules and procedures of each institution or agency is necessary. In addition, specific requirements of some court decisions are that all personnel be provided with a specified number of hours of retraining each year. Most agencies also offer in-service training programs that cover a wide range of topics.

Each agency has its own preservice and in-service training programs. In addition, many colleges and universities offer courses designed to impart specific training skills. The National Academy of Corrections (located in Longmont, Colorado) provides training to numerous corrections and corrections-related professionals each year through its residential training and training-for-trainers programs. The academy "expects to provide training to more than 1,500 participants at its Longmont, Colorado, location and to hundreds more through its training-for-trainers programs at state and local agencies in fiscal year 1989" (Gilley, 1988, p. 30). The curriculum at the National Academy consists of basic, advanced, and specialized training in areas of application including supervision, administration, fiscal affairs, population management, construction, and other specific topics.

SUMMARY

Educational requirements for successful careers in corrections have increased significantly since the mid-1960s. The movement toward professionalization has helped to create a large number of educational facilities. The number of colleges offering criminal justice programs increased from less than 200 in 1967-68 to over 1000 in 1980. In 1985, there were 941 university and college programs in criminal justice in the United States and Canada with a total enrollment of approximately 135,000. Enrollments in criminal justice programs are continuing to increase. The number of individuals in corrections with college degrees continues to increase as agencies become more selective in recruitment, retention, and advancement. Demographic trends, social and political pressures, and court decisions also contribute to the increased professionalization and educational requirements of corrections agencies.

The four categories of personnel—custodial/surveillance, support, treatment, and administrative—require differing levels and types of preparation. The entry level custodial/surveillance position frequently does not require a college degree; however, advancement above entry level usually requires increased amounts of education either as a prerequisite to promotion or as a practical matter of competition. Support roles may or may not require significant occupational or professional preparation, depending upon the actual role performed. Treatment roles usually require advanced skills attainable only through professional education. Administrative roles also usually require professional preparation as well as refined conceptual skills.

Continuing education and training are critical to the maintenance and advancement of professional skills, and to professional development and career progression. Education and training each serve a different purpose. Education imparts specific knowledge at a more abstract level (the body of theory) and concentrates on the development of conceptual skills, whereas training concentrates on skill development for specific techniques and purposes.

NOTES

1. This distribution of educational achievement is probably higher than the distribution would be if one considers all correctional employees. It is likely that those with higher

educational status have a greater likelihood of joining professional associations and a higher probability of responding to surveys.

2. "*Management* positions include persons working as wardens, sheriffs, administrators of juvenile programs agencies, institutions, department heads, and other key personnel of middle-management or above. . . . *Correctional officers* positions include persons working as supervisors or as line officers who have direct responsibility for custody, security, and safety of inmates in adult institutions, including state institutions and jails. . . . *Child care worker* positions include persons working as supervisors or as line houseparents, counselors, night supervisors, or other positions which have the primary responsibility of supervising, or providing custody, care, and safety for juveniles in detention centers, training schools, or other juvenile institutions. . . . *Probation or parole officer* positions include supervisory, line, and support personnel (case aides) who have direct responsibility for supervising those on probation or parole or for conducting presentence or preparole investigations and recommendations. . . . *Professional staff* include a broad range of treatment and service specialists including teachers, therapists, social workers, psychologists, psychiatrists, physicians, dentists, nurses, and chaplains among others. . . . *Clerical, craft, and support* positions include a variety of administrative, clerical, maintenance, and service positions" (Archambeault & Archambeault, 1982, p. 20, emphasis in original).

3. This is not to exclude the need for conceptual skills, especially in the treatment program area. The predominant role, however, of custodial and surveillance, support personnel, and, to a lesser extent, treatment personnel is to perform particular specialized functions rather than generalized roles.

6

The Tasks of Corrections and Corrections Professionals

Corrections agencies and programs have unique tasks. No other agencies, programs, or activities (with the possible exception of mental health facilities) are designed to hold people against their wishes in inherently punitive environments and to impose undesired change and control. The goals of a corrections agency are twofold: First, it has an obligation to the community to ensure that its clients, whether in an institution or in the community, are constrained within acceptable—and frequently specified—behavioral parameters. Second, it should do something positive to ensure that clients, when released, will become productive, noncriminal members of society. In the absence of fulfilling the second goal, the agency should, at the very least, not do anything that will make individuals more prone to criminal behavior upon release from supervision.

Professionals who staff correctional programs are morally and legally responsible for effectively and efficiently accomplishing the tasks of corrections. Specific roles defining responsibilities to clients, staff, and political and social interests are frequently limited and clearly defined. There are instances, however, where roles are broad and not clearly defined. Social, political, and human complexities continually impose conditions with conflicting forces that require balanced decision making within the constraints of imposed rules.

The purposes of corrections are usually identified as being retribution, deterrence, incapacitation, rehabilitation, and reintegration. Correctional agencies must classify clients; impose and ensure discipline; provide security of the institution, agency, and public; and provide treatment programs and services to clients. Corrections professionals

are also responsible for leadership in policy formulation and implementation. This chapter discusses those purposes and tasks which, together,
accomplish the goals of protecting society and changing clients.

THE PURPOSES OF CORRECTIONS

The four generally recognized purposes of corrections are retribution, deterrence, incapacitation, and rehabilitation. The fifth purpose,
reintegration, is a recent addition that became accepted after the rehabilitation goal lost popularity. Emphasis on these purposes varies over
time: When judges sentence individuals to correctional programs, they
actually have in mind all of the purposes identified above. Correctional
agencies usually attempt, either explicitly or implicitly, to serve all five
goals. Usually, however, one goal will receive primary emphasis to the
exclusion of the other goals. There are periodic shifts in emphasis
depending upon the state of knowledge at the time, the political environment, the social environment, and other factors. (This book does not
attempt to resolve the differences of opinion regarding the purposes of
corrections.)

Retribution

The concept of retribution is perhaps the oldest of the several purposes of corrections. Biblical sources refer to the concept of *lex tali-
onis*—an "eye for an eye." Retribution, in its most simple terms, means
that punishment is imposed upon persons because they have committed
crimes. These crimes are considered to have upset the social balance,
which can only be restored by the infliction of punishment upon the
offenders. Although being sent to prison or placed under correctional
supervision may indeed be retribution, it is not the function of corrections professionals to exact retribution through the infliction of physical
pain, mental pain, or excessively unpleasant conditions.

> In summary, it means that a crime is a wrong because it has disturbed the
> order of society; matters can be set right only by an equivalent wrong done
> to the offender. (Jenkins, 1984, p. 144)

Arguments for retribution include: (1) it respects free will and responsibility; (2) it has religious backing; and (3) it prevents vigilantism (Jenkins, 1984). The argument about whether or not man has free will is a philosophical argument that defies absolute resolution. Many believe that individuals do have free will and can choose to commit any acts that they so desire. Others believe that the circumstances and conditions of life that persons encounter determine patterns of behavior and perhaps even specific acts of behavior. The idea of retribution assumes that individuals have free will and must accept full responsibility for their actions; to impose retributory punishment upon persons who have no control over their actions is illogical.

The religious backing of retribution is alluded to above. Biblical passages can be found that support the idea of retribution if interpreted in a literal fashion. The argument that retribution prevents vigilantism is based upon the idea that humans seek revenge and wish to see punitive harm come to those who break the law. If society efficiently imposes punishment, people will refrain from taking the law into their own hands. Additionally, philosophers have argued that it is humanity's "right to be punished" if punishable acts are committed. This is based upon the recognition of humans as having free will and responsibility. Under this argument, if we deny people the right to be punished, we have denied them the honor of being human.

Retribution is a backward-looking act. It does not claim any preventive, treatment, or deterrent rationale. Many claim that it is (or has the great potential to be) a barbarous act. Some oppose retribution as a goal on religious grounds; some also argue that there is a great deal of evidence which supports the idea of external causes of behavior. If behavior has external causes, man does not have free will, and we are therefore not justified in exacting retribution on anyone. There is also a metaphysical and mystical component to retribution (Jenkins, 1984): Exactly what social order has been disturbed, to what extent, and how can it be restored? How much punishment is enough? How much punishment is too much? What kind of "pain" is necessary to avenge a particular act? These are questions that cannot be answered easily. Any attempt to reach agreement upon these questions among civilized people is virtually impossible. Even with discounting the philosophical arguments related to these questions it is easy to see that, as a practical matter, the courts have precluded the imposition of barbaric acts[1] even upon those who themselves have committed such acts.

We cannot measure the effectiveness of retribution, because it is not intended to "work" (Jenkins, 1984). Although going to prison or being punished through fines or probation may be retribution—and, indeed, even the mildest form of punishment is retribution to some people in some circumstances—it is not the function of the correctional agency to exact that retribution. Merely being subjected to the agency control is the retribution. Retribution, then, is a function of the courts, not of correctional agencies.

Deterrence

A sentence to a corrections institution or community program may also serve as a deterrent to the commission of crime. The two types of deterrence are *specific* and *general*. Specific deterrence refers to the belief that the individual who is punished will be deterred from committing future criminal acts. General deterrence refers to the belief that others, coming to know of the plight of the convicts, will refrain from committing similar or other criminal acts.

Deterrence is a utilitarian idea based upon a hedonistic view of man, which presumes that individuals seek to maximize pleasure and avoid pain. Therefore, if the pain (disadvantages) associated with crime outweighs the pleasure (advantages), individuals will refrain from criminal activity. Deterrence therefore serves a purpose—that of reducing the incidence rate of present and future criminal acts. We are justified in administering only that amount of punishment that serves the purpose; too much or too little is equally wrong. It is obviously difficult to determine the appropriate length of sentence, for example, to serve as a deterrent for the particular act because human beings differ so much. We commonly think of the fact that we, as law-abiding citizens, are deterred from such acts as speeding if we see a policeman. We therefore conclude that all that is necessary to reduce crime is to impose enough punishment on enough people.

The fallacy in that argument is twofold: First, it assumes rational behavior in all cases. There is considerable evidence that suggests that criminals do not engage in cost/benefit analysis when considering particular acts (Walker, 1989); therefore, their behavior is frequently irrational. "The fact that their [criminals'] lives are very disorganized undermines the central assumption . . . that criminals . . . make a rational choice" (Walker, 1989, p. 127).[2] Second, it assumes that we can identify, apprehend, and impose punishment on all or most who commit criminal acts. The evidence does not support this. We know from various sources that only about 50% of all crime is reported; of that reported, only about 26% results in clearance by arrest; of those cleared by arrest, only about 69% are convicted (Silberman, 1978; Walker, 1989). In order for punishment of any type to serve as a deterrent, the punishment must be swift, sure, and of appropriate severity. Punishment that is long in coming, if at all, either has no effect on human behavior or may have a negative effect on future behavior. Punishment of inappropriate severity often has the reverse effect of that intended: If punishments are too severe, juries will not convict, police will not arrest (depending upon the type of crime), and individual criminals will commit even more hostile acts to avoid perceived excessive punishment for a less hostile act.

Perhaps the most significant arguments regarding deterrence are heard in regard to the death penalty. There are scientific studies that argue that the death penalty deters, and there are equally valid studies that argue that it does not deter. In the 1950s, Sellin (1980) examined the deterrent effect of the death penalty in contiguous (adjoining) states where one had the death penalty and the other did not. Sellin also examined data from states that had the death penalty, deleted it, and then reinstated it. Analyzing the results, he found that the death penalty had no deterrent effect.

In 1830 there were about 200 offenses for which you were likely to be hanged [in England]; by 1880 it was difficult to be hanged for anything other than murder or treason. Between 1830 and 1880 the number of offenses reported per 100,000 of the population fell from 331 to 33. If deterrence theory is true, surely the decline in the severity of punishments should have meant much more crime, not much less. (Jenkins, 1984, p. 155)

Ehrlich (1975) stated that each execution prevents seven or eight murders. Bowers and Pierce (1975), however, reexamined Ehrlich's data and found that, if the data for selected years were removed, the deterrent effect of the penalty disappeared. These researchers further advanced an idea referred to as "brutalization theory" wherein they suggested that each execution caused two or three more homicides during the months that followed (Bowers & Pierce, 1980). Walker (1989) summarizes the current state of our knowledge regarding the deterrent effect of punishment by stating that "the safest conclusion one can draw from the available research is that the deterrence argument has not been proved" (p. 103). However, neither has it been disproved. If deterrence is a legitimate goal, it is a function of the courts. Corrections programs, including prisons, are very limited in their ability to do anything specific to achieve deterrence. If corrections is a deterrent, merely being in the controlled environment is the deterrent factor. History shows that excessive punishments and unpleasant, unsanitary conditions do not contribute to the deterrent effect of correctional programs.

Incapacitation

Incapacitation is also a function of criminal sanctions. The idea behind the concept is to restrict individuals' behavioral or situational choices such that they are incapable of committing criminal acts upon an unsuspecting public. Imprisonment does not keep inmates from committing criminal acts in the institution, but it does preclude the offender from committing crime in the community during the period of incarceration. Recent emphasis has been placed on the concept of selective incapacitation. Because it is not possible to incarcerate everyone who commits a crime, the idea here is to select those who commit the most criminal behavior—career criminals—and selectively incarcerate them for lengthy periods of time, thereby realizing a significant decline in criminal activity.

Several studies have been conducted which purport to show that, by identifying the relatively small number of all criminals who commit the majority of criminal acts, we could eliminate much criminal activity. Wilson (1975) suggested that crime could be reduced by one third by imposing a three-year sentence on each person convicted of a serious crime; Wilson (1983) was less optimistic in his later work. Greenwood (1982) suggests that robbery can be reduced by 15% while increasing the prison population by only 5%. Other studies (see Walker, 1989) have indicated significant increases in the prison population given mandatory sentences of five years to reduce crime by 26.7%. Walker (1989) summarizes the effect of these policies as follows:

> Thus over five years we would incur combined construction and operating costs of $120 billion to achieve an estimated 26.7 percent reduction in violent crime. (p. 79)

The problem quickly becomes a practical one. The costs are very high for a minimal return, and we cannot predict with any accuracy who it is that will commit crime in the future. The few studies that have been able to predict with greater than 50% accuracy all contained prediction elements that could not be used to incarcerate individuals. For example, the RAND study (Greenwood, 1982) achieved a 51% prediction rate by including several background elements including employment within the last two years. It is not illegal nor necessarily immoral to be unemployed. Therefore, to enhance punishment based on employment history is considered by some to be immoral and would likely be determined to be illegal.

Prisons are effective at incapacitation for the relatively short period of time that the individual is incarcerated. Recent court activity in sending more and more criminals to prison for longer periods of time has had the paradoxical effect of causing prisoners to be released after serving shorter periods of time than would have been the case under more selective incarceration policies. In some cases, violent offenders are released after serving a short period of time in order to make room for nonviolent offenders. Sometimes those violent offenders have committed further crimes. Walker (1989) states that selective incapacitation is ineffective as a policy for reducing serious crime for the following reasons:

(1) The difficulties of correctly estimating the amount of crime reduction;

(2) the difficulties of accurately identifying the chronic offenders. . . ;

(3) the monetary cost of increased prison populations and the political cost of reducing prison terms for low-risk offenders in order to offset increased prison terms for high-risk offenders;

(4) the difficulty of implementing the policy without gross violations of constitutional rights; and

(5) other unpredictable side effects. (p. 72)

Rehabilitation

Rehabilitation as a goal of corrections gained popularity in the 1960s. It is based on the medical model of diagnosis and treatment. The idea is that individuals who have committed criminal acts are in some way deficient in social skills, personal skills, or other attributes, which contributed to their decisions to commit the criminal acts. This model calls for diagnosing the deficiencies and treating the offenders through various programs designed to remove the deficiencies. When they return to the community, they will then be able to interact socially, obtain and retain employment, and be able to function normally without resorting to criminal activity.

In institutions, rehabilitation programs include medical programs, psychological programs, academic and vocational education, religious programs, and other programs not institutionally required. For example, food service and basic health care are institutionally required and would not be considered to be rehabilitation programs. A cooking school and medical programs such as elective plastic surgery and hair transplants, however, would be considered to be rehabilitation. Rehabilitation programs in communities include probation, parole, diversion, and counseling, and other types of programs designed to remove offenders from institutional environments but provide supervision and assistance at the same time.[3]

Rehabilitation is a controversial subject, and came into disfavor in the mid- to late 1970s. Martinson (1974) argued that rehabilitation did not work as effectively as was claimed by its proponents; he did find, however, that 48% of the programs he studied actually were effective for some people. Several other studies (Bailey, 1966; and others) have also found some rehabilitation programs to be effective. Today, most corrections administrators still believe in rehabilitation but do not see it as a panacea to the crime problem. Perhaps Walker (1989) sums it up best when he says that "the most accurate thing we can say about rehabilitation, then, is that some programs work for some offenders" (p. 220). Correctional agencies will continue to offer rehabilitation programs into the foreseeable future for three reasons: First, these programs do work for some people under some circumstances. Second, it is the humane thing to do for both society and the offender. Third, courts will continue to require it. Therefore, treatment based on the concept of rehabilitation will continue to be a primary function of corrections.

Reintegration

Reintegration as a goal of corrections came to prominence after the demise of the rehabilitation model. The rationale is that offenders must learn to function in society, and that they can best learn this in community settings. Therefore, the primary concentration is on working with offenders in the community, helping them to successfully reenter society as law-abiding citizens. There are many similarities between rehabilitation and reintegration; both models employ many of the same processes and programs. The primary difference is in the voluntariness of program participation, and in the expected outcomes. We have come to realize that no individual can be forced to be rehabilitated. It is up to the individual to change his own behavior. We must have the program available, however, to assist those who wish to change. While rehabilitation has primary concern for the client, the reintegration model has high concern for both the offender and society. Some of the programs that have begun in accordance with this model are weekend jail programs, halfway houses, work release, and similar programs.

BEHAVIOR CONTROL AND BEHAVIORAL CHANGE

Corrections professionals are faced with two behavioral goals regarding clients. The most immediate goal is the control of inmate and/or client behavior to assure that the institution and community are safe. The second goal, although some would place it as first priority, is to change long-term behavioral patterns. The first goal is accomplished through mechanisms of control whereby unwanted behavior is discouraged by punishment or other methods. The second goal is accomplished through rehabilitation or treatment programs. Correctional institutions accomplish these tasks through processes of classification, discipline, security, and treatment.

Classification

Classification is a formal process that begins upon entry into a prison system or correctional agency and continues until such time as the individual is released from supervision of the agency. Probation and parole agencies usually only classify individuals as to level of supervision and treatment needs; other types of classification are usually nonexistent in those agencies because they have no real need for them. The primary area where the concept of classification is a significant factor is institutions. Therefore, the information presented below is most relevant to prisons. The process in prisons is designed to make maximum use of scarce program and institutional resources and, at the same time, ensure that each inmate receives the care, custody, and program needs appropriate to that individual.

Upon entry into a prison system, inmates are usually given batteries of tests, including medical, vocational, psychological, academic achievement, and others. The purpose is to determine individuals' strengths, weaknesses, traits, and needs. They will then be placed in particular institutions where they can best be controlled and have access to the most relevant treatment programs for their particular needs. Most prison systems classify according to medical, offender, security, and treatment needs, and by time-earning status.

Inmates are also classified at the institutional level according to their important traits, job and/or treatment programs assignments, security risk, and other factors. Housing assignments are made to utilize space most effectively and provide the degree of security required for each individual. Dormitory assignments and other assignments involving relative freedom of movement are given only to inmates who warrant such assignments.

Medical classification involves a determination of individuals' physical health and capacities. It determines the type of work that they may be required or allowed to do, the type of care, diet, and services they will receive, and the particular prisons to which they will be assigned. If individuals are in need of constant medical care at major hospital units or have special problems, such as AIDS, they will be placed at the locations best suited to provide that particular care.

Offender classification usually involves separation, or selective integration, by age and by criminal history. Those who have committed other crimes in the past and/or are particularly violent will usually be separated from those who are younger and/or have committed nonviolent offenses.

Security classifications involve making judgments about the particular risk posed by each inmate for such things as escape or institutional misbehavior. Inmates who have a history of violence, escapes, and general troublemaking during previous incarcerations are usually separated from those who do not pose such risks. The result is assignment to a minimum, medium, or maximum security institution. Rules, regulations, routines, and procedures vary at these institutions based upon the security risks of the inmates.

Treatment classification involves determination of special needs such as education, psychological treatment, and so forth. This category of classification relies heavily upon vocational and aptitude tests to determine the particular vocational program best suited to and desired by each inmate. Those who need particular types of educational treatment (e.g., special education) or who desire and qualify for particular training programs may be placed at locations where they will have access to the desired or needed programs.

Time-earning classification is based upon the concept of good time—additional credits for time served, awarded for good behavior. Most prison systems grant several categories of good time. For example, in Texas an inmate may receive the following credits for each 30 days served: 30, 40, 50, 60, or 90 days. The actual formulas vary by state, and some inmates are precluded by law from earning good time. The extra time may or may not apply toward parole depending upon the state, the crime, and the offender status of the individual (recidivist or first offender).

Discipline

Discipline in an institution is extremely important. Inmates live in congested conditions and have scarce resources and limited commodities. They are necessarily deprived of many amenities that free individuals routinely enjoy. The typical prison has many rules to ensure the orderly flow of services to all individuals and to protect the lives, property, and safety of inmates, employees, and the public. In such an environment, discipline is a crucial element without which the prison would become a chaotic environment.

Discipline involves the obeying of rules and the self-control and commitment required to accomplish goals. This section is primarily concerned with the rule-breaking behavior and the maintenance of order in the institution. Court action in recent years has changed the processes by which the correctional officer must maintain discipline; officers can no longer impose summary punishment without following due process guidelines that have been specified by the courts. Inmates have the right to know the charges against them, to be notified 24 hours in advance of hearings, to have assistance in their defense, to call witnesses (unless doing so would create additional problems), to have impartial boards determine their guilt or innocence, and to have written findings of facts. Institutions have devised standard procedures to comply with these requirements.

Most inmates do not commonly engage in serious rule-breaking behavior. However, rule breaking does exist at a sufficiently high frequency to cause great concern in prisons. Wheeler (1961) found that inmate rule-breaking behavior follows an inverted-U pattern. That is, when inmates first enter prison, they refrain from rule-breaking behavior, perhaps from fear and lack of knowledge. During the middle part of their sentences, they engage in rule-breaking more frequently. As they near their parole dates, inmates again conform and avoid rule-breaking behavior. MacKenzie (1987) found that younger inmates have more conflict with both guards and inmates. Long sentences, restricted eligibility for—and in some states abolition of—parole, and other factors make it much more difficult for prisons to maintain discipline. Loss of discipline and failure to control inmate populations give rise to conditions that can lead to gang activity and other forms of disruptive behavior.

It is important that the correctional officer recognize that authoritarianism is not necessarily the best way to maintain discipline and control. As noted in Chapter 7, honesty, fairness, objectivity, humaneness, and other attributes are necessary to maintain control of inmates. It is necessary for officers to use discretion when enforcing rules; not all rules are enforced absolutely under all circumstances. Circumstances of events always dictate individual interpretations of rule-breaking behavior. Even so, rules must be applied consistently over time and to all inmates. The art of knowing which rules to bend and how far to bend them is sometimes not easily learned. Taking disciplinary action against an inmate whom one has just awakened, however, for saying "huh" instead of "sir" is not appropriate, although some may interpret this as disrespectful behavior.

Security or Custody

The security, or custodial, function involves maintenance of order and is closely related, in many ways, to the disciplinary function. It is broader, however, and encompasses much more activity. Inmates who are in institutional custody must remain in custody and be kept safe.

There is a high degree of concentration on the physical aspects of security such as locking all doors, counting all inmates at the proper times, restraining inmates in appropriate fashions when transporting them, and so forth. The relationship to discipline is perhaps best exemplified by the emphasis on controlling inmate theft and inmate assaults.

Keys, tools, weapons, and other articles require constant control. Failure to control these items adequately may result in death, escape, or other misuse of the items. Inmates may steal keys, make soap or wax impressions of them and subsequently escape. Tools can be used as weapons, to make weapons, or to facilitate escape attempts. Other articles such as cigarette lighter fluid, ball-point pens, chewing gum, and other seemingly innocuous items can be used for illicit purposes.

The security function involves the use of many physical processes designed to control inmates and contraband. Electronic monitors of various kinds may be used in various places to observe inmate movements and actions. Bars, steel, concrete, fences, and concertina (razor) wire are used to preclude escapes. Weapons and restraining devices are used to control individual inmate behavior if other controls fail.

The security processes and functions can be quite challenging, but most frequently are boring and repetitious activities. Constant alertness and awareness is necessary to preclude inmate abuses of each other or of the system.

Treatment

The treatment function includes the delivery of basic services such as dental, medical, psychological and other required health or personal needs. In addition, other programmatic activities (see Chapter 7) are conducted as treatment processes. Educational programs (both basic and advanced), religious programs, and casework and counseling programs are important to treatment.

Treatment assumes that behavioral change is an important goal. Because 95% of those incarcerated will be released from prison at some point, it is important that constructive programs designed to facilitate behavioral change be implemented. Treatment programs are central components of both rehabilitation and reintegration. The relationship to rehabilitation is clear in that the programs are designed to induce behavioral change in inmates. The relationship to reintegration, though not so clear, is equally as strong as that to rehabilitation. Reintegration takes as its focus both the inmate and society. Perhaps the most significant difference between treatment programs from each of the perspectives is that the rehabilitation approach places primacy on treatment regardless of whether participation is voluntary or involuntary, whereas the reintegration approach recognizes that voluntary participation is the most important and most critical. Individuals cannot be forced to change basic behavioral patterns without their consent or desire. The goals of treatment programs under the reintegration model are more modest than the goals of such programs under the rehabilitation model.

POLICY TASKS OF CORRECTIONS PROFESSIONALS

Corrections professionals share a policy-making role with other professionals and with politicians. The role is incumbent upon both specialists and administrators. Nonadministrative employees must communicate requirements for acceptable professional practice that, in turn, affect policy decisions. Administrators have the primary role of making policy decisions. Archambeault and Archambeault (1982) define policy as

> any statement or set of statements that are written, expressed verbally, or presumed operative that outline the goals, objectives, purpose, scope, principles of organization and operation, values, beliefs, and ideology that justify the continued existence of that organization. (p. 138)

They further identify the following as functions of policy:

(1) The organizational policy of any agency or institution defines for the organization its particular mission.
(2) Policy defines for the organization the particular organizational and management theory and principles which are to guide the processes of decision making, motivation of employees, delegation of authority, and related matters.
(3) Policy defines the organization's value system.
(4) Policy is the foundation for organizational rules and procedures.
(5) Policy justifies the existence of an organization.

(6) Policy serves as a standard by which the success or failure of the correctional organization and that of its personnel are determined.

(7) Policy is the basis for the legal compliance in dealing both with employees and with offenders. (pp. 138-140)

Corrections professionals, including all levels but especially administrative personnel, also have a broader role involving the formulation of policies external to their agencies that affect the agencies' functions. This is a political realm of activity that requires deliberate action on the part of knowledgeable individuals.

Internal Policy Formulation and Implementation

No agency can function without guidelines. The roles of policy that are indicated in the preceding section must be considered carefully, and individual policies developed to ensure that each role is fulfilled effectively. The policy formulation role involves thorough knowledge of the organization, its internal and external working environment, the limitations and capabilities of its employees, and other organizational and environmental factors. The complexities of bureaucratic structure involved in the broad range of activities typical of correctional programs are such that policies must be written and communicated clearly throughout the various levels of command.

The responsibility for implementation of internal policy is shared by both administrative and supervisory personnel. Administrators must ensure that supervisors are knowledgeable regarding policies, their purposes, reasons for being developed, and methods for implementation. Supervisory personnel are responsible for ensuring that the policies are implemented, that policymakers know of needed changes and potential conflicts with other policies, and so forth. They must also ensure that employees understand the policies, the reasons for their existence, and methods for implementation. Supervisors, in addition, must maintain awareness regarding the effectiveness of policies and the manner in which they are being implemented by line personnel. Problems must be communicated to appropriate administrative personnel on a timely basis.

Policies rarely remain in the form in which they are initially formulated. Constant feedback regarding the problems of implementation and evaluations of the effectiveness of policies are needed. Adjustments must be made to accommodate conflicts of unforeseen consequences. Policies, however, are generally stable in that new decisions are made within the framework of past decisions (Katz & Kahn, 1978). Each policy statement will have differing impacts on various parts of the organization; those with interest in the policy will affect its formulation and implementation. For this reason, Katz and Kahn (1978) state that "policies are the outcome of organizational infighting, mutual concessions, and coalition formation" (p. 481). In addition, Katz and Kahn conclude that "The consideration of organizational goals by policy makers may sharpen and clarify organizational purposes and exclude irrelevant activities, add new objectives, shift priorities among objectives or shift the mission of the organization" (pp. 479-480).

External Policy Formulation and Implementation

The fact that corrections agencies are significantly affected by their environments has been well established and documented (see Chapter 2). It is necessary for correctional administrators to formulate policies that relate to the external environment and to ensure that policies imposed by external agencies (such as legislatures, governors, etc.) are reasonable, appropriate, and within the capabilities of their agencies. This has required effective liaison with those external agencies and thorough analysis of proposed policies. For example, many corrections agencies maintain legislative liaison offices which have the responsibility of informing legislators and keeping the agency administrators abreast of laws that have potential impact on the agency. Agencies also employ individuals whose responsibility it is to analyze proposed legislation and to develop impact statements regarding proposed changes.

Most correctional agencies are reactive in the sense that they respond to the actions of others. In the future, it will be necessary for correctional leaders to take a proactive approach to external policy formulation. This will require political wisdom and thorough knowledge of correctional practices, social justice, and all agents and agencies affected by corrections policy.

SUMMARY

The purposes of corrections include retribution, deterrence, incapacitation, rehabilitation, and reintegration. The purposes of correctional programs, including both prisons and community agencies, are not to cause undue hardship and pain unrelated to the express purpose of maintaining control of individuals. Commitment to the program or facility is, in itself, the deterrent factor. Incapacitation is an inherent factor of all corrections programs. Some programs, such as prison facilities, incapacitate to a greater degree than do other programs, but all serve an incapacitative function as they limit the freedom of individuals. Both rehabilitation and reintegration, as purposes of corrections programs, provide guidance regarding correctional programs. Some argue that the exact purpose of any program has little to do with the day-to-day functioning of the agency. Rather, daily activities are determined by a process of accommodation to immediate problems facing administrators and employees. It becomes a matter of expediency rather than goal-directed activity.

The behavior control and behavioral change roles of corrections professions are accomplished through the processes of classification, discipline, security or custody, and treatment programming. Classification ensures that the inmate or client is placed in the best environment to be provided the services necessary for control and/or change. Discipline is necessary to ensure the safety and order of the institution. Discipline, order, and safety are primary roles of the security, or custody, function. Security, or custodial personnel, also are responsible for maintaining individuals in custody or under supervision. Finally, treatment programs include a wide array of activity designed to affect long-term behavioral change in inmates or clients.

Corrections professionals also have primary responsibility in the area of policy formulation and implementation. Internal policy refers to the rules, regulations, and procedures that determine the daily activities of those in the agency. External policy refers to the relationship of the agency to external agencies such as legislatures, courts, governors and their staffs, other criminal justice agencies, other correctional agencies, and other influential and interested groups.

NOTES

1. Exactly what it is that constitutes a "barbaric" act is an evolving standard. U.S. Supreme Court decisions continue to define acceptable and unacceptable punishment. Excessive punishments, as defined by the courts, cannot be imposed. Corporal punishments and physical torture have long been illegal in the United States. In 1977, the Court ruled, in the case of *Coker v. Georgia*, that capital punishment for the rape of an adult woman was disproportionate to the crime and therefore could not be imposed. "Barbaric" acts are defined by the acceptable behavior of the time period.

2. Petersilia, Greenwood, and Lavin (1978) found that 40% of juvenile and 25% of adult robbers had not planned their crimes. Only 40% had visited the scene of the crime, and only 22% had bothered to check on police patrol (see also Walker, 1989).

3. When new programs are instituted—such as diversion programs—the aim is usually to avoid imprisonment or other punishments more severe or harsh than the new program. In reality, this approach usually expands the net of total criminal justice control by placing into the new program those who would have, in the past, not received any type of punishment. The net effect is that instead of reducing the number of individuals subjected to harsh punishment, the total number of persons subjected to correctional control actually increases.

7

Correctional Role Responsibility

As indicated in Chapter 5, correctional roles generally can be categorized as: (1) custodial and surveillance; (2) support; (3) treatment; or
(4) administrative personnel. This chapter looks at these various roles
and defines them in general terms. While the general movement toward
professionalization has affected all roles, some are more professionalized than others. The professionalization movement in corrections has
resulted in two response patterns used by almost all agencies. First,
most agencies use the services of professionals educated and trained in
other fields. Second, most agencies are placing greater emphasis on
professionalization of roles that are specific to corrections.

CUSTODIAL AND SURVEILLANCE PERSONNEL

Because all corrections programs involve constraints being placed
upon unwilling clients, all persons working in those programs have
some responsibility for custody and surveillance. Those whose primary
roles are custody and surveillance, however, are actually performing
paraprofessional roles involving interpersonal and technical skills. Corrections is a service industry and, as such, usually requires that all
personnel (except those in highly specialized and professionalized
roles) begin their careers at entry level positions—for example, custody
and surveillance. This period of practical training at the entry level can
be viewed as an apprenticeship period.

Correctional officers in institutions sometimes experience tension
from lack of definition regarding their roles. The technical tasks associated with entry level work are not difficult; however, relationships

with inmates can become a source of problems for some officers (see Chapter 8).

Probation and parole officers also experience a great amount of role conflict. They serve as police officers (in surveillance roles), caseworkers, counselors, and prosecutors (in revocation proceedings). Whitehead (1987) found that probation officers spend less than 50% of their time in actual contact with probationers; more than 50% is spent on paperwork and other chores associated with their various roles.

Institutional Custody

Archambeault and Archambeault (1982) identify the following as goals of institutional custody:

(1) To confine offenders legally and humanely
(2) To prevent escapes and to ensure that all confined offenders are accounted for at all times
(3) To maintain order and control
(4) To protect the lives, health, persons, and property of offenders, employees, and the general public
(5) To provide a positive climate of control. (pp. 350-351)

"The job description of correctional officers involves a high degree of responsibility for people, genuine threats to personal safety, rotating shifts, and unpleasant physical and interpersonal surroundings" (Lasky, Gordon, & Srebalus, 1986, p. 318). Wicks (1980) identifies the various role components of prison correctional officer as including the following: (1) security officer; (2) disciplinarian; (3) link between inmates and staff; (4) behavioral technologist; (5) milieu setter; (6) educator; (7) administrative officer; (8) blue-collar worker; and (9) consultant to inmates and staff. The job often is perceived as monotonous and boring. The pay is low, power is ambiguous, and managerial philosophies often clash with reality and create additional pressures and stress. Lombardo (1981) found that 50% of the respondents in his survey identified physical danger and mental strain as dissatisfying features of their work.

The security role involves the observation and controlling of inmates to ensure that no one escapes, that there is minimal conflict among inmates, and that inmates are where they are assigned to be and doing what they are assigned to do at all times. The disciplinarian role involves correcting inmates when they do things that are against the rules and, in many cases, taking formal actions that may result in relatively severe penalties being imposed upon inmates. The role as link between inmates and staff involves communicating to both administration and inmates in terms of policy implementation and formulation. The behavioral technologist role involves conducting activities to elicit appropriate behavior from inmates. The milieu setter role involves the creation of an environment within the institution that is conducive to appropriate behavior among inmates. As educator, the officer sets examples for inmates and communicates appropriate information and attitudes. As administrative officer, the correctional officer is responsible for completing reports and ensuring that activities are conducted in accordance with rules and policy. As a blue-collar worker, the officer's role involves the actual completion of tasks such as key control, cell door control, tool control, and other technical tasks related to the operation of institutional environments. As a consultant to inmates and staff, the officer's role involves providing assistance and merely listening to inmates and staff, suggesting alternative solutions to those with problems.

Effectiveness as a correctional officer in the custody role requires the ability to be observant, to evaluate human behavior accurately, and to direct the activity of inmates in an impartial manner. The ability to gain voluntary cooperation from inmates is also necessary (Wahler & Gendreau, 1985). Glaser (1964) found that inmates described effective officers as those who were friendly, accommodating, fair, dependable, predictable, nice, flexible, and sociable. On the other hand, those who were viewed as ineffective by inmates were described as being stupid, rigid, weak, hostile, and aggressive. Homant (1979) found that officers viewed positively by inmates were described as "extremely good with making men feel they are genuinely concerned about their welfare and problems. They are fair, consistent, and in every sense of the word humane" (p. 59). Those receiving poor ratings were "disrespectful, insensitive, mechanical, and to a large degree without much of a positive personality to display to the residents" (p. 59).

Being an effective correctional officer does not necessarily involve being an extremely authoritarian individual. The qualities that generally are required are alertness, sensitivity, fairness, firmness, objectivity, and reasonable reactions. Overreacting, blustery behavior, inability to make decisions, and inconsistency will always create problems for correctional officers supervising inmate populations. It is very important that officers be able to judge human behavior appropriately and that they be able to interact with almost all types of personalities. Some inmates are hostile; others are not hostile. Some are straightforward individuals, while others are always looking for some way to "beat the system." It is very important that officers recognize that maintaining order in prison institutions involves much more than merely opening and closing doors. It involves the supervision of human beings who, although they are in a secure environment, still have many options regarding the particular behaviors that they exhibit.

Most prison correctional officers, with the possible exception of the very youngest, are interested in expanding the role of their jobs to include human service roles as well as the traditional security and order-maintenance roles (Toch & Klofas, 1982). Klofas and Toch (1982), in a study of New York correctional officers, found that "most officers were interested in expanding their roles through the addition of human service functions to their jobs" (p. 241). Others (Cullen, Link, Wolfe, & Frank, 1985; Cullen, Link, & Wolfe, 1989; Teske & Williamson, 1979) also have found that guards support rehabilitation programs.

> While officers work in a paramilitary organization marked by explicit lines of authority and a host of formal regulations, their task of managing inmates demands flexibility, the judicious application of discretionary justice, and the ability to secure inmate compliance through informal exchanges which deviate from the written rules (Sykes, 1958). In a sense, officers are expected to exercise professional expertise within a bureaucratic setting in which they are not granted the formal authority to be professional (Jurik and Musheno, 1985). Consequently, knowledge of which rules can be bent, how far they can bent, and under what circumstances is not always apparent or understood. Ambiguous and conflicting expectations are a likely result and potential source of stress. (Cullen, Link, Wolfe, & Frank, 1985, p. 508)

Hepburn and Albonetti (1980) found that role conflict among correctional staff, both custody and treatment personnel, was more likely to be a product of organizational goals than the position of staff in the institution. They determined that custody staff usually experience greater stress than treatment staff because of dual role expectation; treatment staff experience stress because their requirements are usually secondary to those of security.

The officer subculture in prisons has significant influence upon the individual officers. Many officers do not evaluate the orientation of their peers accurately; they frequently see each other as being antagonistic toward inmates and treatment programs. This is the opposite of reality. Klofas and Toch (1982) state that

> in peer opinion estimates by correctional officers, the officers underestimated the professional orientation and overestimated the cynicism of fellow officers. . . . The largest officer subtype is that of professionally oriented accurate estimator of nonsubcultural peer opinion. (p. 238)

Poole and Regoli (1981) maintain that there is no strong subculture among guards because their contacts with fellow officers are minimal and their job duties are performed alone. Poole and Regoli point out that there are several types of alienation experienced by officers (see also Katz & Kahn, 1978; Seeman, 1972): (1) powerlessness; (2) normlessness; (3) meaninglessness; (4) social isolation; and (5) self-estrangement that destroys intrinsic motivation. Guards often feel powerless to control their institutions, because courts have intervened to constrain prison procedures, eliminate draconian measures used for control, and ensure prisoner rights. Normlessness means that the officers frequently do not know exactly what is expected of them or what to do in various circumstances. Meaninglessness refers to the tendency of some officers to feel that their jobs have no real value and that they are merely "doing time in shifts."

Social isolation can be a result of performing tasks alone and having limited interaction with other officers during the completion of those duties. It also can result from shift work that causes individuals to alter their life styles in such a way that they no longer are able to socialize with their friends in desired manners. Self-estrangement can result when officers are called upon to do things that are against their basic natures. Being in institutional environments requires that officers interact with others (inmates) in negativistic ways; they constantly encounter and are forced to control situations in which they feel uncomfortable. Disciplinary roles involve imposing punitive sanctions on individuals and officers sometimes have second thoughts regarding the negative sanctions they have caused to be imposed on inmates.

Community Corrections

Probation and parole officers supervise approximately 80% of the total offender population (Thomas, 1983). Probation officers serve as surveillance officers, social caseworkers, and counselors; they supervise parolees and probationers to ensure compliance with general and specific rules regarding behavior, associations, employment, and so forth.

> A probation sentence entails a much greater loss of liberty than we have led the public to realize. It is punishing. It is, to a degree, isolating and incapacitating. It can enforce an enormous range of sanctions and controls, beside the economic sanctions already discussed.

> Probation conditions can govern the residence of the offender, inhibit his movements, require him to report regularly, avoid improper companions, persons or areas; forbid him from drinking or drinking to excess; require his participation in antialcohol treatments; compel participation in antinarcotic [sic] testing; regulate his installment purchases; require psychiatric treatment and even—in California, at least—can include a period in jail as a condition of probation. (Barkdull, 1987, p. 52)

The surveillance role of the probation/parole officer involves supervising clients to ensure that they are in compliance with the conditions specified by the judge or parole authority. In addition, officers must physically see their clients on a regular basis to ensure that they have not absconded; they must verify attendance at special classes and meetings, and ensure that clients are meeting curfew and other requirements. Some probation and parole officers may administer drug tests to ensure compliance with conditions of probation/parole. Offenders are supervised in differing degrees; some may be seen only once a month, or only required to check in by telephone. New programs, such as intensive supervision, may require that the officer actually see the client every day.

The caseworker role of probation/parole officers involves conducting presentence and prerelease reports. Most judges require that a presentence report be completed prior to imposing sentencing on a convicted offender. Probation officers conduct investigations and prepare these reports by talking with others who know the individuals, checking various records to ensure the existence or absence of certain elements, and by interviewing the convicted offenders. Prerelease plans are frequently required by paroling authorities to ensure that inmates have jobs and places to live, and that they will reasonably be able to enter society and to refrain from committing crimes. Some institutions have parole officers assigned to them to perform this function; other institutions have members of their own staffs—who are not parole officers—to assist inmates in the preparation of prerelease plans. Regardless of how the plans are originated, parole officers in the communities must verify the truth of the plans and supervise the inmates when they arrive. The caseworker role also involves assisting offenders to obtain the services of other private, community, or governmental agencies.

The counselor role of the probation/parole officer involves communicating with clients to assist them with personal problems or to refer them to appropriate individuals, programs, or agencies. Clients frequently need to be "taught" how to live in free society. They need assistance in making decisions regarding perhaps the most mundane things, such as where to live, what time to get up, what to eat, where to work, and how to avoid temptation and inappropriate influences.

The probation/parole officer's roles may sometimes be inconsistent. The surveillance role is basically that of a policeman—to ensure that the client is meeting the requirements of probation or parole. The caseworker and counselor roles require mutual trust, empathy, and communication that is sometimes difficult for officers to establish because of their roles as policemen. Clients will not reveal information that will place them at risk, even when that information is necessary for the casework or counseling roles. To overcome this problem, some jurisdictions have established practices of assigning two officers to clients—one to serve in the surveillance role, and the other to serve in the roles of caseworker and counselor.

SUPPORT PERSONNEL

This category of personnel is quite large. Those who provide these functions range from occupational to highly professionalized groups; clerical workers, truck drivers, accountants, engineers, are all included in this category. Correctional agencies responsible for institutions frequently have very large staffs. It is not uncommon for the largest agencies to employ 15,000 or more. The Federal Bureau of Prisons now employs approximately 13,000 but expects to almost double its staff within 10 years (Landon, 1989). A review of Appendix F, which contains a list of job categories available in the Federal Bureau of Prisons, will reveal the range of occupations and professions employed in large correctional agencies.

Occupational Groups

The acquisition, distribution, and utilization of resources to provide a wide range of services to large incarcerated populations involves many occupational specialties. Facilities must be constructed, maintained, and repaired. Raw materials must be acquired, stored, and prepared for use or used to create products. Employees must be recruited, trained, supervised, evaluated, and paid.

The number of various occupational groups, the number of persons in each group, and the particular job descriptions of each will vary depending upon the size and scope of the organization in question. Small jails, for example, do not offer the wide range and scope of services offered by large prison systems. Larger systems may vary in their goals and functions; Appendix F provides a good example of the types of occupations in large correctional agencies. This book does not attempt to differentiate between all professional and occupational groups. Further, the following list of occupations includes some groups which may be considered by some to be professional. However, as identified in Appendix F, the following are some of the occupational groups involved in correctional practice:

Safety Management
Correctional Officer (entry)
Personnel Clerical and Assistant
Secretary
Computer Clerk and Assistant
Electronic Technician
Medical Record Technician
Practical Nurse
Paralegal Specialist
Legal Clerk and Technician
General Business and Industry

Industrial Specialist
General Facilities and Equipment
Facility Management
Laundry Plant Management
Training Instruction
Inventory Management
Electronic Equipment Installation and Maintenance
Electrical Installation and Maintenance
Fabric and Leather Work
Machine Tool Work
Structural and Finishing Work
Metal Processing
Metal Working
Painting and Paperhanging
Plumbing and Pipefitting
Printing
Quality Assurance and Control
Wood Work
General Maintenance and Operations Work
Plant and Animal Work
Industrial Equipment Maintenance
Industrial Equipment Operation
Transportation/Mobile Equipment Maintenance
Warehousing and Stock Handling
Food Preparation

The categories listed above are not necessarily job titles; they are categories. Each category may contain several different specific job titles and job requirements.

Professional Groups

A major response to the professionalization movement and to court actions has been the increased utilization of traditional professional groups and members of other emerging professions. This section, prepared from the information contained in Appendix F, contains a partial list of professional groups in corrections (refer to Appendix F for a brief explanation of each category):

Correctional Institution Administration
Chaplain
Correctional Officer (above entry)
Social Science
Psychologist
Recreation Specialist
Personnel Management
Employee Development
General Accounting/Administrative
Financial Management
Accounting
Accounting Technician
Budget Administration
Medical Officer
Physician's Assistant
Nurse
Pharmacist
Health System Administration
General Attorney
Education

Like the occupational groups, the categories listed above may contain several different job titles, each requiring different education, training, and experience.

TREATMENT PERSONNEL

The traditional definition of the treatment function is limited to those programs directed at the change of long-term behavioral patterns, not merely the immediate control of overt behavior while incarcerated or under supervision. These programs typically include vocational and academic education, individual and group counseling, and similar activities. Treatment personnel are those who work in these areas and in such areas as social casework and medical services.

The traditional professions—psychologists, psychiatrists, physicians, surgeons, counselors, teachers, and others—function within the limits imposed by obligations, standards, and ethics of their individual professions. The practice of these professions in correctional settings, however, sometimes requires modification based on the unique environment in which they practice.

Medical

Agencies charged with responsibility for institutions require a wide range of medical personnel to service the inmate populations. Physicians, surgeons, dentists, nurses, physician's assistants, medical records technicians, laboratory technicians, and other types of personnel work in the institutional medical services area. Inmates, generally, are not the type of individuals who cared for themselves when in free communities, as a result, the inmate population is usually in greater need of medical care than free populations of the same size. In addition, the congested nature of the prison environment creates additional concerns regarding the spread of contagious diseases, and so forth.

Courts have forced correctional agencies to develop qualified medical staffs and to provide quality medical care to all inmates at all times. Most health care personnel must be licensed by licensing agencies in order to work in corrections. Physicians, surgeons, dentists, and certain other practitioners (specialists such as radiologists, neurologists, and the like) must hold either Doctor of Medicine or the Doctor of Osteopathy degrees and be licensed to practice in their states. Nurses, depending upon their particular positions, must also be licensed as Registered Nurses or as Licensed Vocational Nurses (LVN—also called LPN in some places). Technicians must be certified in accordance with the requirements of the medical field and appropriate governing agencies. Pharmacists must also meet state and federal guidelines and be certified and/or registered in accordance with state and federal laws.

Many large correctional agencies have sophisticated health care delivery systems, some of which are affiliated with major state teaching hospitals. There is a need for the full range of health care workers at about the same level of demand as that experienced in free communities. It is frequently difficult to attract health care workers—especially doctors—to corrections because of the low pay and poor working conditions.

As stated earlier, inmates usually have neglected to care for their health while in their communities. As a result there is "a high incidence of all sorts of diseases, including venereal disease, tuberculosis, and epilepsy, as well as poor dental health" in institutions (Fox, 1983, p. 74). There is also a high incidence of corrective and cosmetic surgery that is needed in prisoner populations. Scars, gunshot wounds, tattoos, and other disfigurements occur at higher rates than in normal free populations.

Small institutions such as jails usually contract with local physicians, hospitals, and other health care personnel and agencies to provide necessary care on contractual bases. Larger institutions, however, almost always have full-time permanent staffs that perform these services. Individual units of a prison system do not always have fully operational hospitals, but all units have access to such facilities. Courts have gone so far as to specify the number of physicians, dentists, nurses, and so forth, needed for prison populations of various sizes.

Psychological

Prison systems employ psychiatrists, psychologists, counselors, and caseworkers to perform various duties. It is has been estimated that 10% (Brown & Courtless, 1971) of the inmate population are mentally retarded. In addition, many inmates experience episodes of psychological problems including psychoses, neuroses, depression, and suicidal behavior. Estimates are that 20% to 35% of the inmate population have serious psychological problems (see Chapter 3).

Psychiatrists are licensed physicians who have specialized in the area of mental illnesses. They must hold medical degrees and be certified and licensed by appropriate licensing agencies. Psychologists, on the other hand, are not medical doctors. They are individuals who specialize in psychological testing and in treating psychological disorders with therapies not involving drugs. Psychologists, especially clinical psychologists, must possess Doctor of Philosophy degrees in Psychology and be certified by appropriate licensing bodies prior to being allowed to treat individuals. There are exceptions to these educational and licensing requirements, depending upon the states in which individuals function and the particular jobs to be performed.

Counselors who do not use drugs in therapy and who do not prescribe therapy for patients may not be required to hold doctoral degrees or to be certified. They may be able to work under the direction of psychologists or psychiatrists if all they do is lead group sessions, counsel, or assist individuals regarding prescribed treatments.

Some agencies have intensive care psychiatric units, while others transfer inmates to other psychiatric treatment facilities in their communities. The intensive care units usually treat psychotic individuals and are staffed with psychiatrists and other medical staff to prescribe treatment, administer drugs and therapy, and so forth.

Correctional agencies also have psychologists who administer and interpret various psychological tests designed to reveal information about inmates. These psychologists usually are required to hold master's degrees in the field but are not required to be clinical psychologists. Some states may require licensing of all psychologists, including those who only administer and interpret tests.

Educational

Several prison systems in the United States, including the Federal Bureau of Prisons, have compulsory educational programs. Challenges to mandatory educational program participation, however, have been upheld in court decisions. Functional illiteracy is a problem and costs the nation $237 billion in unrealized lifetime earnings as well as $224 billion in social costs such as welfare, unemployment, crime, and other problems (Coffey, 1987).

> One of the most significant areas beginning to affect corrections heavily is special education for the handicapped. . . . Federal law requires that educational and related services be provided to those defined as educationally handicapped. This includes the learning disabled, the emotionally disturbed, and the mentally retarded, among others. (Steurer, 1987, p. 6)

All prison systems are required by Public Law 94-142 to provide special education to those inmates under 21 who have learning deficiencies. The law requires that handicapped inmates up to age 21 receive free appropriate public education; "nondiscriminatory testing, evaluation and placement; placement in the least restrictive educational environment; and the development of an individualized education plan" (Buser, Leone, & Bannon, 1987, p. 17). In a study by Bell (1983), at least 42% of inmates had some form of learning deficiency wherein they were functioning below the fifth grade level. Schwartz (1987) estimates that the number of handicapped (e.g., learning disabled) among delinquents ranges between 30% and 60%.

> The law applies to all individuals identified as deaf, deaf-blind, hard-of-hearing, mentally retarded, orthopedically handicapped, other health impaired, seriously emotionally disturbed, specific learning disabled, speech impaired, visually handicapped, and those with multiple handicaps. (Buser, Leone, & Bannon, 1987, p. 17)

A study of a juvenile delinquent population by Podboy and Mallory (1978) found that approximately 13% of those who enter the juvenile justice system are intellectually substandard, and approximately 50% are learning disabled; only 38.2% of their sample was not learning disabled in some degree. They did not compare the sample to a non-delinquent group, but estimates of the learning disabled in the general population "cluster around 10-20 percent (e.g., Myklebust, 1968)" (Podboy & Mallory, 1978, p. 32).

The full range of academic services is usually provided to inmates. Preparatory classes for general-equivalency diplomas (GED) are provided, as well as regular high school, vocational, and college courses. The average inmate in a prison has less than a high school education, having dropped out at the ninth grade (Fox, 1983). Six percent of those in prison have no formal schooling at all (Bureau of Justice Statistics, 1988c). A study by the Law Enforcement Assistance Administration (LEAA) in 1973 found that the average educational achievement among inmates was 4.9 years (Fox, 1983). Those who read below the 5.0 grade level are considered to be functionally illiterate. It is estimated by Duffy (1988) that 75% of all inmates are functionally illiterate. Therefore, most institutions require that inmates attend school until they reach a certain age, or achieve a score of 5.0 on appropriate educational achievement tests.

Some agencies have separate school systems that serve only the inmates. These school systems offer full academic course offerings and vocational training. In addition, many colleges and universities offer academic and vocational courses in prison environments. It is theoretically possible that an inmate could enter an institution with no education and obtain a college degree—in some cases a graduate degree—prior to being released.

Caseworkers and Counselors

> With the base of knowledge about the causes of human behavior growing, nonmedical therapists began offering their services for newly perceived or newly developed social problems. Moreover, the use of psychological concepts has not been restricted to psychiatrists, psychologists, and social workers. Today, probation and parole officers, psychiatric paraprofessionals, court service workers, juvenile guardians and caretakers, and counselors with a variety of academic backgrounds are assigned to work with clients who would never have been deemed candidates for therapy, counseling, or psychological treatment, or public supervision twenty years ago. (Harris & Watkins, 1987, p. vii)

> Casework includes professional services in (1) obtaining case histories and description, (2) solving immediate problems involving family and personal relationships, (3) exploring long-range problems of social adjustment, (4) providing supportive guidance for inmates about to be released, and (5) providing supportive guidance and professional assistance to probationers and parolees. (Fox, 1983, p. 71)

Most agencies have social caseworkers who deal with inmates in a variety of ways. Some may collect and analyze information relating to classification systems and processes. Others may assist inmates in preparing pre-parole plans and in seeking to obtain the benefits of various treatment and educational programs. Still others may counsel inmates during times of crisis such as the death of a family member or other critical situations involving inmates' families. Psychotherapy, transactional analysis, reality therapy, and behavior modification are some of the techniques used by counselors. Individual and group therapy involve group psychotherapy, psychodrama, group counseling, milieu therapy, and alcohol and drug groups.

Caseworkers may or may not be required to have advanced education. The primary determinants of educational requirements are the specific job description and the states in which they are located. In order to provide therapeutic treatment designed to induce behavioral change, a caseworker usually must possess a clinical degree and be certified by an appropriate licensing agency. Many caseworkers, however, act in roles assisting inmates to acquire the services of other agencies—such as the Veterans Administration, the Social Security Administration, or welfare agencies; in these roles, a bachelor's degree in a related area usually is all that is required. In some instances, depending upon the state, Bachelor of Social Work or Master of Social Work degrees may be required along with appropriate board certification.

A related position is often referred to as counselor. Counselors may work with clients in a number of ways. Some conduct programs in drug and alcohol abuse. Counselors also may conduct other types of activities designed to induce behavioral change or alter behavior without the use of drugs or other strong therapeutic techniques. Most counselors serve in the primary role of collecting and interpreting information, assisting clients in making decisions regarding particular courses of action, and assisting clients participating in particular programs. Bartollas and Miller (1978) provide a good explanation of some counselor roles:

> Some of the specific job responsibilities of correctional counselors are: to open a folder on each new resident; to discuss and determine program objectives and career routes; to enter objectives, methods, effective dates, completion dates, quarterly review dates, and long-range goals on Program Agreement forms; to contact members of program team and determine place and time for meeting; to assist parole board and resident with anything needed for parole hearing; and to assist resident with data and format of rehearing request letter to parole board. In addition, correctional counselors interview residents for work release, explain the program, determine eligibility and openings, set a program team meeting, and write up the recommendation to the department. Home furloughs follow the same procedures as work release. In many facilities, correctional counselors also chair the disciplinary meeting. Furthermore, once they determine the needs and/or wishes of residents, counselors intercede for residents in the vocational and academic schools and on institutional assignments. They also become involved in the grievance procedure as they explain the procedure, discuss the particular inmate grievance, and help the inmate evaluate the possibilities and probabilities. If the inmate is intent on filing a grievance, the counselor assists in the write-up and may even participate in the grievance sessions. (pp. 190-191)

Religious Programs

Most prison inmates do not practice religion; however, the freedom to do so is protected by the U. S. Constitution. Many inmates do experience depression and other emotional crises upon entry into prison, and seek out the advice of chaplains. The chaplain serves to assist those in need of religious counseling and frequently serves as grief counselor and spiritual advisor to sincere inmates. Although some of those inmates who turn to religion while in prison are insincere, there are many who honestly embrace religion.

Religious programs in prisons include almost all of those of any church in a free community. Worship services, Bible study, and other religious services are held regularly. A unique problem associated with prison religious programs is that multiple religious groups must be served by a relatively few practitioners. Courts have required that inmates be allowed the opportunity to practice their own religions, so long as they are sincere and recognized. Meeting space, materials, and religious advisors or ministers must be provided within reasonable limits. Most prisons have a Protestant chaplain, a Catholic priest, and access to other major religious leaders such as Jewish rabbis, Muslim ministers, and others.

> The basic responsibility of the prison chaplain is to provide for specific denominational needs of residents. Duties entail leading the worship service each week; teaching Christian Education classes; performing funeral services and marriages; celebrating communion or the Eucharist, hearing confessions; spiritual counseling of residents; interviewing all new residents; visiting residents in isolation, in segregation, and in the hospital; representing the prison with religious groups in the community; and coordinating the religious program with other prison activities. (Bartollas & Miller, 1978, p. 197)

Many religious groups external to correctional agencies operate outreach programs in correctional facilities. In small facilities such as jails, the entire religious program often is provided by volunteers from the community. Religious services will be held by members of the clergy who represent each major religious group (e.g., Jewish, Christian) according to schedules determined by interest, need, and opportunity.

Other Programs

The scope and magnitude of many correctional organizations require that large numbers of professionals be employed. In addition to the medical, social, psychiatric, educational, and other professionals already discussed, large prison systems employ individuals such as engineers, tradesmen, and industrial workers of differing skill levels in various program activities. These programs are multifaceted; they serve as income producing programs and cost reduction programs. They also serve significant treatment functions, however, in that they provide inmates with opportunities for constructive employment while in prison and with increased opportunities for skilled employment upon release.

Many prisons, especially those in the southern United States, have extensive agricultural operations. The primary purposes of these programs are to provide work therapy and to serve as cost reducing programs. Most prisons, including those in the South, also have extensive industrial operations that produce a wide range of products.[1] The UNICOR program which operates within the Federal Bureau of Prisons employs 33% of all federal inmates, and 45% of those qualified to work. There were 78 factories in 43 institutions that generated $300 million in sales in 1987 (Meese, 1988). There are 35 prison industries with private sector involvement in 12 states (Meese, 1988).

MANAGEMENT AND ADMINISTRATIVE PERSONNEL

Paraphrasing Keegan (1987), Cohn (1987) states that effective leaders must be empathetic, decisive, able to communicate clearly and effectively, willing to give rewards and impose negative sanctions, know when and how to act, be willing and able to do those things that they ask their staffs to do, and subscribe to participative management ethics. Archambeault and Archambeault (1982) identified the functions of correctional administration and management as follows:

(1) Formulating policies and setting goals and objectives for the organization
(2) Implementing policies, goals, objectives, and standards
(3) Supervising personnel
(4) Supervising programs and operations
(5) Planning, budgeting, allocating and controlling resources and research
(6) Maintaining physical plant and equipment
(7) Protecting the organization from litigation
(8) Maintaining public relations

(9) Decision making

(10) Structuring and organizing

(11) Coordinating inter- and intra-agency or systems interfacing

(12) Surviving politically. (pp. 51-52)

Administration of correctional agencies is influenced by general factors related to all areas of public administration and by specific factors related to corrections. Administrators' roles are leadership roles. The changes in corrections during the last 20 years have made administration a complex activity. In addition to daily management of programs, administrative functions associated with planning, policy formulation and implementation, and leadership activities are increasingly necessary. The acquisition, allocation, and control of resources that is necessary to service unpredictable populations, in varied circumstances and using diverse methods, are not easy tasks. Lack of consensus among correctional administrators, legislators, judges, other politicians, diverse interest groups, and the public compounds the difficulty of an already difficult role.

The primary obligations of correctional administrators are to exercise leadership in reconciling these diverse forces and to formulate rational correctional policies that respond humanely and realistically to present and future demands of specified populations in an efficient and effective manner. These all-encompassing obligations require special skills (both political and administrative), deep commitment, high educational achievement, refined personal skills, and the ability to "see the big picture" (conceptual skills) and function effectively in ambiguous environments.

Personnel costs in correctional programs are high. Bostick (1988) indicates that, in small jails, the personnel costs sometimes reach as high as 70% of total costs. The relationships between management and staff personnel are significant factors in the effectiveness of organizations. Correctional leadership and management "must move beyond the realm of traditional management into creative leadership if we are to deal effectively with our rapidly changing world" (Evans, 1988, p. 6). There is significant evidence that guards (and others) comply with the goals set by the organization (Farmer, 1977; Jurik, 1985; Jurik & Winn, 1987). Cacioppe and Mock (1984) found that the quality of work and communication between management and staff was related and important:

Public sector managers should give more emphasis to staff development
that is oriented toward career and personal development and programs that
will enhance work and organizational pride. (p. 937)

Public organizations are not all the same. They differ in organizational styles, histories, and capacities to change. They differ in degrees
of stability regarding the demand for their services or products, in the
uncertainty of their environments, and in external support of their
agencies (Brudney & Hebert, 1987). For these and other reasons, it is
important that correctional supervisors and administrators have specific
knowledge and experience in the area of corrections and its relationship
to the broader society and other agencies. With very few exceptions,
correctional employees are supervisors of human behavior; those who
move up the career ladder become managing supervisors who oversee
the work of other supervisory personnel. Corrections employees must
function in dynamic, ambiguous, and somewhat negative environments.
Supervisors must be constantly aware of the necessity to create environments conducive to good correctional practice and of the professionals employed in correctional service. Peterson, Houston, Bosshardt, and
Dunnette (1977), in a study of correctional officers at Marion Correctional Institution in Ohio, found that the primary reasons for leaving
were: (1) no feeling of accomplishment; (2) low pay; (3) accepting other
jobs; (4) poor promotion opportunities; (5) boredom; (6) few incentives for good work; (7) poor relationships with supervisors; (8) lack
of support from supervisors; (9) unfair treatment by supervisors;
(10) overly critical supervisors; and (11) management that did not treat
employees fairly. Archambeault and Archambeault (1982) point out that
with the exception of "low pay" and "accepting other jobs" all reasons
were connected to employee-supervisor relations. Of 26 categorical
responses to 10 open questions in the survey, 10 dealt with supervisory
and 10 with management related concerns.

Supervisory Personnel

Archambeault and Archambeault (1982) identify the objectives of
correctional supervision, the managerial functions of supervisors, and
the skills and competencies required of supervisors. The objectives of
supervision include the following: (1) to effect legal and humane
control over the offender population; (2) to reinforce positive change

among offenders; (3) to ensure safety of all persons and property; (4) to coordinate with other components in and out of the organization for personnel resources and support services; (5) to motivate subordinates to accomplish tasks; and (6) to engender a sense of cooperation, personal commitment, and positive discipline in employees and inmates. The managerial functions of supervisors include: (1) planning; (2) staffing; (3) communicating; (4) training subordinates; (5) delegating authority and responsibility; (6) organizing subordinates' actions; (7) directing and controlling subordinates' activities; and (8) evaluating subordinates. The skills and competencies required of supervisors include: (1) job knowledge; (2) the ability to communicate with all involved parties; (3) the ability to motivate employees and inmates; (4) the ability to lead both employees and inmates; and (5) the ability to make effective, efficient, and timely decisions and judgments.

Culture emanates from an organizational center and develops over time (Shils, 1974). Supervisory staff play an important role in developing the organizational culture. Many authors have recognized that supervisors' relationships with employees are significant in creating positive feelings toward the job among correctional officers (Gardner, 1981; Jacobs, 1978; Jurik & Halemba, 1984; Lombardo, 1981; Merker, Rhodes, & Vito, 1984; Poole & Regoli, 1980a, b; Veneziano, 1984). Supervisory support mitigates both work stress and job dissatisfaction (Cullen, Link, Wolfe, & Frank, 1985).

Prison supervisors and other correctional program supervisors strongly believe in autonomy (that is, they believe that they, or their peers, are the only ones qualified to judge their work). Supervisory personnel, however, must also believe in and be dedicated to their work as an end in itself—a calling, in short. Poole and Regoli (1983) underscore the necessity of belief in self-regulation by stating that "commitment to a professional ideology lowers role conflict, work alienation, and anomie among correctional supervisors" (p. 67).

Supervisors have one of the most demanding positions in correctional institutions. They are cast in the role of interpreting top management's policies and must do so in a manner convincing to their subordinates. They must be able to coordinate the activities of many below them who may not agree with the philosophy of top management. Middle managers, perhaps even more than top executives, are responsible for developing effective communication networks throughout the organization.

Supervisors must be generalists and systems managers in much the same manner as their superiors. Even though they do not make policy decisions, they should be aware of how broad policy decisions affect their actions. They should also know how personnel above, under, and on their same level do their jobs. Although they are not directly concerned with the environmental constraints of public opinion, state legislatures, and other outside pressure groups, middle managers should be aware of how these external forces are influencing the correctional organization. (Bartollas & Miller, 1978, p. 143)

Administrative Personnel

Administrators increasingly face an unstable environment. In the face of such complexity, ambiguity, and rapid change, conventional methods of coping are not very useful. Public managers must more and more rely on a combination of strategic planning and contingency management to adapt to the unsure conditions they face. (Cayer & Weschler, 1988, p. 31)

Administrative personnel are charged with the responsibility of co-ordinating massive efforts to manage large, complex organizations—with ambiguous, divergent, and sometimes conflicting goals—effectively and efficiently. They must give reasonable consideration to public beliefs, to professional tenets, and to organizational realities.

The public interest can become an abstraction that is pursued regardless of public views. Professional practices can too easily become an end pursued without change in a world in which both circumstances and public attitudes are changing and where a new professional response is demanded. The public service orientation still requires the consideration of the public interest, political purposes and professional requirements. Needs have to be assessed as well as expressed. Service *for* the public means, however, that needs should not be regarded as separable from the views, wishes, and "felt" needs of those for whom they are provided. (Stewart & Clarke, 1987, p. 168, emphasis in original)

Administrators must meet the public's needs without catering to them. They also must create environments where those with professional orientations will be able to practice. This requires the establishment of goals, objectives, and operating procedures consistent with professional practice and the development and implementation of realistic performance and evaluation measures. Jurik and Winn (1987) found that "three factors are of primary importance in distinguishing continuing from terminating officers—race, opportunities to influence institutional policy decisions, and most important, satisfaction with perceived working conditions" (p. 5). Jurik (1985) further states that "the significant direct effects for organizational-level factors suggest the need for reformers to exhibit greater future concern with the institutional selection and socialization processes that shape officer attitudes toward inmates. . . . In summary, the findings suggest that without due attention to the significant influence of organizational conditions on officer attitudes and behavior, current correctional reform efforts will most certainly fail to reduce tensions in today's prisons" (p. 537).

Organizational culture is critical in the development of an effective organization. Because organizational cultures emanate from the center (Feldman, 1985; Shils, 1974), administrators have a critical responsibility to see that cultures conducive to effectiveness, efficiency, and professionalism are developed. Feldman's (1985) study of a telephone company culture which emphasized conformity to idiosyncratic desires of superiors indicated that

> the resulting cultural development that was characterized by these strong demands for conformity would not only attract security-interested managers, it would naturally repel independent and autonomous types of managers. It is more likely that these latter individuals would gravitate toward organizations whose cultures signaled a belief in management autonomy and challenge. (p. 354)

Demands for routinized job conformity in highly bureaucratic settings can be detrimental to the development of a professional atmosphere in institutions. "Highly centralized and highly formalized organizational structures are characterized by greater work alienation and greater alienation from expressive relations" (Aiken & Hage, 1966, p. 506).

Correctional administrators are concerned with both the external and the internal environments of their agencies; the two environments are symbiotic in that each affects the other. Administrators must influence the broad social and political policies that determine agency policies. The organizational structure of the agencies must be designed to ensure consistency with both external and internal influences and demands. Agency policies must be clearly articulated, communicated, implemented, and enforced. The tasks of the correctional administrator are clearly complex, difficult, and critical.

Cohn (1987) states that the critical problems and issues facing correctional administrators are:

(1) The need to reassess the organization in terms of its goals and priorities; to re-examine mandates and requirements; and to evaluate required resources to mount effective delivery systems of services.

(2) The need to develop processes for accountability for all staff, regardless of hierarchical position in the organization; and to develop fair but appropriate means for evaluating performance as such relates to organizational mission and goals.

(3) The need to develop program evaluation strategies to determine which programs and services are effective, which indeed do or do not meet established programmatic objectives, and to be prepared to discard those programs which do not meet defined needs in a cost-effective manner, even though they may be popular services. In short, the administrator must learn how to husband scarce resources in order to utilize them as efficiently as possible without sacrificing the clients, courts, or communities.

(4) The need to say "No" when it is not possible to take on new assignments without appropriate resources, when such a declination would be received unpopularly, or when the proposed new service does not fall within the mandate or priorities of the organization.

(5) The need to insist on consistent, quality services from all staff.

(6) The need to reject old dogmas—old ideas, simply because "that is the way we have always been doing it."

(7) The need to develop a style of management that reflects participation and an organizational team effort that results in commitment to service, willingness to take risks, and an atmosphere which provides mutual support.

(8) The need to develop support groups and constituencies among staff, judges, legislators, elected political officials, and critical community-based groups and organizations.

(9) The need to resist change that is inappropriate, create change where it is appropriate, to innovate where indicated, and to seek renewal when needed.

(10) The need to relate to other units and components of the administration of justice in a collegial manner in order to enhance systematization efforts.

(11) The need to deal with, if not embrace, private correctional efforts in order to develop a coordinated and effective delivery system of services in the community.

(12) The need to develop responsible training—and more training—at the inter- and intra-organizational level, not only in substantive areas of concern, but especially for middle and top management personnel in process areas of concern.

SUMMARY

Correctional roles generally can be categorized as custodial and surveillance, support, treatment, and administrative. Custodial officers in institutions are primarily concerned with the security of the facilities, keeping prisoners incarcerated, and maintaining order and safety within the institutions. Community corrections officers (e.g., probation and parole officers) engage in surveillance roles in their supervision of offenders. Their goals are to ensure that the offenders do not violate the conditions of their release, that they do not abscond, and that they attend any special functions (such as drug programs) assigned as conditions of release.

Support personnel perform many functions. Large correctional agencies with responsibility for institutions have needs for many types of employees. Basically, a large prison facility will require the services needed in almost any city of its size, plus some specialized roles unique to the prison environment. Many occupational groups engaged in traditional trade activities are present in large numbers. Other professional groups whose specialities are other than corrections are also employed in large numbers. Examples of support personnel include clerical staff, records clerks, truck drivers, welders, accountants, lawyers, and other groups.

Treatment personnel form a large contingent of any prison facility. These individuals are present in large numbers regardless of the particular orientation of the facility—retribution, deterrence, incapacitation, rehabilitation, or reintegration. Medical personnel of almost all types are employed in primary and secondary health care facilities serving prison populations. Psychological services employees, including therapists, psychiatrists, psychologists, and noncertified counselors provide various psychological services to the inmate population. Vocational and academic teachers provide services in primary, secondary, vocational, and higher educational facilities serving prison populations. Caseworkers and counselors assist inmates in effectively utilizing the services of the institution or agency and the services of other agencies. Religious workers, both paid and voluntary, provide a limited but full range of religious services to those incarcerated.

Management and supervisory personnel form a large contingent of correctional employees. In fact, it could be said that almost all correctional employees are supervisors in the sense that the basic function of entry level employees is to supervise inmates. The key obligation of correctional supervisors is to exercise leadership in the implementation of appropriate policy and to ensure that employees perform their functions in such ways as to ensure the safety and order of their institutions and to ensure maximum attainment of program goals.

Administrative personnel are charged with the responsibility of setting goals and determining policies in ambiguous and ever-changing environments influenced by the social, political, legal, and institutional environments. They must balance diverse forces and ensure formulation of appropriate policies to create environments conducive to inmate and employee interests. They are concerned with both the internal and the external environments of their agencies.

NOTES

1. Various types of industrial operations in prisons include: license plate manufacture; printing; furniture manufacture and refinishing; tire recapping; garment production; shoe and leather products manufacture; lumber, brick, and other building material manufacture; automotive repair, refinishing, and rebuilding; food processing and canning; meat processing; box manufacture; sign manufacture; records microfilming; broom, mop, soap, and janitorial supply manufacture; electronic equipment assembly; and textile manufacture.

8

Organizational and Human Factors Contributing to Stress

Correctional officers experience higher rates of hypertension, heart disease, ulcer, gout, and gall bladder problems than patrol officers. Their divorce rate is twice the average rate of blue-collar workers (Cheek & Miller, 1983). While correctional officers display higher than average rates for some stress-related illnesses, along with alcohol and other health problems, many deny feeling any debilitating effects. (Mobley, 1985, p. 18)

Correctional officers have twice the national average divorce rate and one of the highest heart attack rates of state employees. One study soberly reported correctional officers' life expectancy to be 59 years. (Moracco, 1985, p. 22)

As indicated in Chapter 3, human service occupations or professions are practiced in stressful environments. Correctional officers have been specifically identified as a stressed group (e.g., Cheek and Miller, 1982; Cheek and Miller, 1983; Harris, 1983; Lasky, Gordon & Srebalus, 1986; Mobley, 1985; Moracco, 1985). The factors that contribute to stress—and the related phenomenon of burnout—include both organizational and human factors. The effect of these factors on individuals are determined, in part, by individual characteristics, reactions, career and life stages, and professional accomplishments. It is critical that corrections professionals understand the impact of the corrections environment on their mental and physical health and well-being. They also need to understand how their job may affect their interpersonal relationships. Uncontrolled stress causes a state of exhaustion, called burnout, which results in depersonalization and feelings of low personal accomplishment (Jackson, Schwab, & Schuler, 1986) and low self-esteem.

Stress is a necessary component of life; without it, we cannot function effectively. Too much stress, however, is severely debilitating. Researchers who initiated the study of dysfunctional stress include Herbert J. Freudenberger (1974), Hans Selye (1976), and Thomas H. Holmes and Richard H. Rahe (1967). Cournoyer (1988) indicates that

> stress becomes distress when (1) the perceived stressors are so extreme, occur so often, or for such a long duration that the person becomes overwhelmed and exhausted, (2) the person's cognitive appraisal of the stressful situation is dysfunctional, (3) the persons's coping skills are inadequate to address the perceived stressors or to moderate the individual distress, or (4) the external resources available to the person are either not available or insufficient. (p. 260)

Cournoyer (1988) provides an excellent discussion of stages of stress. The first stage involves a stress response, but is not dysfunctional. The second stage is the initial stage of distress and involves several biological and psychosocial responses including worries, restlessness, stomach disorders, and other significant symptoms. The third stage represents serious distress, with more serious symptoms such as sleep disorders, ulcers, anxiety, sexual dysfunction, and other more serious symptoms. The fourth and final stage is the most serious and results in complete exhaustion and perhaps major psychological breakdown or major physical illness.

This chapter identifies and discusses the organizational and human factors contributing to stress. It also discusses briefly the relationships and effects of such factors as life stage, career stage, and professional growth and development. Finally, it identifies common reactions to stress and suggests ways to mitigate the negative effects of chronic and acute stress situations.

ORGANIZATIONAL FACTORS

The previous chapters have served to establish that corrections agencies and the roles of various corrections professionals are frequently characterized by conflict, ambiguity, and overload. Katz and Kahn (1978) suggest that these are primary factors contributing to stress.

Further, they state that those with responsibility for the futures of others are more prone to health difficulties (which can be a symptom of stress).

Conflict in corrections agencies is created by tension between and among inmates and staff, inmates and administrators, and staff and administrators. It is also generated to a significant extent from relationships with individuals, agencies, and groups external to each agency. Role conflict involves two or more sets of pressures requiring different reactions or behavior (Shamir & Drory, 1982). Many correctional officers—often undereducated and undertrained—who face complex and difficult tasks requiring interpersonal and leadership skills may feel helpless and develop a sense of failure.

Ambiguity regarding role definition has been discussed earlier. It is caused primarily by lack of leadership, goals, and definition of job responsibilities. Interference by external agencies (courts, legislatures, governors, and others) also contributes to confusion regarding purposes and methods. Individuals become unsure of what they are trying to accomplish and the methods that they should be using to conduct the business of their agencies.

There are two types of overload that individuals can experience (Katz & Kahn, 1978). Objective overload involves having too much to do or too much interference by external factors. For example, trying to supervise 300 inmates/clients in a dynamic environment with continuous interruptions by telephone and individual conversations results in the inability to do the job well. The individual may be able to perform any particular function with extraordinary effectiveness and efficiency but, because of too many demands on time and attention, is unable to perform satisfactorily. Subjective overload involves work tasks being too difficult for the individual to perform. This is seldom a continuing problem, because such individuals simply cannot do the work. They are usually transferred to jobs more suited to their abilities, are terminated, or they resign.

A related source of stress from the organizational environment is underload. Employees, especially at the entry level, are assigned to roles that are narrowly defined and do not utilize a broad range of their individual abilities. The demands, though perhaps high in an objective sense, require only limited utilization of one or more skills. Underload is related to role definition; for example, security officers frequently are discouraged from interacting with inmates in any way except to ensure their physical presence and good behavior. Shamir and Drory (1982) state that "low job scope [underload] can therefore be assumed to become a source of stress in custodial officers" (p. 85). Some attempts to broaden the role of security officers have been made, and some agencies encourage security officers to engage in limited, but important, counseling of inmates.

Cheek and Miller (1982) stated that the inability to see positive results from work, negative job stigma, and lack of administrative support contribute to low staff morale and, thereby, to stress.[1] Whitehead and Lindquist (1986) found a dramatic relationship between "administrative practices and job stress and burnout" (p. 37). It is important to note that these factors are controllable. The ability to see positive results from work can be achieved with proper role definitions and realistic expectations, careful observation of inmate behaviors, and broader time perspectives. Subtle changes in behavior often require extended periods of time before they are observable. Negative job stigma can be changed by effective public relations and increased effectiveness and efficiency by agencies. Lack of administrative support can be resolved by organizational training and effective internal procedures. Staff morale will improve as a result, and stress will be reduced.

> Correctional officers are also subject to specific stressors including unfavorable attitudes held by the public toward correctional officers, daily crisis situations, daily situations posing a threat or overwhelming officers emotionally, racial situations, confrontations among officers and minority groups, and court rulings that make it seem almost impossible not to violate someone's human or civil rights. (Morris, 1986, p. 124)

The bureaucratic nature of criminal justice organizations emphasizes standardization and impersonality (Thomas, 1988); this emphasis conflicts with the human service orientation of many corrections professionals. As indicated in Chapter 4, concern for the outcome of individual cases is replaced with concern for due process, equal treatment, and standardization. Bureaucracies are often rigid and uncompromising, which causes stress in some individuals.

> Environmental and organizational factors in human service settings may also cause stress: (1) role or case overload with few structured "time outs," (2) institutional disregard for needs of clients in favor of administrative, financial, and bureaucratic needs, (3) inadequate leadership, supervision, or both, (4) lack of training and orientation specific to the job, (5) lack of a sense of impact on and control over one's work situation, (6) lack of social

interaction and support among staff, (7) caseloads consisting predominantly of extremely difficult clients, and (8) majority of time spent on administration and paperwork tasks. (Ratliff, 1988, p. 149)

The Work Environment

Corrections agencies are complex bureaucracies that exist in complex environments (see Chapter 2). Narrow role definitions, ambiguous role expectations, and internal and external conflicts are characteristic of many agencies. The dynamic nature of the everyday environments (especially in prisons) is such that predictability of events is difficult at best. The total work environment has been identified by many as being a source of stress. Long, Shouksmith, Voges, and Roache (1986), in their New Zealand study comparing correctional officers to Army personnel, found that high stress among correctional officers is a result of occupational pressures, staff relations, inmate relations, and concern with promotions.

Conflicts among staff factions also contribute to the stressful nature of the work environment. For example, security staff and treatment staff often perceive each other as interfering with their abilities to perform their duties effectively. Lower level staff may find that the demands of their jobs at times exceed their abilities. As previously indicated, this often leads to feelings of helplessness and failure.

The following description of a correctional officer's job is taken from Hawkins and Alpert (1989):

A candid job description for a correctional officer position would read something like this: Excellent employment opportunity for men and women who are willing to work eight-hour shifts at varying times (early morning, afternoon, and late nights) on a rotating basis. Applicants must enforce numerous rules with few guidelines. They must be willing to risk physical harm, psychological harassment, and endure the threat of inmate law suits, which could involve civil liability. They must be willing to spend eight hours each day among people who do not like them. They will not be allowed to fraternize with these people, but are expected to control as well as help them. Applicants must accept that they have little or no input into the rules they will be asked to enforce, nor will they be privy to the policy rationale for these rules. They should realize that management will probably not listen to their complaints. Work superiors, located in a military chain of command, are likely to have a great deal of time invested in organizational rules and therefore will resist employee innovations. The person at the top of the chain of command is likely to be a political appointment, but applicants are not allowed to engage in political activity. Promotion is infrequent and opportunities for advancement in the organization are very limited. Most of the training will be on the job—often from inmates. All applicants are considered untrustworthy: frequent questioning and searches of private possessions are designed to reduce corruption. Applicants must give up some civil rights for employment to continue. Women and minority group members are encouraged to apply, but will be discriminated against once on the job.[2] (pp. 338-339)

The above description is an attempt by Hawkins and Alpert to indicate the stressful, ambiguous, and less than desirable nature of entry-level corrections positions. Some would argue that positions above entry level could be described similarly. This description, however, while accurate if taken as a general indicator of the role, is an exaggeration of the actual experience of most employees (this author included). The inclusion of this description is important in that it should give adequate notice to correctional administrators that changes are needed in many instances to ensure adequate and qualified staff in the future. The closer an organization approximates the above description, the greater the need for change.

As indicated in Chapter 2, the environments within which corrections must function contribute significantly to the stress that correctional officers must endure. Bureaucratization, intervention by the courts and other agencies of government, and the rapidly increasing size of the inmate population create an ambiguous environment. As Hawkins and Alpert (1989) indicate:

Correctional officers are [often] caught in the middle; pressured by superiors concerned with procedural niceties which often lack any substantive guidance, on the one hand, and prison inmates who seek to test their newly won freedoms, on the other, the staff is confronted with a two-edged powerlessness. (p. 345)

The work environment is the single largest contributor to stress in correctional officers (Brown, 1987). At the entry level, it has negative emotional, physical, moral, and social implications for the officer (Kauffman, 1988). Although other factors, such as individual characteristics and reactions, contribute to the amount of stress experienced, these factors have been found to be less significant contributors than the work environment. Gerstein, Topp, and Correll (1987) found that "generally . . . the nature of the correctional institution environment contributes more to burnout experienced by correctional staff than does personal information about such staff members" (p. 359).

Higher level officers do not experience the same degree of stress as lower level correctional officers. Roles generally produce stress inversely to the degree of professionalization, because professional roles are better defined and the incumbents are generally better educated and capable of functioning in the dynamic environments of correctional agencies. Higher level officers and professionals do not experience powerlessness to the degree experienced by lower level officers.

Unions

The many problems faced by corrections employees, the lack of concern on the part of politicians, and the inability or lack of desire on the part of correctional leadership to adequately provide safe, secure, and professional environments have prompted the rise of employee unions. Of course, the unions were partially prompted as well by self-serving motivations, but the rise of unions in corrections cannot be explained merely as a result of greedy employees.

"Unions of correctional workers, particularly guards' unions, have been strong in some states, like New York, since just before World War II" (Fox, 1985, p. 435). Fox (1985) indicates that the largest union representing correctional workers is the American Federation of State, County, and Municipal Employees, but that there are many different unions that represent employees. For example, different unions may represent "teachers, nurses, craftsmen, blue-collar and non-building trades, social workers, and the clerical staff" (p. 435). In 1974, officials in Ohio signed agreements with 40 different unions representing five different employee groups (May, 1980).

Unionization has been viewed as reducing the capacity of the administration to manage the system. Higher salaries, time-and-a-half for overtime during escapes and other emergencies, compensation for call-in and standby time, protection against abuse of extra-duty requirements, scheduling, and many other areas have been affected. The traditional autocratic authority of the administrator in personnel matters has given way to a new system of government by shared decision-making power, negotiation, and review of management decisions. (Fox, 1985, p. 436)

Among the factors contributing to the unionization movement is lack of support by administrative and supervisory personnel. Hawkins and Alpert (1989), however, indicate that correctional unions grew from the general trend toward unionization of public employees. Guards were the last group of public employees to unionize; currently, over half the states have guard unions (Hawkins & Alpert, 1989).

Unions have not been as effective as correctional officers had hoped. They have improved working conditions somewhat; working conditions, safety, and security of institutions are the primary concerns of correctional unions. Unions have also helped to secure due process rights (grievance procedures) for employees. The autocratic administrator who summarily dismisses employees for little or no reason can no longer function in most correctional agencies. Unions—and other forces such as courts—have precluded this type of activity.

Hawkins and Alpert (1989) point out that unions have failed correctional officers for several reasons. First, there is too much competition for representation when guards form a union. The result is that guards are confused, and the competing interest groups have limited power as a result of numerous parties to the action. Second, unions have failed to represent the diversity of correctional employees. Minority groups are unrepresented or underrepresented in union membership and in union leadership positions. Third, the potential lawlessness of unions contributes to their ineffectiveness. Unions are controlled by law and not allowed to strike; therefore, the effectiveness of union representation is significantly diminished. Illegal strikes do occur, but the existence of replacement forces such as the National Guard undermine their effectiveness.

The only legal means for union activity in most states are negotiation by union leadership with correctional administrators, political influence through legislators and other politicians, and informal job actions such as work slowdowns, the performance of all instructions to the letter (which results in work not getting done in many cases and creating additional problems in others), and sick-outs (which may be technically illegal).

HUMAN FACTORS

Human relationships can be a source of stress, or they can be a significant factor in dealing with stress effectively. Corrections professionals must interact continuously with inmates or clients, with colleagues, and with others external to their particular organizations but significant in their lives. Individuals both affect and are affected by others. Effectiveness in establishing and maintaining responsible human relationships requires accurate and adequate communication; individuals under extreme stress seldom communicate either accurately or adequately.

Ratliff (1988) points out that many sources of stress are within individuals themselves and that "some human service workers possess personality characteristics that make them more prone to burnout" (p. 150). Among those characteristics are neurotic anxiety and flexibility. Neurotic individuals will set goals that are unattainable, and in addition may be emotionally unstable, impulsive, lacking in perserverance, or may develop low self-esteem. Flexibility may create stress, because those individuals who are flexible may find it difficult to set limits and have broader ranges of understanding or interpretation of events. Flexibility, however, may make it easier for individuals to effectively deal with stressful situations (Kahn & Rosenthal, 1961; Ratliff, 1988).

Inmates/Clients

As indicated earlier in this book, inmates and clients do not usually welcome the services provided by corrections professionals. They frequently are self-serving individuals who look out for themselves to the exclusion of all others. Their relationships with each other, with employees, and with others are frequently exploitive. The inability to determine accurately the motives of inmates/clients frequently causes professionals to react to everyone in a suspicious and cynical manner, and to attribute the worst motives to everyone involved in each interaction.

The changed environment of corrections has forced officers to alter the traditional uses of power. There are generally five types of power that can be utilized in correctional environments. *Referent* power is that power gained from association with a powerful individual, group, or agency. *Coercive* power is the power to force an individual to do something. *Reward* power is the ability to grant favors, desired items, or favorable situations in return for good behavior or compliance with expectations. *Expert* power is the power gained as a result of unique knowledge which grants special ability to the professional. *Legitimate* power is that power which is affiliated with position and usually granted, in this case, by laws or organizations. While coercive, reward, and legitimate power are formal bases of power, referent and expert power are informal bases. The changes in correctional institutions, the granting of rights to inmates, oversight by external agencies, and other factors have eroded the significance of referent, coercive, and reward power. Therefore, officers must rely upon legitimate and expert power to control individual inmates and inmate groups. Hepburn (1985) found legitimate and expert power to be the most important power bases:

> Prisoners do not comply with directions on a routine basis because guards exercise coercive power. Instead, prisoners expect that reasonable instructions and directions related to their daily activities will be given by guards and followed by prisoners. (p. 160).

As stated at several points in this text, a significant contributor to guards' stress is powerlessness in regard to inmates. Hawkins and Alpert (1989) identify a major source of stress in relationships with inmates as corruption of authority:

> The corruption of a correctional officer's authority is more likely to occur than a physical attack; it contributes to high staff turnover and low employee morale. More critically, the loss of authority leaves staff members open to more psychological and physical victimization, as inmates gain power over line officers . . .

> Gresham Sykes (1958) has suggested three forms of corruption of guards by inmates. Corruption through friendship refers to the potential problems which arise when guards get too close to one or more inmates. . . . When authority is corrupted by reciprocity, it means that correctional officers have delegated some of their power to the inmate. . . . Corruption by default refers to the loss of authority which results when a guard does not take action to enforce the rules. (p. 344)

Whitehead and Lindquist (1986) found, in their study of Alabama correctional officers, that inmate contact did not contribute to officer burnout. In another article, they indicate that 63% of the officers in the study "reported at least one inmate stressor" (Lindquist & Whitehead, 1986, p. 12). Kauffman (1988) and many others have identified inmate contact as a source of correctional officer stress. Therefore, the weight of the evidence is such that we must believe inmate contact to be stressful.

Whereas contact with inmates in prison may be a source of stress for institutional correctional officers, it does not appear to be stressful for probation officers. Whitehead (1987), in his study of probation officers, found that those with greater client contact had more frequent feelings of accomplishment. He indicates that "the officer's perception of overload or excessive demands is much more important than the simple amount of offender contact inherent in the job" (p. 13). Moreover, 51% of the probation officers felt that they had a positive impact on the lives of offenders. One third reported feelings of exhilaration after contact with offenders. In another study, Whitehead and Lindquist (1985) found that 49% of probation and parole officers rated their jobs as stressful, but 44% indicated that they were satisfied.

Colleagues

The work environment, role expectations and definitions, professional status, and individual characteristics often have significant effects on relationships with colleagues. As referred to in Chapter 4, a sense of community is an important characteristic of professionalization. In several areas of this book, references are made to the correctional officer subculture. There are differing opinions as to whether or not it exists and, if it does exist, as to its influence. Hawkins and Alpert (1989) indicate that earlier studies found the existence of such a subculture, but that those studies which relied upon data collected within the last ten years (Kauffman, 1981; Klofas & Toch, 1982; Lombardo, 1981; Poole & Regoli, 1981) have found that there is no strong guard subculture. Hawkins and Alpert (1989) further explain the reasons for the weakening of the subculture as follows:

> Correctional staff members today are much more heterogeneous than ever before. Active recruitment campaigns for minorities, and the entrance of

female guards into male correctional facilities, have reduced the "good old boy" sense of community. The increasing powerlessness of the occupation has promoted cynicism and anomie—both destructive of the subculture. The bureaucratization of prisons and increased pressure of law suits has split supervisory staff from line officers. Unlike the police, where subcultural norms stretch across the ranks from patrolman up to captain, the break between supervisors and guards has retarded the subcultural response. We have seen that line officers have as many problems with their superiors as they do with inmates—if not more (Poole and Regoli, 1981; Fox 1982). Also contributing to this division was the rise of employee unions for correctional officers. Union issues came to "divide the guard subculture horizontally" (Jacobs, 1977:198). The unionization of correctional workers was to have an impact not only on the guard subculture, which it partially replaced, but on relationship [sic] with inmates and superiors. Unions would alter work relationships in the prison in very distinct and irreversible ways. (p. 353)

Several studies have found that supervisory support mitigated work stress and job dissatisfaction among correctional employees (Cullen, Link, Wolfe, & Frank, 1985); several, however, have also found that peer support is positively associated with stress (Cullen et al., 1985). Jurik and Halemba (1984) and Lombardo (1981) found that peer relationships were not necessarily rewarding. One reason for the negative influence of peer relationships may be the self- fulfilling nature of the relationships. Cynicism, anger, frustration, and hostility are not mitigated when continuous and exclusive associations are with individuals who are also cynical, angry, frustrated, and hostile. The demise of the "good old boy" subculture may be a necessary prerequisite to the development of a professional subculture.

Others

An individual's entire self-definition and life style should not be built around the work environment. Relationships with other people are very important to the mental, physical, and social health and well-being of everyone. There is an interactive effect between stressful situations not adequately dealt with and all relationships in one's life. For example, stress on the job can have negative consequences for relationships with spouses, children, friends, or others with whom persons must interact in nonwork situations. Likewise, stressful relationships in nonwork environments can have negative consequences for work relationships.

Healthy relationships with and support by family members have been found to mitigate stress (Cullen et al., 1985). Morris (1986) suggests that close family members (such as spouses) be included in correctional officers' training. The purpose is to provide family members with knowledge of the environment in which the officers work, thereby providing the family members with better understanding of the officers' behavior and information through which they can better support the officers.

CAREER STAGES, GROWTH, AND DEVELOPMENT

Psychologists and psychiatrists have long recognized the relationship between life stages and individual reactions. Where persons are located on the continuum from birth to normal death has a significant effect on their interpretations of situations and their reactions.

Entry into a profession is usually accompanied by high expectations regarding effectiveness and ultimate achievement. Most individuals, in any profession, do not reach the levels of aspiration that they held upon entry into the profession. Individual reactions to this difference between aspirations and reality range from acceptance to complete rejection. We hear frequently of people who quit their high-paying jobs, abandon established relationships, and start over in other fields of endeavor. Most individuals probably accept with reluctance that they will not achieve their initial high aspirations; many become cynical and merely go through the motions of work. Others seek to develop outside interests that fill the void created by lack of accomplishment in their professions. Still others are encouraged to make new and concerted efforts to accomplish more and to continue to progress in their chosen fields.

It is not possible for anyone to specify a correct course of action for anyone else. What is important is that individuals recognize that life and career stages are significant factors in their perceptions of events. They can then evaluate, perhaps with proper guidance, the courses of action available to them and choose appropriate alternatives.

Mental, social, and professional growth does not stop until death. Physical growth, involving increased height of the body, stops in the late adolescent stage; for other types of growth to cease prior to actual death, however, is a negative response to stress and life situations. Continued growth and development requires a conscious effort on the part of the individual. Interests and perceptions may change, but the process of growth and development must continue.

Regoli, Poole, and Schrink (1979) indicate that anomie (confusion, lack of direction, and feelings of alienation) in organizations leads to cynicism. They further found that the degree of cynicism varies during individuals' careers. They identified six career stages and found low cynicism in the early stages, followed by increased cynicism during the middle stages and lowered cynicism during the latter stages of careers.

The first stage (entry to six months) is the initial exposure to the professional and organizational ideology. Differences between the ideal and reality create the seeds of cynicism, but it is not observable at this stage. The second stage (6 to 24 months) results in individuals' total accommodation to the demands of their institutions; they experience the relationships and differences between the professional ideology and the actual job tasks. Cynicism now becomes detectable in the individuals' behavior. The third stage (2 to 6 years) is the period in which officers are thoroughly integrated into organizational cultures; jobs become more routine and officers become more cynical. The fourth stage (7 to 10 years) is perhaps the most critical:

> It is during this fourth career stage that the worker is particularly ripe and vulnerable for cynicism. This is not only because he is disillusioned with the occupation, but also because during this period his aspirations are the greatest and his frustrations the most intense. Simply, the worker reflects upon what he has done with his life and contemplates his future. If he decides to stay in the corrections occupation, he more than likely feels he deserves a promotion. But he knows from experience that this is unlikely. (Regoli, Poole, & Schrink, 1979, p. 186)

During the fifth stage (10 to 15 years), employees resign themselves to stay for retirement. They become less cynical, partially because they see some rewards forthcoming (retirement). During stage six (16 years and over) employees become even less cynical. Retirement can be a reality, but

> · being closer to retirement is only part of the reason these workers renew their commitment to the occupation. An additional element fostering

renewed commitment is the retiring worker's assessment of postretirement job opportunities. This worker quickly discovers that even though he is not "old" (most often retiring workers in progressive correctional systems do not exceed 50 years of age), the outside employment opportunities that do exist are at best "second-rate" (e.g., warehouse security guard or elementary school crosswalk guard). The net effect of this perceived situation is for these workers to further renew their commitment to the occupation. (Regoli, Poole, & Schrink, 1979, p. 186)

The findings of Regoli, Poole, and Schrink (1979) are consistent with Whitehead's (1985) findings regarding burnout among probation officers: "Burnout is worst for employees past their initial period of employment and lowest for newly hired and for the most experienced" (p. 91).

The life stages of individuals also have significant effects on their perceptions and experiences of stressful situations. The adult psyche is not static, but continues to unfold and develop throughout life (Schott, 1986): "Regardless of one's particular personality structure, the individual encounters during the lifespan a certain progression of psychological and psychosocial growth" (p. 659). This growth is not automatic and not experienced by all. Retarded growth can result in an individual remaining fixed at some point along the continuum of development.

The life stages of adults have been identified generally as early adulthood, middle adulthood, and late adulthood. "The cluster of issues . . . that characterize early adulthood [mid-20s to mid-30s] revolve about forming intimate bonds with others and establishing a profession or career" (Schott, 1986, p. 659). Middle adulthood consists of two stages—the stage of transition (mid-30s to mid-40s) and the true stage of middle adulthood. The transition period is characterized by the "midlife crisis" wherein individuals are discontented with accomplishments, searching for meaning to their lives, coming to terms with the inevitability of death, and establishing realistic goals that can be accomplished. The transition period can be defined as a period of disillusionment (Levinson, 1978; Schott, 1986). The true stage of middle adulthood (mid-40s to 60) is characterized by calmness, a sense of direction, and creativity. Late adulthood is the time, after age 60, when most individuals are approaching retirement or are indeed retired.

Job and organization satisfaction rise rapidly during the 30s, a period of "socialization and growth." . . . Job satisfaction plummets from the mid-to-late 30s to the mid-40s, a period identified as the mid-career crisis. . . . Organization and job satisfaction increase again from the mid-40s to the 50s, a phase which the authors term "acceptance." . . . Job satisfaction declines again beginning in the 50s, a period of "pre-retirement." (Schott, 1986, p. 664)

O'Connor and Wolfe (1987) also point out that adult life is characterized by periods of instability and change: "Perhaps a key message to those responsible for themselves, for organizations, and for others' careers is one of tolerance for hiatus and change" (p. 814). They indicate that the processes of growth and development are characterized by ambiguity and confusion. "Tolerance for self directedness is another message of this study" (p. 815). Autonomy, a coveted element of professionalism, requires that individuals be self-directed to at least some degree. The message seems to be that we can expect nothing less than periods of instability during growth and change. Individuals must recognize the nature of adult growth and capitalize on the advantages provided by it.

Awareness of these life stages and their impact on individuals and their perceptions of events is imperative. Individuals can better deal with stress if they fully understand the sources of it and the alternatives to influence the stressors. Agencies must practice true personnel management and take advantage of employee interests, desires, and life stage influences. The organization will then be less stressful, and individuals will be less stressed.

COPING WITH STRESS

Individuals differ in their tolerance for different kinds of stresses and in their ways of handling them. It seems likely also that the effects of stress at work are moderated or conditioned by other interpersonal resources available to the individual, or at least by the interpersonal context in which the stress is experienced. (Katz & Kahn, 1978, p. 609)

The negative effects of stress are related to individual characteristics, personality, life style, and other personal relationships. "The issue is not general tolerance or intolerance for stress, but specific responses to specific stressors" (Katz & Kahn, 1978, p. 604). The negative effects of stress can be mitigated with adequate understanding and appropriate action.

Latack (1986) identifies three categories of response to stress—action, cognitive reappraisal, and symptom management. Action involves actually doing something in regard to the stressor to cause it to cease being a stressor. Cognitive reappraisal involves a reinterpretation of the stressful event or situation. Symptom management concentrates on psychophysiological characteristics of stress and treats them with drugs, diet, exercise, and so forth. Several authors have suggested increased training and improved relationships with inmates as being significant factors in stress reduction (Gerstein, Topp, & Correll, 1987; Shamir & Drory, 1982). Shamir and Dory (1982) also point out that social support by prison management, peers, and the community serves to reduce stress among correctional officers.

> Perhaps the finding of this study that deserves the most emphasis is the importance of the contribution of social support toward reducing the level of tedium. Lack of social support can contribute to tedium directly by transmitting to the individual messages that can damage his self-image and self-esteem. (p. 95)

Healthy relationships with individuals outside the work group can also serve to reduce stress. Exclusive association with individuals from the work group can create narrow mindsets and promote "us-them" types of thinking among officers. Cynicism is increased, and noncorrectional employees are seen as uninformed individuals who are either "bad guys" or, at best, individuals who are well-meaning but cannot be trusted. Too often, law enforcement and security personnel withdraw into their own worlds and do not communicate with people outside those worlds—even with family members such as spouses and children. The lack of communication contributes to increased strain from external relationships.

Morris (1986) suggests that organizations may implement "an effective and comprehensive stress management program . . . [which should] include" (p. 126) at least the following components:

(1) A definition of the components of stress.
(2) An explanation of the warning signals and effects of stress.
(3) A method of overcoming, reducing, and dealing with stress.

(4) A health maintenance program, including physical fitness.

(5) An analysis of the physical environment.

(6) An analysis of the organizational structure.

(7) The inclusion of families in stress management programs.

Several studies (Carroll & White, 1982; Link & Dohrenwend, 1980; Shapiro, 1982) have found that education helps to reduce stress. Thomas (1988) "found that officers who underwent a stress management orientation program reported less stress than those who did not or those who were still waiting for the program" (p. 54). Therefore, education and training—both general and specific—are important in controlling the negative effects of stress.

Walsh (1987) indicates that values can hinder the ability of an individual to deal effectively with stress. Values provide an anchor in times of ambiguity and they provide us with a sense of direction when dealing with problems and situations. If they fail in particular situations, however, they can preclude the development of effective coping strategies. "A second burdensome form of values is when the social service professional equates his or her personal goodness with a degree of professional success" (Walsh, 1987, p. 281). Walsh (1987) further suggests that four complementary perspectives must be considered in order to fully understand burnout:

(1) *The holistic perspective*: Appreciating the interactive impact of burnout on the physical, psychological, social, intellectual, and spiritual dimensions of life.

(2) *The ecological perspective*: Recognizing that burnout is seldom experienced only in oneself but also infects others, the work environment, and the life situation in general.

(3) *The interactive perspective*: It is in the alterations of mode and effect found in everyday exchanges with other people that awareness of burnout is most acutely experienced.

(4) *The state/stage-of-life perspective*: Where one is in life's developmental struggle contributes to the impact of burnout. If one's life is one's work, the impact is different from what it is when work is one of several equally weighty anchors on which one finds stability. (p. 28)

Walsh suggests that, to effectively deal with stress, individuals should have contacts with broad ranges of people both inside and outside the organizational environment. They should use people external to their organizations as touchstones in accurately defining situations and problems. They must fully understand their roles in their organizations and work actively to solve problems. They should also communicate effectively, take all of their vacation days, and live balanced life styles.

Prevention of burnout is a better approach than dealing with it once it has occurred. Ratliff (1988) suggests that life enrichment, cognitive approaches to coping, self-awareness and philosophy, and agency interventions are necessary in preventing burnout. Life enrichment involves living a balanced, active life with a wide range of interests. Cognitive approaches to coping involve redefining situations and events that create undue stress, paying attention to gains and successes instead of losses and failures, and developing realistic perceptions of events, individuals' roles in those events, and methods of altering stressful events. Self-awareness and philosophy is closely related to cognitive redefinition in that it involves the development of a thorough understanding of the self and those things that are important to the individual. Agency interventions can be numerous actions designed to change the stressful environment. Support groups, variety in job assignments, improvement of working conditions, holistic concern for individuals, and continuous training are examples of agency interventions.

Cournoyer (1988) identified the following as important elements of effective coping with distress: (1) positive self-talk; (2) positive imagery; (3) proper breathing; (4) muscle relaxation; (5) exercise; (6) nutrition; (7) hobbies; (8) money; (9) time; (10) knowledge; and (11) support. Moracco (1985) suggests that individuals and organizations can develop activities centering around the following approaches for dealing with stress: (1) advanced planning; (2) relaxation techniques; (3) life style assessment; (4) cognitive restructuring; (5) time-outs; (6) time management; (7) diet; (8) exercise; (9) varied activities; (9) social support; (10) prescreening; (11) organizational policy; (12) job rotation; and (13) organization-sponsored stress reduction plans. Cheek (1984) outlines several methods in her book *Stress Management for Correctional Officers and Their Families* that are effective in coping with stress. The reader is referred to any of these excellent sources for more information regarding stress management.

SUMMARY

The daily summary of their jobs and the existence of chronic work stresses such as working with involuntary "clients," the existence of never-ending emergency situations, the daily confrontation with human suffering, hostility, and cruelty, the existence of dangers and fear of escapes and riots, the working conditions, the conflicts inherent in the roles, and the incompatibility of work and family roles all lead to a state of tedium. (Shamir & Drory, 1982, p. 95)

Stress is a very complex and important topic for correctional employees and administrators, and cannot adequately be dealt with in a single chapter in one book. There is an expansive and rich literature on the subject and the reader is encouraged to pursue further study through other sources. Stress is caused by organizational factors and by human factors, and must be reduced through the efforts of both organizational and human activities.

The work environment contributes significantly to stress. The bureaucratic nature of organizations, the ambiguity of role definitions, and the nature of physical facilities contribute significantly to negative stress. Continuous contact with inmates, though not as stressful as some other stressors, can contribute significantly to the feelings of helplessness, powerlessness, and low self-esteem that are experienced by many. Relationships with colleagues can be either sources of stress or sources of support. Negative relationships, "gripe" sessions without constructive suggestions, and continuous and exclusive interaction with cynical and burned-out individuals tend to exacerbate the effect of stressful situations. Relationships with other significant individuals—such as children, spouses, parents, and others—can contribute to stress on the job. Likewise, stress on the job can contribute to negative relationships with others.

Career and life stages, professional growth and development, and life styles also contribute significantly to stress. Perceptions of events and expectations tend to change as individuals move along the life and professional continuums. Older individuals in corrections tend to experience less stress; it may be that they have learned to cope better than younger individuals or that (through the process of attrition) only those with good coping skills and abilities remain in corrections.

Coping with the negative effects of stress calls for intentional effort on the part of the individual. There are many ways that individuals attempt to cope with stressful events and situations. Some are dysfunctional—that is, they are not effective or may even exacerbate the problem—and some are functional. Although much research needs to be conducted and the literature regarding coping mechanisms needs to be synthesized, it is clear that a well balanced life style with realistic expectations and progressive, professional environments is necessary for the individual to be most effective. Individuals and organizations must realize the nature of the profession and take positive steps, both individually and collectively, to counteract the negative and stressful nature of corrections environments.

NOTES

1. Lack of administrative support is a significant factor in employee dissatisfaction and stress. Kauffman (1988) reports that, in her study, Massachusetts correctional officers were given little or no support by the administration.

2. "This hypothetical but nonetheless accurate job description is suggested in part by David Duffee (1980:205-6). Other contributing sources for the employment listing include Crouch (1980), Jacobs and Retsky (1980), and Jurik (1985)." (Hawkins & Alpert, 1989, p. 339)

9

Future Directions of Professionalization in Corrections

Corrections has not reached the state of a profession at this point in its development; however, it is clearly an emerging profession that will continue to develop. Some correctional roles are more professionalized than others. Archambeault and Archambeault (1982) state that, in corrections, "progress toward a higher degree of professionalism has been occurring slowly since the 1930s. Comparatively great strides were made during the 1960s and early 1970s; these, however have slowed down since the mid 1970s" (p. 252). The dramatic expansion of corrections has caused a setback for professionalization at the entry level, because agencies have been forced to hire those who marginally qualify for employment. Professionalization in the upper ranks continues, however, and will resume at the entry level.

> Achievement of correctional programs staffed with those who are highly motivated, well educated, and oriented toward the mission of reintegration is still far down the line. . . . It is ironic that just as the movement is being made toward improvement, the population crunch is causing the hiring of personnel to be done on a crisis basis—no doubt setting back progress in this area. (Allen & Simonsen, 1986, p. 472)

Many professionals do work in corrections, and more will continue to join the ranks. In addition, many correctional roles are being professionalized. "The occupational group of the future will combine elements from both the professional and bureaucratic models, [and] the average professional man will combine professional and non-professional orientations" (Wilensky, 1964).

171

The next decade promises to be one of the most exciting and challenging in correctional history. Never has there been such a demand for professionally competent and motivated staff. The Federal Bureau of Prisons predicts that the next five years will bring the greatest growth in its history. Twenty-nine new federal facilities will open and some existing institutions will be expanded. (Rosetti, 1988, p. 34)

Landon (1989) indicates that the Federal Bureau of Prisons expects to double its current 13,000 employees within 10 years. Landon further states that statistics show that corrections is one of the ten fastest growing occupations in the United States.

The 1970s and 1980s were decades in which a major problem for correctional agencies was a shortage of space. In the 1990s, the space shortage may be replaced by a shortage of qualified and motivated personnel. In the past, such shortages have generally existed only in certain institutions, such as rural prisons distant from a sufficiently large labor pool, or urban and suburban prisons and jails unable to compete with higher paying jobs. Competition for a qualified, motivated workforce will increase in the 1990s, and corrections will have to respond not only by increasing compensation and benefits, but also by rethinking many correctional jobs to enhance satisfaction, career opportunity, and worker productivity. (Benton, 1988, p. 108)

The nature of America's correctional population is constantly changing. Continued competition for limited space will result in increasingly hard-core prison populations. "Thus, we must recognize that by the year 2000, only the hard-core cases, offenders extremely difficult to treat, will be committed to prison" (Fenton, 1973, p. 187).

The professionalization movement in corrections must expand to include more than merely increasing the education of employees. Education has had little influence on changing the guard role in corrections (Jurik & Musheno, 1986). Jurik, Halemba, Musheno, and Boyle (1987) state that

with regard to future correctional policy, our own findings tentatively suggest that narrow definitions of professionalization limited simply to increasing the educational level of line officers is an inadequate solution to the problems of modern prisons. (p. 121)

Corrections will remain a public service profession regardless of the influences of privatization. The characteristics of a profession (see Chapter 4) will continue to be further defined and refined as corrections develops. "The degree of professionalization is measured not just by the degree of success in the claim to exclusive competence, but also by the degree of adherence to the service ideal and its supporting norms of professional conduct" (Wilensky, 1964, p. 141).

Several factors will combine to force continued professionalization. Administrators, legislators, and others will continue to seek higher qualified employees as the correctional process continues to increase in complexity. Courts will continue to require professional standards of conduct and service. Robey (1985) identified three demographic trends that will also be important in the professionalization of corrections: the middle-aging of America; further advancement for women; and advances in education.

> As these factors interact in the coming decade, the nature of corrections in the United States will change profoundly. As the demand for correctional workers rises, the traditional sources of correctional workers will be inadequate to meet the demands, and new correctional workers will expect more from their employers. (Benton, 1988, p. 108)

Mangrum (1981) indicates the importance of a positive self-image which, he states, promotes self-esteem, is critical to success, and reduces fears, anxiety, and defensive behaviors. Mangrum suggests that though there is not much that average correctional officers can do about their external environments, they can change their self-images, gain pride, and place emphases on professional behavior. Officers must be committed to professionalism and must be competent, credible, and confident. Commitment comes from action, perseverance, and attitude. Competency must be gained and maintained. Credibility must be earned internal and external to the individual and the organization. Confidence, Mangrum says, flows from these other attributes and characteristics. It is a widely accepted belief that the officer who has a solid educational background, professional supervision, ongoing in-service training, and continuous professional development will be better able to cope with the environmental influences that will have a continuing impact on corrections.

Archambeault and Archambeault (1982) identify several trends in correctional employment. First, larger numbers of employees will be younger and better educated. Second, there will be an increase in the number of minorities and women in corrections. Third, if the economy expands, it will be harder to fill vacant positions. Fourth, turnover is too high and will likely remain too high. Fifth, a major factor contributing to manpower problems in corrections is low quality and ineffective supervisory management. Sixth, agencies do not develop human resources and do not provide adequate feedback and reinforcement. Most of these negative points, however, can be dealt with in positive ways.

The more highly professionalized are likely to be less loyal to employers and to pursue personal interests (Cayer, 1986). Intense specialization, which will become more prevalent in corrections, also creates a narrow view in employees. Even so, corrections will be competing strenuously for qualified and motivated workers. Agencies will need to increase "compensation and benefits . . . [and rethink] many correctional jobs to enhance motivation, satisfaction, career opportunity and worker productivity" (Benton & Nesbitt, 1988, p. 4).

> The role of the administrator has likewise changed. It is more than supervising subordinates and preparing the budget. It now involves contracting for services, space, and equipment, protecting the agency from lawsuits initiated by clients and staff, negotiating with the public and media on the value of community programming, and monitoring monies collected from probationers and parolees. . . . [The changes that are] occurring today and continuing tomorrow are not internally sponsored, but forced upon the system, primarily by legislative initiatives. (Thomas, 1988, p. 49)

> Corrections administrators who are politically astute, sophisticated, and powerful are the exceptions. Too many managers and administrators in corrections are politically naive or ineffective when judged against other public sector managers. Correctional agencies are generally not good at initiating necessary legislation and they are seldom known for their close, positive working relationships with the legislative branch. (Schwartz, 1989, p. 40)

Allen, Latessa, and Vito (1987) project that privatization will continue in the area of community corrections. They are less optimistic, however, regarding privatization in the area of correctional institutions. They suggest that electronic monitoring of offenders will be more important and that other factors such as the graying (aging) of the general and correctional populations will affect corrections in both predictable and unpredictable ways. They also indicate that there will be more minority incarceration, more intensive supervision in communities, and improved classification systems. A higher percentage of juveniles will be tried as adults, and the focus will be upon the serious juvenile offender. There will be increased prison construction, expanded victim compensation programs, and crime insurance. Urban redesign and redevelopment patterns will be affected by the crime problem experienced in this country. Allen, Latessa, and Vito predict the demise of mandatory parole and suggest that there will be a gradual erosion of individual rights as society tries to deal with the problems of crime and corrections. They state also that community-based corrections will remain the best hope of corrections in general.

Fox (1985) states that "the future of corrections lies in an increased awareness of its function and its value to society" (p. 441). Increasing complexity of society will necessitate stronger controls. More prisons are being built and community programs are being expanded. Although parole as a discretionary function of parole boards may decline, it is doubtful that postrelease supervision of institutionalized inmates will be abolished.

Although some experts predict that prisons will become less attractive to idealistic college graduates "with the facade of idealistic purpose [rehabilitation]" (Jacobs, 1978, p. 94) being eroded, others (Cullen, Lutze, Link, & Wolfe, 1989) find that correctional officers still believe in the reformation value of prison treatment programs:

Indeed, the level of officers' support for rehabilitative ideology is remarkably high, when one considers the past decade's pervasive assault on the treatment ideal by politicians, criminal justice policy makers, and academic criminologists. (p. 40)

The stressful nature of correctional work will likely continue; complexity will increase, and new challenges will arise. Those organizations that are successful will continue to professionalize, and the working conditions and career progression possibilities will improve. Personnel management—in its truest and most professional sense—will become increasingly necessary in all correctional organizations. Those who take responsibility for their own professional development and growth will do well through all stages of their careers. Corrections is a challenging and satisfying profession for those who are prepared adequately and who continue to maintain professional status through professional growth and development. Much remains to be done by administrators, politicians, employees, professionals, and others to make the correctional environment less negative—especially at the entry level. Descriptions of the environment are unfavorable for line correctional officers. Those above entry level and in professional roles also experience less than desirable environments. Given that government policies are slow, deliberate, and the result of compromise, however, it will take more time in order for the full potential of the professional environment to be realized. There is reason for hope.

For Further Reading

Allen, H. E., & Simonsen, C. E. (1989). *Corrections in America: An introduction* (5th ed.). New York: Macmillan.

American Correctional Association (1982). *Classification as a management tool: Theories and models for decision makers*. College Park, MD: American Correctional Association.

Binder, A., Geis, G., & Bruce, D. (1988). *Juvenile delinquency: History, cultural, legal perspective*. New York: Macmillan.

Blankenship, R. L. (Ed.). (1977). *Colleagues in organizations: The social construction of professional work*. New York: Wiley.

Braswell, M., Dillingham, S., & Montgomery, R., Jr. (Eds.). (1985). *Prison violence in America*. Cincinnati, OH: Anderson.

Carroll, L. (1988). *Hacks, blacks, and cons*. Prospect Heights, IL: Waveland.

Cherniss, C. (1980). *Staff burnout: Job stress in the human services*. Beverly Hills, CA: Sage.

Clements, C. B. (1985). *Offender needs assessment*. College Park, MD: American Correctional Association.

Cord, R. C., Medeiros, J. A., Jones, W., & Roshkin, M. (1985). *Political science: An introduction* (2nd ed.). Englewood Cliffs, NJ: Prentice-Hall.

Cressey, D. (1961). *The prison: Studies in institutional organization and change*. New York: Holt, Rinehart, and Winston.

Guy, M. E. (1985). *Professionals in organizations: Debunking a myth*. New York: Praeger.

Harris, G. A., & Watkins, D. (1987). *Counseling the involuntary and resistant client*. College Park, MD: American Correctional Association.

Hatcher, H. (1978). *Correctional casework and counseling*. Englewood Cliffs, NJ: Prentice-Hall.

Irwin, J. (1980). *Prisons in turmoil*. Boston: Little, Brown.

Langworthy, R., & McCarthy, B. (1988). *Older offenders: Perspectives in crime and criminal justice*. College Park, MD: American Correctional Association.

Lipsky, M. (1980). *Street-level bureaucracy*. New York: Russell Sage Foundation.

Lorch, R. (1986). *State and local politics*. Englewood Cliffs, NJ: Prentice-Hall.

McCarthy, B., & McCarthy, B. (1984). *Community based corrections*. Monterey, CA: Brooks/Cole.

Moore, W. E. (1970). *The professions: Roles and rules*. New York: Russell Sage Foundation.

Neubauer, D. (1988). *America's courts and the criminal justice system* (3rd ed.). Monterey, CA: Brooks/Cole.

Peters, B. G. (1978). *The politics of bureaucracy: A comparative perspective*. New York: Longman.

Pfeffer, J., & Salancik, G. R. (1978). *The external control of organizations: A resource dependence perspective*. New York: Harper and Row.

Pollock-Byrne, J. (1989). *Ethics in criminal justice: Dilemmas and decisions*. Pacific Grove, CA: Brooks/Cole.

Quay, H. C. (1984). *Managing adult inmates: Classification for housing and program assignment*. College Park, MD: American Correctional Association.

Saenz, A. (1986). *Politics of a prison riot*. College Park, MD: American Correctional Association.

Santamour, M. B. (1989). *The mentally retarded offender and corrections*. Laurel, MD: American Correctional Association.

Seigel, L., & Senna, J. (1988). *Juvenile delinquency: Theory, practice, and law*. St. Paul, MN: West.

Steadman, H. J., McCarty, D. W., & Morrissey, J. P. (1989). *The mentally ill in jail: Planning for essential services*. New York: Guilford.

Toch, H., Adams, K., & Grant, J. D. (1989). *Coping: Maladaptation in prisons*. New Brunswick, NJ: Transaction.

Vollmer, H. M., & Mills, D. L. (Eds.). (1966). *Professionalization*. Englewood Cliffs, NJ: Prentice-Hall.

Walker, S. (1983). *The police in America*. New York: McGraw-Hill.

Ward, R. H., & Webb, V. J. (1984). *Quest for quality*. New York: University.

Webb, G. L., & Morris, D. G. (1978). *Prison guards: The culture and perspective of an occupational group*. Fayetteville, GA: Coker.

Wilson, J. Q. (1986). *American government: Institute and policies* (3rd ed.). Lexington, MA: D. C. Heath.

Woolfolk, R. L., & Lehrer, P. M. (1984). *Principles of stress management*. New York: Guilford.

Zimring, F. E., & Hawkins, G. J. (1973). *Deterrence: The legal threat in crime control*. Chicago: University of Chicago Press.

References

Abadinsky, H. (1977). *Probation and parole: Theory and practice*. Englewood Cliffs, NJ: Prentice-Hall.

Abney, G., & Lauth, T. P. (1983, January/February). The governor as chief administrator. *Public Administration Review, 43*, 40-48.

Adams, K. (1983, September). Former mental patients in a prison and parole system: A study of socially disruptive behavior. *Criminal Justice and Behavior, 10*, 358-384.

Adams, K. (1985a, December). Addressing inmate's mental health problems: A new direction for prison therapeutic services. *Federal Probation, 49*, 27-33.

Adams, K. (1985b). *Pathology and disruptiveness among prison inmates*. Paper presented at the annual meeting of the American Society of Criminology, San Diego, CA.

Aiken, M., & Hage, J. (1966). Organizational alienation: A comparative analysis. *American Sociological Review, 31*, 497-507.

Allen, H. E., Eskridge, C., Latessa, E. J., & Vito, G. F. (1985). *Probation and parole in America*. New York: Free Press.

Allen, H. E., Latessa, E. J., & Vito, G. F. (1987, April). Corrections in the year 2000. *Corrections Today, 49*, 92-96.

Allen, H. E., & Simonsen, E. (1986). *Corrections in America: An introduction*, (4th ed.). New York: Macmillan.

American Correctional Association (1975). *Code of ethics*. College Park, MD: Author.

American Correctional Association (1983). *Correctional officer resource guide*. College Park, MD: Author.

American Correctional Association (1988). *Juvenile and adult corrections departments, institutions, agencies, and paroling authorities*. College Park, MD: Author.

American Correctional Association (1989a, September). *On the Line, 12*, 5.

American Correctional Association (1989b). *Vital statistics in corrections*. Laurel, MD: Author.

American Heritage Publishing Company (1970). *The American Heritage dictionary of the English language*. New York: Author.

Archambeault, W. G., & Archambeault, B. J. (1982). *Correctional supervisory management: Principles of organization, policy, and law*. Englewood Cliffs, NJ: Prentice-Hall.

Bailey, W. (1966, June). Correctional outcome: An evaluation of 100 reports. *Journal of Criminal Law, Criminology, and Police Science, 57*, 153-160.

Baker, J. N., Hutchison, S., Joseph, N., Manley, H., Pedersen, D., Springen, K., & Zeman, N. (1989, February). Learning to live with AIDS in prison. *Newsweek*, pp. 27-28.

Barber, B. (1965). The sociology of professions. In K. S. Lynn (Ed.), *The professions in America*. Boston: Houghton-Mifflin.

Barkdull, W. L. (1987, June). Probation: Call it control—and mean it. *Federal Probation*, *51*, 50-55.

Baro, A. (1988, September). The loss of control over prison administration. *Justice Quarterly*, *5*, 457-473.

Bartol, K. M. (1979). Professionalization as a predictor of organizational commitment, role stress, and turnover: A multidimensional approach. *Academy of Management Journal*, *22*(4), 815-821.

Bartollas, C., & Miller, S. J. (1978). *Correctional administration: Theory and practice*. New York: McGraw-Hill.

Bateman, T. S., & Strasser, S. (1984). A longitudinal analysis of the antecedents of organizational commitment. *Academy of Management Journal*, *27*(1), 95-112.

Beck, A. J., Kline, S. A., & Greenfeld, L. A. (1988). *Survey of youths in custody, 1987*. Washington, DC: U.S. Department of Justice, Bureau of Justice Statistics.

Bell, R. (1983). *Learning deficiencies of adult inmates*. Washington, DC: National Institute of Corrections.

Benton, F. W., & Nesbitt, C. A. (Eds.). (1988). *Prison personnel management and staff development*. College Park, MD: The American Correctional Association.

Benton, N. (1988, August). Personnel management: Strategies for staff development. *Corrections Today*, *50*, 102-108.

Bentz, W. K., & Noel, R. W. (1983). The incidence of psychiatric disorder among a sample of men entering prison. *Corrective and Social Psychiatry and Journal of Behavior Technology, Methods, and Therapy*, *29*(1).

Bostick, B. A. (1988, December). Facing the future: Challenges for small jails. *Corrections Today*, *50*, 6.

Bowers, W. J., & Pierce, G. L. (1975). The illusion of deterrence in Isaac Ehrlich's research on capital punishment. *Yale Law Journal*, *85*, 187-208.

Bowers, W. J., & Pierce, G. L. (1980, October). Deterrence or brutalization: What is the effect of execution? *Crime and Delinquency*, *26*, 453-484.

Bromberg, W. (1961). *The mold of murder*. New York: Grune and Stratton.

Brown, B., & Courtless, T. (1971). *The mentally retarded offender*. Washington, DC: National Institute of Mental Health.

Brown, P. W. (1986, March). Probation officer burnout: An organizational disease/an organizational cure. *Federal Probation*, *50*, 4-7.

Brown, P. W. (1987, September). Probation officer burnout: An organizational disease/an organizational cure, part II. *Federal Probation*, *51* 17-21.

Brudney, J. L., & Hebert, F. T. (1987, February). State agencies and their environments: Examining the influence of important external actors. *The Journal of Politics*, *49*, 186-206.

Bucher, R., & Stelling, J. (1977). Characteristics of professional organizations. In R. L. Blankenship, (Ed.), *Colleagues in Organizations: The Social Construction of Professional Work*. New York: John Wiley.

Bucher, R., & Strauss, A. (1961). Professions in process. *American Journal of Sociology*, *66*(4), 325-334.

Bureau of Justice Statistics. (1984). *1983 jail census.* Washington, DC: U.S. Department of Justice.

Bureau of Justice Statistics. (1988a). *Prisoners in 1987.* Washington, DC: U.S. Department of Justice.

Bureau of Justice Statistics. (1988b). *Probation and parole, 1987.* Washington, DC: U.S. Department of Justice.

Bureau of Justice Statistics. (1988c). *Report to the nation on crime and justice* (2nd ed.). Washington, DC: U.S. Department of Justice.

Bureau of Justice Statistics. (1989). *Profile of state and local law enforcement agencies, 1987.* Washington, DC: U.S. Department of Justice.

Bureau of the Census. (1987). *Statistical abstract of the United States* (107th ed.). Washington, DC: U.S. Department of Commerce.

Bureau of the Census. (1988). *Statistical abstract of the United States, 1988* (108th ed.). Washington, DC: U.S. Department of Commerce.

Bureau of the Census. (1989). *Statistical abstract of the United States* (109th ed.). Washington, DC: U.S. Department of Commerce.

Buser, C. A., Leone, P. A., & Bannon, M. E. (1987, June). Segregation: Does educating the handicapped stop here? *Corrections Today, 49,* 17-18.

Cacioppe, R., & Mock, P. (1984, November). A comparison of the quality of work experience in government and private organizations. *Human Relations, 37,* 23-40.

Carlson, K. A. (1988, April). Understanding community opposition to prison siting: More than fear and finance. *Corrections Today, 50,* 84-90.

Carroll, J. F., & White, W. L. (1982). Theory building: Integrating individual and environmental factors within an ecological framework. In W. Paine (Ed.), *Job stress and burnout: Research, theory and intervention perspectives.* Beverly Hills, CA: Sage.

Cayer, J. F., & Weschler, L. F. (1988). *Public administration: Social change and adaptive management.* New York: St. Martin's Press.

Cayer, N. J. (1986). *Public personnel administration in the United States.* New York: St. Martin's Press.

Cerrato, S. (1984, March). Politically appointed administrators: An empirical perspective. *Federal Probation, 48,* 22-28.

Chambliss, W., & Seidman, R. (1971). *Law, order, and power.* Reading, MA: Addison-Wesley.

Cheek, F., & Miller, M. (1982). *Prisoners of life.* Washington, DC: American Federation of State, County, and Municipal Employees.

Cheek, F. E., & Miller, M. D. (1983). The experience of stress for correctional officers: A double-bind theory of correctional stress. *Journal of Criminal Justice, 11*(2), 105-120.

Cherniss, C., & Egnatios, E. S. (1978, Winter). Is there job satisfaction in community health? *Community Mental Health Journal, 14,* 309-318.

Cherniss, C., & Kane, J. S. (1987, March). Public sector professionals: Job characteristics, satisfaction, and aspirations for intrinsic fulfillment through work. *Human Relations, 40,* 125-136.

Clemmer, D. (1958). *The prison community.* New York: Holt, Rinehart, and Winston.

Coffey, O. D. (1987, June). Book 'em: No read, no release. *Corrections Today, 49,* 116-118.

Cohn, A. W. (1987, December). The failure of correctional management—the potential for reversal. *Federal Probation, 51,* 3-7.

Cole, G. F (1989). *The American system of criminal justice* (5th ed.). Pacific Grove, CA: Brooks/Cole.

Corothers, H. (1987, October). Crisis is another word for opportunity. *Corrections Today, 49,* 58-62.

Corrections Compendium (1983). *National survey of correctional staff turnover.* Lincoln, NB: Contact.

Cournoyer, B. (1988, May). Personal and professional distress among social caseworkers. *Social Casework, 69,* 259-264.

Crouch, B. M. (1980). *The keepers: Prison guards and contemporary corrections.* Springfield, IL: Charles C. Thomas.

Cullen, F. T., Link, B. G., Wolfe, N. T., & Frank, J. (1985, December). The social dimension of correctional officer stress. *Justice Quarterly, 2,* 505-533.

Cullen, F. T., Lutze, F. E., Link, B. G., & Wolfe, N. T. (1989, March). The correctional orientation of prison guards: Do officers support rehabilitation? *Federal Probation, 53,* 33-41.

Duffee, D. (1980). *Correctional management.* Englewood Cliffs, NJ: Prentice-Hall.

Duffy, J. E. (1988, October). Illiteracy: A national crisis. *Corrections Today, 50,* 44-45.

Duncan, R. B. (1972). Characteristics of organizational environments and perceived environmental uncertainty. *Administrative Science Quarterly, 17*(3), 313-327.

Edelwich, J., & Brodsky, A. (1983). *Burnout: Stages of disillusionment in the helping professions.* New York: Human Sciences Press.

Ehrlich, I. (1975, June). The deterrent effect of capital punishment: A question of life and death. *American Economic Review, 65,* 397-417.

Evans, David C. (1988, June). Leadership and vision in a world of change. *Corrections Today, 50,* 6.

Farmer, R. E. (1977). Cynicism: A factor in corrections work. *Journal of Criminal Justice, 5,* 237-246.

Feldman, S. P. (1985, April). Culture and conformity: An essay on individual adaptation in centralized bureaucracy. *Human Relations, 38,* 341-356.

Fenton, N. (1973). *Human relations in adult corrections.* Springfield, IL: Charles C. Thomas.

Fisher, C. D., & Gitelson, R. (1983, May). A meta-analysis of the correlates of role conflict and ambiguity. *Journal of Applied Psychology, 68,* 330-333.

Fox, J. (1982). *Organizational and racial conflict in maximum-security prisons.* Lexington, MA: D. C. Heath.

Fox, V. (1983). *Correctional institutions.* Englewood Cliffs, NJ: Prentice-Hall.

Fox, V. (1985). *Introduction to corrections* (3rd ed.). Englewood Cliffs, NJ: Prentice-Hall.

Friedrich, C. J. (1935). Responsible government service under the American constitution. Commission of Inquiry on Public Service Personnel. *Problems of the American Public Service.* New York: McGraw.

Freudenberger, H. J. (1974). Staff burnout. *Journal of Social Issues, 30*(1), 159-164.

Gardner, R. (1981, October). Guard stress: Resentments focus on the brass, not the inmates. *Corrections Magazine, 7,* 7-14.

Gerstein, L. H., Topp, C. G., & Corell, G. (1987, September). The role of the environment and person when predicting burnout among correctional personnel. *Criminal Justice and Behavior, 14,* 352-369.

Gill, H. B. (1958, July/August). Training prison officers. *American Journal of Corrections.*

Gilley, K. (1988, October). NIC update. *Corrections Today, 50*, 30.

Glaser, D. (1964). *Effectiveness of a prison and parole system*. Indianapolis, IN: Bobbs-Merrill.

Goffman, E. (1961). *Asylums*. Garden City, NY: Doubleday.

Goldstein, I. L. (1986). *Training in organizations: Needs assessment, development, and evaluation* (2nd ed.). Monterey, CA: Brooks/Cole.

Greenwood, E. (1957). Attributes of a profession. *Social Work, 2*(3), 45-55.

Greenwood, P. (1982). *Selective incapacitation*. Santa Monica, CA: RAND Corporation.

Gulick, L. (1937). Notes on the theory of organization. In L. Gulick and L. Urwick (Eds.), *Papers on the science of administration* (pp. 1-45). New York: Columbia University, Institute of Public Administration.

Gurin, G., Veroff, J., & Feld, S. (1960). *Americans view their mental health*. New York: Basic Books.

Guy, E., Platt, J., Zwerling, I., & Bullock, S. (1985, March). Mental health status of prisoners in an urban jail. *Criminal Justice and Behavior, 12*, 29-53.

Haas, K. C., & Alpert, G. P. (Eds.). (1986). *The dilemmas of punishment: Readings in contemporary corrections*. Prospect Heights, IL: Waveland Press.

Hall, R. H. (1968). Professionalization and bureaucratization. *American Sociological Review, 33* 92-104.

Hammond, T. H., & Miller, G. J. (1985, February). A social choice perspective on expertise and authority in bureaucracy. *American Journal of Political Science, 29*, 1-28.

Harris, G. (1983). *Stress in corrections*. Boulder, CO: National Institute of Corrections.

Harris, G. A., & Watkins, D. (1987). *Counseling the involuntary and resistant client*. College Park, MD: The American Correctional Association.

Hawkins, R., & Alpert, G. P. (1989). *American prison systems: Punishment and justice*. Englewood Cliffs, NJ: Prentice-Hall.

Hepburn, J. R. (1985). The exercise of power in coercive organizations: A study of prison guards. *Criminology, 23*(1), 145-164.

Hepburn, J. R., & Albonetti, C. (1980). Role conflict in correctional institutions: An empirical examination of the treatment-custody dilemma among correctional staff. *Criminology, 17*(4), 445-459.

Hollenbeck, J. R., & Williams, C. R. (1986). Turnover functionality versus turnover frequency: A note on work attitudes and organizational effectiveness. *Journal of Applied Psychology, 61*(4), 606-611.

Holmes, T. H., & Rahe, R. H. (1967, August). The social readjustment rating scale. *Journal of Psychosomatic Research, 11*, 213-218.

Homant, R. J. (1979). Correlates of satisfactory relations between correctional officers and prisoners. *Journal of Offender Counseling, Services, and Rehabilitation, 4*, 53-62.

Houle, C. (1980). *Continuing learning in the professions*. San Francisco: Jossey-Bass.

Hudzik, J. K., & Cordner, G. W. (1983). *Planning in criminal justice organizations and systems*. New York: Macmillan.

Hughes, E. C. (1965). Professions. In K. S. Lynn (Ed.), *The professions in America*. Boston: Houghton-Mifflin.

Hummel, R. (1987). *The bureaucratic experience* (3rd ed.). New York: St. Martin's.

In brief. (1988, September 28). *Chronicle of Higher Education, 35*, 2.

Jackson, S. E., Schwab, R. L., & Schuler, R. S. (1986). Toward an understanding of the burnout phenomenon. *Journal of Applied Psychology, 4*, 630-640.

Jacobs, J. B. (1977). *Stateville: The penitentiary in mass society.* Chicago: The University of Chicago Press.

Jacobs, J. B. (1978, April). What prison guards think: A profile of the Illinois force. *Crime and Delinquency, 24,* 185-196.

Jacobs, J. B. (1983). *New perspectives on prisons and imprisonment.* Ithaca, NY: Cornell University Press.

Jacobs, J. B., & Retsky, H. G. (1980). Prison guard. In B. Crouch (Ed.), *The keepers: Prison guards and contemporary corrections.* Springfield, IL: Charles C. Thomas.

Jamieson, K. M., & Flanagan, T. J. (Eds.). (1987). *Sourcebook of Criminal Justice Statistics—1986.* Washington, DC: Bureau of Justice Statistics.

Jenkins, P. (1984). *Crime and justice: Issues and ideas.* Monterey, CA: Brooks/Cole.

Johnson, R. (1987). *Hard time: Understanding and reforming the prison.* Monterey, CA: Brooks/Cole.

Johnson, R., & Price, S. (1981, September). The complete correctional officer: Human services and the human environment of prison. *Criminal Justice and Behavior, 8,* 343-373.

Johnson, R., & Toch, H. (Eds). (1982). *The pains of imprisonment.* Prospect Heights, IL: Waveland.

Jurik, N. C. (1985a). An officer and a lady: Organizational barriers to women working as correctional officers in men's institutions. *Social Problems, 32,* 375-388.

Jurik, N. (1985b, September). Individual and organizational determinants of correctional officer attitudes toward inmates. *Criminology, 23,* 523-539.

Jurik, N., & Halemba, G. J. (1984, Autumn). Gender, working conditions and job satisfaction of women in non-traditional occupations: Female correctional officers in men's prisons. *The Sociological Quarterly, 25,* 551-566.

Jurik, N., Halemba, G. L., Musheno, M. C., & Boyle, B. V. (1987, February). Educational attainment, job satisfaction, and the professionalization of correctional officers. *Work and Occupations, 14,* 106-125.

Jurik, N. C., & Musheno, M. (1985). *The professionalization of corrections: Diffusing organizational reforms.* Paper presented at the annual meeting of the Society for the Study of Social Problems.

Jurik, N. C., & Musheno, M. C. (1986, December). The internal crisis of corrections: Professionalization and the work environment. *Justice Quarterly, 4,* 457-479.

Jurik, N., & Winn, R. (1987, March). Describing correctional-security dropouts and rejects: An individual or organizational profile? *Criminal Justice and Behavior, 14,* 5-25.

Kahn, R. L., & Rosenthal, R. A. (1961). *Organizational stress: Studies in role conflict and ambiguity.* New York: Basic Books.

Karmen, A. (1984). *Crime victims: An introduction to victimology.* Monterey, CA: Brooks/Cole.

Katz, D., & Kahn, R. L. (1978). *The social psychology of organizations.* New York: John Wiley.

Kauffman, K. (1981, July). Prison officers' attitudes and perceptions of attitudes: A case of pluralistic ignorance. *Journal of Research in Crime and Delinquency, 18,* 272-294.

Kauffman, K. (1988). *Prison officers and their world.* Cambridge, MA: Harvard University Press.

Kearney, R. C., & Sinha, C. (1988, January/February). Professionalism and bureaucratic responsiveness. *Public Administration Review, 48,* 571-579.

Keegan, J. (1987). *The mask of command.* New York: Viking.

Kennedy, D. B., & Homant, R. J. (1988, September). Predicting custodial suicides. *Justice Quarterly, 5,* 441-456.

Klofas, J. (1986). Discretion among correctional officers: The influence of urbanization, age, and race. *International Journal of Offender Therapy and Comparative Criminology, 30,* 111-124.

Klofas, J., & Toch, H. (1982, July). The guard subculture myth. *Journal of Research in Crime and Delinquency, 19,* 238-254.

Landon, M. D. (1989). Letter dated January 3, 1989. Washington, DC: U.S. Department of Justice, Federal Bureau of Prisons.

Lasky, G. L., Gordon, B. C., & Srebalus, D. J. (1986, September). Occupational stressors among federal correctional officers working in different security levels. *Criminal Justice and Behavior, 13,* 317-327.

Latack, J. (1986). Coping with job stress: Measures and future directions for scale development. *Journal of Applied Psychology, 71*(3), 377-385.

Lawrence, R. (1984, December). Professionals or judicial servants? An examination of the probation officer's role. *Federal Probation, 48,* 14-21.

Lawton, H. W., & Magarelli, A. (1980). Stress among public child welfare workers. *Catalyst, 2*(3), 57-65.

Levinson, D. (1978). *The seasons of man's life.* New York: Knopf.

Lillyquist, M. J. (1980). *Understanding and changing criminal behavior.* Englewood Cliffs, NJ: Prentice-Hall.

Lindquist, C., & Whitehead, J. (1986, Summer). Burnout, job stress and job satisfaction among southern correctional officers: Perceptions and causal factors. *Journal of Offender Counseling, Services and Rehabilitation, 10,* 5-26.

Link, B. G., & Dohrenwend, B. P. (1980). Formulation of hypotheses about the true prevalence of demoralization in the United States. In B. P. Dohrenwend, B. S. Dohrenwend, M. S. Gould, B. G. Link, R. Neugebauer, & R. Wunsch-Hitzig (Eds.), *Mental Illness in the United States: Epidemiological Estimates* (pp. 114-127). New York: Praeger.

Locke, E. A. (1976). The nature and cause of job dissatisfaction. In M. D. Dunnette (Ed.), *Handbook of individual / organizational psychology* (pp. 1297-1349). Chicago: Rand McNally.

Lombardo, L. X. (1981). *Guards imprisoned: Correctional officers at work.* New York: Elsevier.

Long, N., Shouksmith, G., Voges, K., & Roache, S. (1986, May). Stress in prison staff: An occupational study. *Criminology, 24,* 331-345.

Lynn, K. (Ed.). (1965). *The professions in America.* Boston: Houghton-Mifflin.

MacKenzie, D. L. (1987, December). Age and adjustment to prison: Interaction with attitudes and anxiety. *Criminal Justice and Behavior, 14,* 427-447.

Mangrum, C. T. (1981, June). A positive self-image for corrections. *Federal Probation, 45,* 10-14.

Mannheim, B. (1975). A comparative study of work centrality, job rewards, and satisfaction. *Sociology of Work and Occupations, 2,* 79-102.

Manning, W. (1983, February). An underlying cause of burnout. *Corrections Today, 40,* 20-22.

Martinson, R. (1974, Spring). What works? Questions and answers about prison reform. *Public Interest, 35,* 22-54.

May, E. (1980). Prison guards in America—the inside story. In B. Crouch (Ed.), *The keepers: Prison guards and contemporary corrections.* Springfield, IL: Charles C. Thomas.

Mayhew, L. B. (1971). *Changing practices in education for all professions.* Atlanta, GA: Southern Regional Education Board.

McArdle, A. (1988). Personal letter to the author, December 28, 1988. Laurel, MD: The American Correctional Association.

McCabe, J. M. (1986). *The relationship of burnout, coping methods, and locus of control among probation and parole officers.* Unpublished doctoral dissertation, University of Missouri, Kansas City.

McDougall, E. (1985). Foreword. In M. Braswell, S. Dillingham & R. Montgomery, Jr. (Eds.), *Prison Violence in America.* Cincinnati, OH: Anderson.

McGowan, R. A. (1982, Winter). The professional in public organizations: Lessons from the private sector. *American Review of Public Administration, 16,* 337-349.

McGowan, R. A. (1980). *Information preferences and acquisition by public managers: An analysis of New York state agencies.* Unpublished doctoral dissertation, Syracuse, NY, 1980.

Meese, E., III. (1988, April). An equal partner: Corrections and the criminal justice system. *Corrections Today, 50,* 58-60.

Merker, S. L., Rhodes, G. B., & Vito, G. F. (1984). *Elements related to job satisfaction, alienation, and morale among correctional officers.* Paper presented at the Organization Police and Development conference.

Mobley, M. J. (1985, December). Occupational hazard?: Stress has many implications for the administrator. *Corrections Today, 47,* 18-20.

Mobley, M. J. (1986, May). Mental health services: Inmates in need. *Corrections Today, 48,* 12-14.

Monahan, J., & Steadman, H. (1983). Crime and mental disorder: An epidemiological approach. In M. Tonry & N. Morris (Eds.), *Crime and criminal justice: An annual review of research, Volume 4.* Chicago: University of Chicago Press.

Moracco, J. C. (1985, December). Stress: How corrections personnel can anticipate, manage, and reduce stress on the job. *Corrections Today, 47,* 22-26.

Morris, R. M. (1986, August). Burnout: Avoiding the consequences of on-the-job stress. *Corrections Today, 48,* 122-126.

Mosher, F. C. (1982). *Democracy and the public service* (2nd ed.). New York: Oxford University Press.

Mosher, F. C., & Stillman, R. (1977, November/December). The professions in government. *Public Administration Review, 37,* 631-632.

Murphy, A. I. (1988, July). Today's line staff: Tomorrow's leadership. *Corrections Today, 50,* 6.

Myklebust, H. R. (Ed.). (1968). *Progress in learning disabilities, volume 1.* New York: Gune & Stratton.

National Center for Education Statistics. (1988). *Digest of Education Statistics.* Washington, DC: U.S. Government Printing Office.

National Neighborhood Foot Patrol Center. (1988, Fall/Winter). LE degree can pay off. *Footprints, 1,* 2, 13.

Nelson, R. (1988). Cost savings in new generation jails: The direct supervision approach. *Construction Bulletin.* Washington, DC: National Institute of Justice.

Nemeth, C. P. (1986). *Anderson's directory of criminal justice education*. Cincinnati, OH: Anderson.

Nigro, F. A., & Nigro, L. G. (1984). *Modern public administration*. New York: Harper & Row.

O'Connor, D. J., & Wolfe, D. M. (1987, December). On managing midlife transitions in career and family. *Human Relations, 40*, 799-816.

O'Reilly, C. A., III, & Caldwell, D. E. (1980, October). Job choice: The impact of intrinsic and extrinsic factors on subsequent satisfaction and commitment. *Journal of Applied Psychology, 65*, 559-565.

Pavalko, R. M. (1971). *Sociology of occupations and professions*. Itasca, IL: F. E. Peacock.

Petersilia, J., Greenwood, P. W., & Lavin, M. (1978). *Criminal careers of habitual felons*. Washington, DC: U.S. Government Printing Office.

Peterson, N. G., Houston, J. S., Bosshardt, M. J., & Dunnette, M. D. (1977). *A study of the correctional officer job at Marion Correctional Institution, Ohio: Development of selection procedures, training records and exit information program*. Minneapolis, MN: Personnel Decision Research Institute.

Podboy, J. W., & Mallory, W. A. (1978, September). The diagnosis of specific learning disabilities in a juvenile delinquent population. *Federal Probation, 42*, 26-33.

Poole, E. D., & Regoli, R. M. (1980a). Work relations and cynicism among prison guards. *Criminology, 7*, 303-314.

Poole, E. D., & Regoli, R. M. (1980b, August). Role stress, custody orientation, and disciplinary actions. *Criminology, 18*, 215-226.

Poole, E. D., & Regoli, R. M. (1981, August). Alienation in prison: An examination of the work relations of prison guards. *Criminology, 19*, 251-270.

Poole, E. D., & Regoli, R. M. (1983, January). Professionalism, role conflict, work alienation, and anomie: A look at prison management. *The Social Science Journal, 20*, 63-70.

President's Commission on Law Enforcement and the Administration of Justice. (1967). *Task force report on the police*. Washington, DC: U.S. Government Printing Office.

Rainey, H. G., & Backoff, R. W. (1982, Winter). Professionals in public organizations: Organizational environments and incentives. *American Review of Public Administration, 16*, 319-336.

Ratliff, N. (1988, March). Stress and burnout in the helping professions. *Social Casework, 69*, 147-154.

Regoli, R. M., Poole, E. D., & Schrink, J. L. (1979, Summer). Occupational socialization and career development: A look at cynicism among correctional institution workers. *Human Organization, 38*, 183-187.

Reichers, A. E. (1986). Conflict and organizational commitments. *Journal of Applied Psychology, 71*(3), 508-514.

Repetti, R. L. (1987). Individual and common components of the social environment at work and psychological well-being. *Journal of Personality and Social Psychology, 52*(4), 710-720.

Rizzo, J. R., House, R. J & Heitzman, S. I. (1970). Role conflict and ambiguity in complex organizations. *Administrative Science Quarterly, 15*(2), 150-163.

Robey, B. (1985). *The American people: A timely exploration of the population megatrends influencing a changing USA*. New York: E. P. Dutton.

Robin, G. (1987). *Introduction to the criminal justice system* (3rd ed.). New York: Harper & Row.

Rosecrance, J. (1987, June). Getting rid of the prima donnas: The bureaucratization of a probation department. *Criminal Justice and Behavior, 14*, 138-155.

Rosetti, R. (1988, August). Charting your course: Federal model encourages career choices. *Corrections Today, 40*, 34-38.

Sarason, S. B. (1977). *Work, aging, and social change.* New York: Free Press.

Schade, T. (1986). Prison officer training in the United States: The legacy of Jessie O. Stutsman. *Federal Probation, 50*(4), 40-46.

Schott, R. L. (1986, November/December). The psychological development of adults: Implications for public administration. *Public Administration Review, 46*, 657-667.

Schwartz, G. M. (1987, June). Effective special education information exchange is critical. *Corrections Today, 49*, 26-30.

Schwartz, J. (1988, February). Learning and earning. *American Demographics, 10*, 12.

Schwartz, J. (1989). Promoting a good public image: Effective leadership, sound practices make the difference. *Corrections Today, 51*, 38-42.

Seeman, M. (1972). Alienation and engagement. In A. Campbell & P. E. Converse (Eds.), *The human meaning of social change* (pp. 467-527). New York: Russell Sage Foundation.

Sellin, T. (1980). *The penalty of death.* Beverly Hills, CA: Sage.

Selye, H. (1976). *The stress of life* (rev. ed.). New York: McGraw-Hill.

Shamir, B., & Drory, A. (1982, March). Occupational tedium among prison officers. *Criminal Justice and Behavior, 9*, 79-99.

Shannon, M. J. (1987, April). Officer training: Is enough being done? *Corrections Today, 49*, 172-175.

Shapiro, C. (1982). Creative supervision: An underutilized antidote. In W. Paine (Ed.), *Job stress and burnout: research, theory, and intervention perspectives.* Beverly Hills, CA: Sage.

Sheridan, J. J. (1988, August). The juvenile sector: Challenging careers in a unique environment. *Corrections Today, 50*, 84-87.

Shils, E. (1974). *Center and periphery: Essays in macrosociology.* Chicago: University of Chicago Press.

Shover, N., & Einstadter, W. J. (1988). *Analyzing American corrections.* Belmont, CA: Wadsworth.

Silberman, C. (1978). *Criminal violence, criminal justice.* New York: Random House.

Skolnick, J. (1966). *Justice without trial.* New York: John Wiley.

Staufenberger, R. A. (1977, November/December). The professionalization of police: Efforts and obstacles. *Public Administration Review, 37*, 678-685.

Steurer, S. J. (1987, June). Correctional education: Testing new ideas. *Corrections Today, 49*, 6.

Stevenson, L. (1987). *Seven theories of human nature.* New York: Oxford University Press.

Stewart, J., & Clarke, M. (1987, Summer). The public service orientation: Issues and dilemmas. *Public Administration, 65*, 161-177.

Straussman, J. (1986, July/August). Courts and public purse strings: Have portraits of budgeting missed something? *Public Administration Review, 46*, 345-351.

Sykes, G. (1956). The corruption of authority and rehabilitation. *Social Forces, 34*, 257-262.

Sykes, G. (1958). *Society of captives*. Princeton, NJ: Princeton University Press.

Teske, R., & Williamson, H. (1979, March). Correctional officer's attitudes toward selected treatment programs. *Criminal Justice and Behavior, 6*, 59-66.

Thomas, J. (1988a, July). Inmate litigation: Using the courts or abusing them? *Corrections Today, 50*, 124-127.

Thomas, J. (1988b). *Prisoner litigation: The paradox of the jailhouse lawyer*. Totowa, NJ: Rowman and Littlefield.

Thomas, R. L. (1983, March). Professionalism in federal probation: Illusion or reality? *Federal Probation, 47*, 3-9.

Thomas, R. L. (1988, September). Stress perception among select federal probation and pretrial services officers and their supervisors. *Federal Probation, 52*, 48-58.

Toch, H. (1977). *Living in prison: The ecology of survival*. New York: Free Press.

Toch, H., & Grant, J. (1982). *Reforming human services: Change through participation*. Beverly Hills, CA: Sage.

Toch, H., & Klofas, J. (1982, March). Alienation and desire for job enrichment among corrections officers. *Federal Probation, 46*, 35-44.

Travisono, A. (1987a, June). Corrections' most critical factors: Education, education, education. *Corrections Today, 49*, 4.

Travisono, A. (1987b, July). Corrections motto: Be prepared and safe. *Corrections Today, 49*, 4.

Travisono, A. (1988a, February). Celebrating the past; Anticipating the future. *Corrections Today, 50*, 4.

Travisono, A. (1988b, August). Promoting professionalism: Corrections as a career. *Corrections Today, 50*, 4.

U.S. Department of Justice (1978). *National manpower survey of the criminal justice system: Corrections, volume II*. Washington, DC: Superintendent of Documents.

Van Fossen, B. E. (1979). *The structure of social inequality*. Boston: Little, Brown.

Veneziano, C. (1984). Occupational stress and the line correctional officer. *Southern Journal of Criminal Justice, 8* 214-231.

Vold, G., & Bernard, T. J. (1986). *Theoretical criminology*. New York: Oxford University Press.

Von Glinow, M. A. (1983). Incentives for controlling the performance of high technology and professional employees. *IEEE Transactions on Systems, Cybernetics, and Man, 13*, 70-74.

Wahler, C., & Gendreau, P. (1985, March). Assessing correctional officers. *Federal Probation, 49*, 70-74.

Walker, S. (1989). *Sense and nonsense about crime* (2nd ed). Pacific Grove, CA: Brooks/Cole.

Walsh, J. A. (1987, May). Burnout and values in the social service profession. *Social Casework, 68*, 279-283.

Warrick, D. D., & Zawacki, R. A. (1984). *Supervisory management: Understanding behavior and managing for results*. New York: Harper & Row.

Weick, K. E. (1979). *The social psychology of organizing* (2nd ed.). Reading, MA: Addison-Wesley.

Wheeler, S. (1961). Socialization in correctional communities. *American Sociological Review, 26*, 697-712.

Whitehead, J. T. (1985, March). Job burnout in probation and parole: Its extent and intervention implications. *Criminal Justice and Behavior, 12*, 91-110.

Whitehead, J. T. (1987). Probation officer job burnout: A test of two theories. *Journal of Criminal Justice, 15*(1), 1-16.

Whitehead, J. T., & Lindquist, C. A. (1985). Job stress and burnout among probation/parole officers: Perceptions and causal factors. *International Journal of Offender Therapy and Comparative Criminology, 29*(2), 109-119.

Whitehead, J. T., & Lindquist, C. A. (1986, February). Correctional officer job burnout: A path model. *Journal of Research in Crime and Delinquency, 23*, 23-42.

Whitmer, G. (1980, January). From hospitals to jails: The fate of California's deinstitutionalized mentally ill. *American Journal of Orthopsychiatry, 50*, 65-75.

Wicks, R. J. (1980). *Guard! Society's professional prisoner.* Houston, TX: Gulf.

Wilensky, H. L. (1964). The professionalization of everyone? *American Journal of Sociology, 70*(2), 137-158.

Wilson, F. (1980). Who will care for the "mad and bad?" *Corrections Magazine, 6*(1), 6.

Wilson, J. Q. (1975). *Thinking about crime.* New York: Basic Books.

Wilson, J. Q. (1983). *Thinking about crime* (rev. ed.). New York: Basic Books.

Appendix **A**

Professional Associations in Corrections

The major association of corrections professionals is the American Correctional Association; 8025 Laurel Lakes Court; Laurel, Maryland 20707; telephone (301) 206-5100. In 1989, the membership of the ACA was 24,000. In addition, the following professional associations were affiliated with the ACA in 1989:

Professional Associations

American Association of Correctional Psychology
American Association of Correctional Training Personnel
American Correctional Chaplains Association
American Correctional Food Services Association
American Correctional Health Services Association
American Jail Association
American Probation and Parole Association
Association for Correctional Research and Information Management
Association of Juvenile Compact Administrators
Association of Paroling Authorities
Association of State Correctional Administrators
Association on Programs for Female Offenders
Correctional Education Association
Correctional Industries Association, Inc.
International Halfway House Association
National Association of Blacks in Criminal Justice
National Association of Juvenile Correctional Agencies
National Association of Probation Executives

National Correctional Recreation Association
National Council on Crime and Delinquency
National Juvenile Detention Association
North American Association of Wardens and Superintendents
Parole and Probation Compact Administrators Association
Prison Fellowship
The Salvation Army
Volunteers of America

State Affiliates

Alabama Council on Crime and Delinquency
Arizona Probation, Parole, and Corrections Association
Colorado Correctional Association
Connecticut Criminal Justice Association
Correctional Association of Massachusetts
Florida Council on Crime and Delinquency
Illinois Correctional Association
Indiana Correctional Association
Iowa Corrections Association
Kansas Correctional Association
Kentucky Council on Crime and Delinquency, Inc.
Louisiana Council on Criminal Justice, Inc.
Maryland Criminal Justice Association
Michigan Corrections Association
Minnesota Corrections Association
Missouri Corrections Association
Nebraska Correctional Association
Nevada Correctional Association
New Jersey Chapter Association
New Mexico Correctional Association
New York Corrections and Youth Services Association
North Carolina Correctional Association
Ohio Correctional and Court Services Association
Oklahoma Correctional Association
Oregon Corrections Association
South Carolina Correctional Association

Texas Corrections Association
Utah Correctional Association
Virginia Correctional Association
Washington Correctional Association
Wisconsin Correctional Association

Regional Associations

Central States Corrections Association
Middle Atlantic States Correctional Association
Southern States Correctional Association
Western Correctional Association

Source: American Correctional Association. (1989). *Juvenile and adult correctional departments, institutions, agencies, and paroling authorities* (refer to p. 558). Laurel, MD: American Correctional Association. ACA membership number taken from *On the Line* (January, 1989), Vol. 12, No. 1, p. 1.

Appendix B

Criminal Justice Higher Education in the United States, 1983-1984

Region/State	Total Number Programs	Undergraduate Degrees Offered	Graduate Degrees Offered	Number of Faculty	Undergraduates Enrolled	Graduates Enrolled	Undergraduate Degrees Granted	Graduate Degrees Granted
Northeast	172	432	93	1,174	34,636	1,447	8,805	328
Connecticut	13	4	19	84	974	106	184	9
Maine	7	11	—	45	438	225	95	80
Massachusetts	20	45	6	131	8,839	160	5,579	66
New Hampshire	2	19	6	24	248	6	39	2
New Jersey	23	42	6	133	3,877	60	376	24
New York	62	192	41	419	13,271	492	1,370	75
Pennsylvania	38	103	14	287	5,870	358	1,126	72
Rhode Island	4	9	1	37	876	40	4	—
Vermont	3	7	—	14	243	—	32	—
Midwest	242	669	68	1,933	28,476	2,176	4,394	322
Illinois	45	112	15	271	5,035	281	476	61
Indiana	14	48	8	169	1,858	938	435	32
Iowa	20	49	4	231	915	4	144	4
Kansas	14	56	0	56	757	—	53	—

Region/State	Total Number Programs	Under-graduate Degrees Offered	Graduate Degrees Offered	Number of Faculty	Under-graduates Enrolled	Graduates Enrolled	Under-graduate Degrees Granted	Graduate Degrees Granted
Michigan	29	91	10	345	5,245	256	946	55
Minnesota	20	44	6	96	2,419	26	466	48
Missouri	29	96	10	188	3,773	400	455	51
Ohio	30	86	9	269	4,086	94	797	57
Nebraska	9	27	2	41	648	—	84	—
North Dakota	5	12	1	16	501	—	70	—
South Dakota	6	15	1	25	264	—	47	—
Wisconsin	21	33	2	226	2,975	177	421	14
South	341	792	131	2,395	40,127	1,645	6,503	395
Alabama	20	43	9	87	1,848	110	347	46
Arkansas	8	13	1	13	274	16	49	4
Delaware	6	8	—	24	266	—	22	—
Dist. of Col.	2	11	9	18	228	55	65	20
Florida	42	121	17	765	5,647	82	523	29
Georgia	24	35	6	93	1,701	195	380	54
Kentucky	9	32	6	88	1,429	118	283	26
Louisiana	14	24	4	70	2,000	74	226	10
Maryland	20	66	15	110	2,460	224	464	35
Mississippi	10	23	8	29	1,039	29	175	14
North Carolina	47	84	2	214	4,189	—	1,293	—
Oklahoma	22	48	13	108	1,853	129	196	32
South Carolina	18	34	1	96	1,656	80	277	21
Tennessee	16	51	4	111	2,331	130	449	20
Texas	44	104	22	363	8,894	315	1,048	69

Region/State	Total Number Programs	Undergraduate Degrees Offered	Graduate Degrees Offered	Number of Faculty	Undergraduates Enrolled	Graduates Enrolled	Undergraduate Degrees Granted	Graduate Degrees Granted
Virginia	30	64	13	163	3,375	63	519	7
West Virginia	9	31	1	43	937	25	187	8
West	181	511	52	2,121	24,184	958	3,201	141
Alaska	2	2	—	10	147	—	33	—
Arizona	14	47	9	105	2,631	40	118	—
California	77	218	34	1,489	14,113	701	1,758	88
Colorado	15	38	2	101	1,144	77	154	12
Hawaii	6	15	—	15	419	30	50	3
Idaho	3	9	—	9	207	—	39	—
Montana	4	4	2	19	250	37	74	6
Nevada	5	23	—	44	839	—	134	—
New Mexico	8	29	—	45	789	40	194	4
Oregon	18	42	3	137	1,043	15	231	20
Utah	2	13	—	10	439	—	99	—
Washington	21	57	2	110	1,872	18	282	8
Wyoming	6	14	—	27	291	—	35	—
Total	936	2,404	344	7,623	127,423	6,226	22,903	1,196

Source: Nemeth, C. P. (1986). *Anderson's directory of criminal justice education, 1986-1987.* Cincinnati, OH: Anderson.
Note: A new edition of the directory was being prepared at the time of this writing.

Appendix C

Career Information Sources and Job Announcements

Career information can be obtained from job counselors for state employment services, local colleges and universities, and from correctional agencies. In addition, there are several sources from which to obtain job listings in correctional services. Some of these sources are as follows:

The NELS Bulletin
College of Criminal Justice
Sam Houston State University
Huntsville, TX 77341
(409) 294-1692

ACAnet (electronic communications/information)
The American Correctional Association
8025 Laurel Lakes Court
Laurel, MD 20707
(301) 206-5100 or (800) ACA-5646

National Recruiting Office
Federal Bureau of Prisons, Room 438
320 First Street, N.W.
Washington, DC 20534
(202) 724-3204

Federal Job Information Service Centers (located at various places in the United States—see telephone directory for your area)

State Employment Service Bureaus (see telephone book for your area)

In addition to the specific publications and clearinghouses listed above, the agencies may be contacted directly for information regarding job openings. The best sources for obtaining names, addresses, and telephone numbers are as follows:

American Correctional Association. (1989). *Juvenile and adult correctional departments, institutions, agencies, and paroling authorities.* Laurel, MD: American Correctional Association.

American Correctional Association. (1985). *Probation and parole: United States and Canada.* College Park, MD: American Correctional Association.

American Correctional Association. (1986). *National jail and adult detention directory: 1986-88.* College Park, MD: American Correctional Association.

National Police Chiefs and Sheriffs Information Bureau. (Use current edition.) *The national directory of law enforcement administrators, correctional institutions, and related government agencies.* Milwaukee, WI: The National Police Chiefs and Sheriffs Information Bureau.

Appendix **D**

Correctional Employment and Beginning Salaries in the United States

State	Number of Officers	Beginning Salary
Alabama	2,052	$15,350
Alaska	689	26,784
Arizona	2,681	16,172*
Arkansas	1,061	13,832
California	12,261	20,328
Colorado	1,006	20,004
Connecticut	1,866	21,403
Delaware	820	16,211
Florida	7,793	14,261*
Georgia	3,485	16,320
Hawaii	1,036	18,132
Idaho	278	16,620
Illinois	5,645	18,720
Indiana	2,158	14,482
Iowa	986	18,012
Kansas	1,065	16,427
Kentucky	1,153	12,408
Louisiana	3,078	13,227
Maine	391	14,705
Maryland	3,583	19,150
Massachusetts	2,207	23,176
Michigan	4,752	18,803
Minnesota	852	20,379
Mississippi	1,232	12,231*
Missouri	2,239	15,936
Montana	213	13,427
Nebraska	484	15,893
Nevada	911	17,577
New Hampshire	290	16,598
New Jersey	3,038	23,071

State	Number of Officers	Beginning Salary
New Mexico	1,050	14,374
New York	17,197	19,261
North Carolina	4,754	16,968
North Dakota	135	13,932
Ohio	3,507	14,539*
Oklahoma	1,460	14,145*
Oregon	655	20,496
Pennsylvania	2,948	16,120
Rhode Island	616	20,334
South Carolina	3,011	14,082
South Dakota	241	12,700
Tennessee	2,735	12,588
Texas	9,935	14,400
Utah	442	15,952
Vermont	253	10,837*
Virginia	4,141	15,168
Washington	2,093	19,308
West Virginia	418	11,604
Wisconsin	1,691	16,198
Wyoming	205	15,348
Washington, DC	2,142	20,418

Number of correctional officers as of June 30, 1988; beginning correctional officers salaries as of June 1, 1988. Note that this is *beginning* salary for correctional officers only. It does not include nonsecurity staff. Most correctional agencies grant raises within the first six months to one year or as soon as training is completed, and salaries sometimes increase quite rapidly. It should also be noted that no fringe benefits are included in the salaries listed. Although this information was the most recent available at the time this book was written, the reader is cautioned that the salary information may be outdated.

Source: American Correctional Association. (1989). *Vital statistics in corrections.* Laurel, MD: American Correctional Association.
Note: In the survey conducted by the ACA, salaries of correctional personnel were distributed as follows: 38.3% earned $20,000 per year or less, 61.7% earned $20,000 or more per year, and 21.6% earned $30,000 or more per year in 1988.
*The 1989 edition did not contain current salary information for Arizona, Florida, Mississippi, Ohio, and Oklahoma. The salary listed here is that received as of January 1, 1985; it is most likely incorrect for 1990. These figures are from the 1986 edition of *Vital Statistics in Corrections.*

Appendix E

Salary Ranges and Median Salary by Job Title

Job Title	Salary Range	Median Salary*
Chief Administrative Officer	$36,700–104,000	66,410
Assistant CAO	25,000–97,340	56,731
Legal Officer/Consultant	21,756–80,869	40,887
Legislative Liaison	22,572–77,100	40,270
Director/Research	22,001–75,711	39,575
Director/Community Services	19,006–73,620	45,138
Director/Special Services	24,064–59,696	36,329
Director/Institutional Services	20,254–73,751	46,801
Director/Dietary	13,900–55,315	29,840
Line Food Service Staff	8,258–44,444	21,404
Director/Industries	18,100–81,513	43,313
Director/Maintenance–Construction	14,472–74,363	37,155
Plant Maintenance Staff	10,500–45,792	23,443
Line Maintenance Staff	10,500–48,964	23,051
Director/Client Education	19,524–73,062	39,739
Director/Security	19,865–65,317	37,558
Director/Treatment	19,000–76,424	38,490
Regional Director	16,475–85,452	43,830
Ombudsman	19,826–62,127	28,404
Public Information Officer	19,044–70,032	36,092
Grants Manager	18,930–74,303	34,698
Chief of Administration	25,000–100,375	52,327
Chief of Program Services	26,136–88,605	49,855
Chief Chaplain	12,500–77,903	29,344
Chief Personnel Officer	20,520–74,303	41,142
Chief Budget Officer	21,755–82,418	41,424
Chief/Medical Services	20,254–100,963	55,284

Job Title	Salary Range	Median Salary*
Medical Doctor	25,728–108,672	64,199
Dentist	19,676–84,720	48,120
Psychologist	17,172–94,907	34,281
Recreation Staff	11,628–38,800	24,293
Chief/Evaluation–Inspection	16,152–81,513	42,721
EEOC Officer	16,718–81,513	33,921
Administrative Assistant	14,742–62,472	28,259
Executive Assistant	15,312–66,074	35,008
Secretary	11,414–61,700	20,620
Clerk	7,620–29,244	15,222
Warden I/Entry Level Admin.	24,492–69,900	42,716
Deputy Warden	24,552–80,063	41,928
Jail Director	18,806–59,177	31,267
Correctional Officer/Entry	11,604–35,760	19,438
Correctional Officer I	12,204–35,298	20,657
Correctional Officer II	12,636–41,160	22,948
Correctional Officer III	15,072–47,292	25,132
Correctional Officer IV	16,286–55,545	28,031
Probation/Parole Compact Adm.	18,333–75,711	35,307
Chief Probation Officer	19,812–66,043	36,181
Probation Officer/Entry	13,752–59,886	24,104
Chief Parole Officer	16,608–68,490	37,743
Parole Officer/Entry	11,000–41,640	22,884
Parole Board Chairman	12,285–93,000	52,202
Parole Board Member	12,285–87,417	46,880

Source: American Correctional Association. (1989). *Vital statistics in corrections*. Laurel, MD: American Correctional Association.
Note: Contains information for adult correctional agencies only. For information concerning juvenile correctional agencies, refer to source. Pay ranges and medians represent salaries as of June, 1988.
*Computed as midpoint of the median range as stated in the source.

Appendix **F**

Occupations Within the Federal Bureau of Prisons

006—Correctional Institution Administration
This series includes positions which involve responsibility for managing or participating in the overall management of correctional institutions, correctional systems, or correctional programs and positions which involve responsibility for advising on, reviewing, and evaluating the management of such institutions, systems, or programs. Work in this series requires knowledge of (1) penological theories, principles, and techniques and (2) the problems, methods, and techniques of institutional management.

007—Correctional Officer
This series covers positions involving the correctional treatment, custody, and supervision of criminal offenders in correctional institutions or rehabilitation facilities. Positions in this series have as their paramount requirements the knowledge of and application of correctional skills and techniques.

018—Safety Management
This series includes positions which involve technical and management work concerned with occupational safety programs, regulations, and standards. Such work has the object of eliminating or controlling the physical conditions, operating practices, and other factors that may result in injury to persons or damage to property. The work requires application and knowledge of: (1) the principles, standards, and techniques of safety, and (2) pertinent aspects of engineering, psychological, and other scientific and technological factors affecting safety.

060—Chaplain
This series includes all positions that advise on, administer, supervise, or perform professional work involved in programs of spiritual welfare and religious guidance for inmates of government correctional and penal institutions. A position is classifiable to this series when the nature of duties and

responsibilities is such that ordination by a recognized ecclesiastical body is a basic requirement.

101—Social Science

This series includes positions that advise on, administer, supervise, or perform research or other professional and scientific work in one or any combination of the social sciences when such work is not classifiable in other series or this occupation group. This group includes correctional treatment specialist (case manager) positions and research positions.

180—Psychologist

This series includes positions involving professional work relating to the capacities, traits, interests, and activities of human behavior. This work involves applying professional knowledge of psychological principles, theories, methods, or data to practical situations and problems, and providing consultative services or training in psychological principles, theories, methods, and techniques and their appropriate use.

188—Recreation Specialist

This series includes positions where the paramount requirement is for a general knowledge of the goals, principles, methods, and techniques of the broad field of recreation in evaluating recreational needs and in planning, organizing, advising on, and administering recreation activities and programs that promote the physical, creative, and social development of participants.

201—Personnel Management

This series includes positions that either (1) direct or assist in directing a personnel management program, or (2) advise on, supervise, perform, or provide staff leadership and technical guidance for work which involves two or more specialized personnel functions, or (3) perform specialized personnel management work not covered by other series in this group.

203—Personnel Clerical and Assistant

This series includes personnel, clerical, and technical support positions involving supervision or performance of work that requires substantial knowledge of civilian personnel rules, regulations, procedures, and program requirements. These positions do not require the broad knowledge of federal personnel systems or the depth of knowledge about personnel management concepts, principles, and techniques that are characteristic of the recognized personnel management specialist.

235—Employee Development

This series covers positions that involve planning, administering, supervising, or evaluating programs designed to train and develop employees. This series also covers positions that involve providing guidance, consultation, and staff assistance to management concerning employee training and development matters. Positions covered by this series require as their paramount qualifications an understanding of the relationship of employee development objectives, methods, and procedures; analytical ability; and a knowledge of the principles, practices, and techniques of education or training.

303—General Clerical

This series includes positions that perform or supervise clerical, assistant, or technician work for which no other series is appropriate. The work requires a knowledge of the procedures and techniques involved in carrying out the work of an organization and involves application of procedures and practices within the framework of established guidelines. This group also includes security officer positions.

318—Secretary

This series includes all positions that involve assisting one individual, and in some cases the subordinate staff of that individual, by performing general office work auxiliary to the work of the organization. To be included in this series, a position must be the principal clerical or administrative support position in the office. The duties require knowledge of clerical and administrative procedures and requirements, various office skills, and the ability to apply these skills in ways that increase the effectiveness of others.

334—Computer Specialist

This series includes positions involving responsibility for managing, supervising or performing the work necessary to design, implement, maintain, or modify systems for solving problems or accomplishing work processes by the use of digital computers. Positions are included in this series when the primary need is knowledge of computer requirements and techniques. The positions are concerned with functions such as: (1) identification of the nature and scope of subject matter processes and problems to be automated, and organization of such processing by computers; (2) selection or designation of specific kinds of computers and related peripheral devices to be used; (3) organization of plans and programs specifying the nature and sequence of actions to be accomplished by the computers themselves; and (4) performance of specialized activities associated with development and design of data processing systems.

335—Computer Clerk and Assistant

This series covers positions involving performance or supervision of data processing support and services function for users of digital computer systems, including such work as: (1) receiving, maintaining and issuing data storage media for computer operations; (2) collecting and sequentially staging input media with associated program instructions for processing; (3) scheduling the use of computer time for program processing; (4) collecting, maintaining, and distributing program and systems documentation; and (5) collecting raw information, preparing flow charts, and coding in program languages, or (6) other support functions.

501—General Accounting/Administrative
This series includes all classes of positions that administer, supervise, advise on, or perform clerical, technical, or administrative work of an accounting or budgetary nature requiring less than full professional education (or equivalent experience) in the principles, procedures, and techniques of accounting, when such positions: (1) are not classifiable in any other series in the Accounting and Budget Group, GS-500; or (2) consist of combinations of two or more different types of clerical, technical, or administrative work of an accounting or budgetary nature when such combinations are not specifically included in another series.

505—Financial Management Series
This series includes all classes of positions that involve managing or directing a program for the management of the financial resources of an organizational segment, field establishment, bureau, department, independent agency, or any other organizational entity of the federal government, when the duties and responsibilities include: (a) developing, coordinating, and maintaining an integrated system of financial staff services (such as auditing, credit analysis, management analysis, etc.); (b) exercising effective control over the financial resources of the organization; (c) coordinating and synthesizing financial and management data so as to interpret the composite financial resources of operations to all levels of the organization's management; and (d) advising on, developing, coordinating, and carrying out financial policies, procedures, and plans.

510—Accounting
This series includes all classes of positions that advise on, administer, supervise, or perform professional accounting work relating to the transactions of governmental, quasigovernmental, or private business organizations. The work ordinarily is concerned with the design, development, installation, operation, or inspection of accounting systems; the prescription of accounting requirements; the audit of similar examination of accounts and records of transactions; the examination, analysis, and interpretation of accounting data or reports; or providing accounting advice and assistance to management.

525—Accounting Technician
This series includes account-maintenance clerical and accounting-technician support positions requiring a basic understanding of accounting systems, policies, and procedures in performing or supervising the examination, verification, and maintenance of accounts and accounting data. Also included are positions that perform technical audit functions, develop or install revised accounting procedures, or perform similar quasiprofessional accounting work.

560—Budget Administration

This series includes all classes of positions that perform, supervise, administer, or advise on work in one or more phases of budgeting, such as the formulation of budget estimates, the presentation of budget estimates, and the giving of testimony before examining, reviewing, and fund-granting authorities; the execution of approved budgets, and the exercise of management controls over the obligation and expenditure of funds.

602—Medical Officer

This series includes all classes of positions that advise on, administer, supervise, or perform professional and scientific work in one or more fields of medicine. A position is classifiable to this series when the nature of duties and responsibilities is such that the degree of Doctor of Medicine or Doctor of Osteopathy is a fundamental requirement. Most positions in this series require a current license to practice medicine and surgery in a state or territory of the United States or the District of Columbia.

603—Physician's Assistant Series

This series covers positions that involve assisting physicians by providing diagnostic and therapeutic medical care and services under the guidance of the physicians. The work requires knowledge of specific observation and examination procedures, and the ability to perform diagnostic and therapeutic tasks. Physician's assistants assist in the examination and observation of patients by performing such duties as taking case histories, conducting physical examinations, and ordering laboratory studies during hospital rounds and clinic visits. As directed by physicians, physician's assistants carry out special procedures; for example, they give injections or other medication, apply or change dressings, perform lumbar punctures, or suture minor lacerations.

610—Nurse

This series includes positions that require a professional knowledge of nursing. Positions involve providing care to patients in hospitals and clinics; administering anesthetic agents and supportive treatments to patients undergoing surgery or other medical procedures; promoting better health practices; teaching; performing research in one or more phases of the field of nursing; or consulting and advising nurses who provide direct care to patients.

620—Practical Nurse

This series covers positions that involve a variety of nursing care and practices which do not require full professional nursing education, but are represented by the licensing of practical and vocational nurses by states, territories, or the District of Columbia.

660—Pharmacist

This series includes all positions that involve professional and scientific work in the field of pharmacy. The work typically involves the compounding of prescriptions of physicians, dentists, and other licensed practitioners; and the formulation, preparation, bulk compounding selection, dispensing, and preservation of drugs, medicines, and chemicals.

670—Health System Administration

Positions in this series have full line responsibility for the administrative management of health care delivery systems that may range from nationwide networks including many hospitals to major subdivisions of individual hospitals. The fundamental responsibility of health system administrators is to use all available resources effectively to provide the best possible patient care. This requires an understanding of the critical balance between the administrative and clinical functions in the health care delivery system, and ability to coordinate and control programs and resources to achieve this balance.

675—Medical Record Technician

This series includes positions that involve analyzing medical records for completeness, consistency, and compliance with requirements, and performing related functions such as coding medical record information and selecting and compiling medical record data. The work requires applications of practical knowledge of medical terminology, anatomy, physiology, the internal organization and consistency of medical records, medical record references and procedures, and the medical and legal significance of medical records.

809—Construction Control

This series includes positions that involve on-site inspection of construction or the monitoring and control of construction operations. Positions in this occupation require application of: (a) practical knowledge of engineering methods and techniques; (b) knowledge of construction practices, methods, techniques, costs, materials, and equipment; and (c) ability to read and interpret engineering and architectural plans and specifications.

856—Electronic Technician

This series includes positions that require; (a) the knowledge of the techniques and theories characteristic of electronics, such as knowledge of basic electricity and electronics theory, algebra, and elementary physics, (b) the ability to apply that knowledge to duties involved in engineering functions such as design, development, evaluation, testing, installation, and maintenance of electronic equipment, and (c) knowledge of the capabilities, limitations, operations, design, characteristics, and functional use of a variety of types of models of electronic equipment and systems. Such knowledge is related to, but less than, full professional knowledge of electronics engineering.

905—General Attorney

This series includes professional legal positions involved in preparing cases for trial, and/or the trial of cases before a court or an administrative body or persons having quasijudicial power; or rendering legal advice and services with respect to questions, regulations, practices, or other matters falling within the purview of federal government agencies. This may include conducting investigations to obtain evidentiary data; preparing interpretative and administrative orders, rules, or regulations to give effect to the provisions of governing statutes or other requirements of law; drafting, negotiating, or examining contracts or other legal documents required by an agency's activities; drafting, preparing formal comments; or otherwise making substantive recommendations with respect to proposed legislation; editing and preparing for publication statutes enacted by Congress or opinions or discussions of a court, commission, or board; or drafting and reviewing decisions for consideration and adoption by agencies. This work requires admission to the bar.

950—Paralegal Specialist Series

This series includes positions that involve paralegal work not requiring professional legal competence. The work requires discretion and independent judgment in the application of specialized knowledge or particular laws, regulations, precedents, or agency practices based thereon. The work includes such activities as: (a) legal research; (b) selecting, assembling, summarizing, and compiling substantive legal information; (c) case preparation; and (d) analyzing facts and answering legal questions.

986—Legal Clerk and Technician

This series includes all classes of positions that perform or supervise legal, clerical, or technical work. The work requires: (1) a specialized knowledge of legal documents and processes; and (2) the ability to apply established instructions, rules, regulations, precedents, and procedures pertaining to legal activities. Administrative Systems Technician positions are in this series.

1101—General Business and Industry

This series includes all classes of positions that administer, supervise, or perform: (1) any combination of work characteristic of two or more series in this group where no one type of work is controlling, and where the combination is not specifically included in another series; or (2) other work properly classified in this group for which no other series has been provided. This series includes UNICOR Superintendents, Industrial Managers and Industrial Marketing Specialists.

1102—Contract and Procurement

This series includes positions involving work concerned with: (1) obtaining contractual agreements through negotiation with private concerns, educational institutions, and nonprofit organizations to furnish services, supplies, equipment, or other materials to the government; (2) assuring compliance with the terms of contracts; (3) analyzing negotiations; (4) examining and evaluating contract price proposals; and (5) purchasing supplies, services, equipment, or other materials by formally advertised bids and negotiated procurement procedures.

1150—Industrial Specialist

This series includes positions that primarily require practical knowledge of the nature and operations of an industry or industries, and the materials, facilities, and methods employed by the industry or industries in producing commodities.

1601—General Facilities and Equipment

This series covers positions involving: (1) a combination of work characteristic of two or more series in the Equipment, Facilities, and Services Group when no other series is appropriate for the paramount knowledges and abilities required for the position, or (2) other equipment, facilities, or services work properly classified in this group for which no other series has been established. This series includes UNICOR Factory Managers.

1640—Facility Management

This series covers positions that involve managing the operation and maintenance of buildings, grounds, and other facilities such as camps, power plants, and roadways. Such work requires: (1) administrative and managerial skills and abilities; and (2) broad technical knowledge of the operating capabilities and maintenance requirements of various kinds of physical plants and equipment.

1658—Laundry Plant Management

This series includes all positions that advise on or manage and direct the operations of laundries, dry cleaning plants, or combined laundry/dry cleaning plants when the duties require: (1) skill in performing managerial functions associated with the operation of laundries and/or dry cleaning plants, and (2) a combination of practical knowledge of laundry and/or dry cleaning equipment and processing operations.

1667—Food Services

This series includes all classes of positions that manage, supervise, or perform work involved in the operation of food-supply services of government institutions, including storerooms, kitchens, dining rooms, meat shops, and bakeries.

1710—Education

This series includes positions that require the application of full professional knowledge of the theories, principles, and techniques of education and training in such areas as instruction, guidance counseling, education administration, development or evaluation of curricula, instructional materials and aids, and educational tests and measurements. Some positions also require specialized knowledge of one or more subjects in which the education is given.

1712—Training Instruction

This series covers positions concerned with administration, supervision, training program development, evaluation, or instruction in programs of training when the paramount requirement of the work is the combination of practical knowledge of methods and techniques of instruction and practical knowledge of the subject matter being taught.

1910—Quality Assurance

This series includes all positions that perform, administer, or advise on work concerned with assuring the quality of products acquired and used by the federal government. The work of this series involves: (1) the development of plans and programs for achieving and maintaining product quality throughout items' life cycles; (2) monitoring operations to prevent the production of defects and to verify adherence to quality plans and requirements; and (3) analysis and investigation of adverse quality trends or conditions and initiation of corrective actions.

2010—Inventory Management

This series includes all positions that involve technical work in managing, regulating, coordinating, or otherwise exercising control over supplies, equipment, or other material. Control relates to any one or more phases of material management from initial planning (including provisioning and requirements for determination) through acquisition and distribution, up to ultimate issue, consumption, retention, or disposal.

2600—Electronic Equipment Installation and Maintenance

This job family includes occupations involved in the installation, repair, overhaul, fabrication, tuning, alignment, modification, calibration, and testing of electronic equipment and related devices, such as radio, radar, loran, sonar, television, and other communications equipment; industrial controls; fire control, flight/landing control, bombing/navigation, and other integrated systems; and electronic computer systems and maintenance.

2800—Electrical Installation and Maintenance

This job family includes occupations involved in the fabrication, installation, alteration, maintenance, repair, and testing of electrical systems, instruments, apparatus, and equipment.

3100—Fabric and Leather Work

This job family includes occupations involving the fabrication, modification, and repair of clothing and equipment made of: (1) woven textile fabrics of animal, vegetable, or synthetic origin; (2) plastic film and filaments; (3) natural and simulated leather; (4) natural and synthetic fibers; and (5) paper. Work involves use of hand tools and mechanical devices and machines to lay out, cut, sew, rivet, mold, fit, assemble, and attach findings to articles such as uniforms, rainwear, hats, belts, shoes, brief cases, holsters, equipage articles, tents, gun covers, bags, parachutes, upholstery, mattresses, and brushes.

3400—Machine Tool Work

This job family includes occupations that involve setting up and operating machine tools and using hand tools to make or repair (shape, fit, finish, assemble) metal parts, tools, gauges, models, patterns, mechanisms, and machines; and machining explosives and synthetic materials.

3600—Structural and Finishing Work

This job family includes occupations not specifically covered by another family that involve doing structural and finishing work in construction, maintenance, and repair of surfaces and structures (e.g., laying brick, block, and stone; setting tile; finishing cement and concrete; plastering; installing, maintaining, and repairing asphalt, tar and gravel; roofing; insulating and glazing).

3700—Metal Processing

This job family includes occupations that involve processing or treating metals to alter their properties or produce desirable qualities such as hardness or workability, using processes such as welding, plating, melting, alloying, casting, annealing, heat treating, and refining.

3800—Metal Working

This job family includes occupations involved in shaping and forming metal and making and repairing metal parts or equipment. This includes such work as the fabrication and assembly of sheet metal parts and equipment; forging and press operations; structural iron working, boilermaking, shipfitting, and other plate metal work; rolling, cutting, stamping, riveting, and so forth. This series does not include machine tool work.

4100—Painting and Paperhanging

This job family includes occupations that involve hand or spray painting and decorating interiors and exteriors of building structures, aircraft, vessels, mobile equipment, fixtures, furnishing, machinery, and other surfaces; finishing hardwoods, furniture, and cabinetry; painting signs; covering interiors of rooms with strips of wallpaper or fabric; and similar tasks.

4200—Plumbing and Pipefitting

This job family includes occupations that involve the installation, maintenance, and repair of water, air, steam, gas, sewer, and other pipelines and systems and related fixtures, apparatus, and accessories.

4400—Printing

This job family includes occupations involved in letterpress (relief), offset-lithographic, gravure (intaglio), or screen printing, including layout, hand composition, typesetting from hot metal type, platemaking, printing, and finishing operations.

4600—Wood Work

This job family includes occupations involved in the construction, alteration, repair, and maintenance of wooden buildings and other structures, and fabrication and repair of wood products such as furniture, foundry patterns, and form blocks, using power and hand tools.

4700—General Maintenance and Operations Work

This job family includes occupations that: (1) consist of various combinations of work that are involved in constructing, maintaining, and repairing buildings, roads, grounds, and related facilities; manufacturing, modifying and repairing items or apparatus made from a variety of materials or types of components; or repairing and operating equipment or utilities; and (2) require the application of a variety of trade practices associated with occupations in more than one job family (unless otherwise indicated), and the performance of the highest level of work in at least two of the trades involved. This series includes 178 positions involved in utility systems operations.

5000—Plant and Animal Work

This job family includes occupations involved in general or specialized farming operations; gardening (including the general care of grounds, roadways, nurseries, greenhouses, etc.); trimming and felling trees; and propagating, caring for, handling, and controlling animals and insects, including pest species.

5300—Industrial Equipment Maintenance

This job family includes occupations involved in the general maintenance, installation, and repair of portable and stationary industrial machinery, tools, and equipment, such as sewing machines, machine tools, woodworking and metalworking machines, printing equipment, processing equipment, driving machinery, power generating equipment, air conditioning equipment, heating and boiler plant equipment, and other types of machines and equipment used in the production of goods and services.

5400—Industrial Equipment Operation

This job family includes occupations involved in the operation of portable and stationary industrial equipment, tools, and machines to generate and distribute utilities, such as electricity, steam, and gas for heat or power; to treat and distribute water; to collect, treat, and dispose of wastes, to open and close bridges, locks, and dams; to lift and move workers, materials, and equipment; to manufacture and process materials and products; and so forth.

5800—Transportation/Mobile Equipment Maintenance

This job family includes occupations involved in repairing, adjusting, and maintaining self-propelled transportation and other mobile equipment (except aircraft), including any special purpose features with which they may be equipped.

6900—Warehousing and Stock Handling

This job family includes occupations involved in physically receiving, storing, handling, and issuing supplies, materials, and equipment; handling, marking, and displaying goods for selection by customers; identifying and condition-classifying materials and equipment; and routing and expediting movement of parts, supplies, and materials in production and repair facilities.

7400—Food Preparation

This job family includes occupations involved in the preparation and serving of food. The full range of food preparation—including cooking, baking, meat cutting, food handling, storage, and serving—is supervised by these positions.

Note: The above job group descriptions are adapted from *Occupations Within the Federal Bureau of Prisons*, a booklet published by the U.S. Department of Justice, Federal Bureau of Prisons, in December, 1988. The Federal Bureau of Prisons is composed of approximately 50 institutions and is responsible for the care and custody of all federal inmates. It employed over 13,000 people in 1988 and expects to almost double its work force within ten years.

The types of positions described in this appendix can be found in almost all correctional agencies responsible for institutions.

UNICOR is the Industrial Division of the Federal Bureau of Prisons.

Author Index

Subject Index

About the Author

Dr. Harold E. Williamson is Associate Professor of Criminal Justice and Director of the Criminal Justice Program at Northeast Louisiana University in Monroe, Louisiana. He received his bachelor's, master's, and doctoral degrees from the College of Criminal Justice at Sam Houston State University in Huntsville, Texas. He served in the United States Air Force from 1966 to 1970. During ten years of corrections experience with the Texas Department of Corrections, he held positions including security officer, agricultural work supervisor, industrial work supervisor, training instructor, research analyst, and administrator. He taught as an adjunct faculty member at Lee College and Sam Houston State University for two years prior to appointment at Northeast Louisiana University in 1981. He has also served as a consultant to the North Delta Regional Training Academy in Monroe, Louisiana since 1981. He is a member of several professional associations including the American Correctional Association, the Academy of Criminal Justice Sciences, and the American Society of Criminology. Dr. Williamson is married to the former Sharon Ann Clark and has three children—Crystal, Jason, and Travis.